Cyberfactories

Cyberfactories
How News Agencies Produce News

Barbara Czarniawska

Professor of Management Studies, GRI, School of Business, Economics and Law, University of Gothenburg, Sweden

Edward Elgar
Cheltenham, UK • Northampton, MA, USA

Published by
Edward Elgar Publishing Limited
The Lypiatts
15 Lansdown Road
Cheltenham
Glos GL50 2JA
UK

Edward Elgar Publishing, Inc.
William Pratt House
9 Dewey Court
Northampton
Massachusetts 01060
USA

A catalogue record for this book
is available from the British Library

Library of Congress Control Number: 2011931018

ISBN 978 0 85793 912 8 (cased)

Typeset by Servis Filmsetting Ltd, Stockport, Cheshire
Printed and bound by MPG Books Group, UK

Contents

Glossary

Alert	Signals the highest priority news at Reuters (with "Red Alert", i.e., an Alert in red letters at the absolute top). At TT and ANSA called Flash (as it was called before even at Reuters)
Baud	A unit of measure of the velocity of transmission of the news
Beat	A first article on a given topic; news delivered before the competitors
Blue light news	News from police and emergency at TT
Brief	A short and concise summary of a story
Byline	Personal credit, a line indicating authorship of a text
Clip	A quote from another media, rewritten and acknowledging the source
Credit	A provenance of a text (a person or an organization)
Crier	A person that used to read news on the phone to the subscribers
Factbox	A framed panel containing a list of facts
Flash	Signals the highest priority news at TT and ANSA; at Reuters called Alert
Desk	Originally a physical desk, now a desktop dedicated to the editorial functions of assigning, coordinating, and editing
Exclusive	Interview given to one journalist only
Lead	A new opening to a running story
Newswire	A wire service that transmits up-to-the-minute news, usually electronically, to the media and even to the public
Polygraphist	A person that used to convert a typewritten text for use on a teleprinter
Quarantine	Putting files suspected of being infected by viruses or simply being spam into a special directory, to be deleted manually
Rewrite	A final version of the story, called at Reuters Wrap-up
RSS	Really Simple Syndication: shows recently updated

	content on chosen websites, makes it easier to keep up to date with sites in an automated manner
Slug	Previously called catchline, a short phrase or title used to indicate the story content
Snap	A one-line news report, breaking news but not of the same importance as Flash or Alert
Spike	Originally, literally a metal spike on which the refused texts were put
Stringer	A freelance journalist or a local newspaper journalist used by an agency more or less regularly as correspondent
Take	A paragraph of a story; originally a portion of copy assigned to a teletype operator at one time
Wrap-up	A final version of the story at Reuters, at other agencies called a rewrite

1. The places where information overflows

Where does news come from? The answer, much of the time, is from newswires. Many of the stories in newspapers, on television, radio and online are
based on dispatches filed by the big news agencies.
The Economist, 12 February 2009

The idea of studying news agencies was born during a study of management in the city of Rome (Czarniawska, 2002). As part of my fieldwork,
I received for my perusal an enormous collection of press cuttings concerning City Utility – a company I was studying at the time when it was
at the center of media attention. I also received an almost equally large
collection of faxes sent by City Utility to the Italian news agency ANSA.
A simple calculation revealed that Rome's city administration had at least
30 departments and utilities, each with its own press office, and that they
were likely sending the same type of faxes to ANSA. Add to this the rest
of Rome (trade unions, companies, politicians, voluntary organizations),
and – why not? – the rest of Italy and the world. How did ANSA select
"news" from such an overflow? The journalists in the Italian press and the
visual media pay more attention to certain events than to others, but it is
ANSA that makes the first selection. How did it manage to process those
avalanches of information?

MANAGING OVERFLOW

It turned out that several other scholars were asking themselves the
same question, albeit in different contexts. We joined forces in a larger,
ongoing program called "Managing Overflow". The program involves
a team of ethnologists and management scholars from the University of
Gothenburg and Lund University who are examining the conditions of
alleged surplus, overabundance, or overflow, seeking perspectives distant
from the traditional genre of texts on these themes by asking "What is
too much and who defines it?" In the process, we have been scrutinizing
a variety of sites where overflows are supposed to occur: in private and
public domains, in personal and collective situations. If a diagnosis of

overflow has been reached, what are the strategies and tactics for dealing with it? And are they transferable across the domains?

One obvious setting in which the phenomenon of overflow is bound to occur is the production of news. This process can be said to begin with news agencies – organizations employing journalists and established to supply news reports to other organizations in the news trade. But do news agencies play the role of "gatekeepers", as has been assumed in the past, or do they contribute to an even more abundant flow of information? How do they manage the inflow and how do they regulate the outflow?

Some Theoretical and Methodological Frameworks

The phenomenon of overflow or surplus or excess has been noticed, described, and analyzed in various epochs and contexts, but the discussion has almost always had a moral connotation. One can begin in the nineteenth century with Thorstein Veblen, who depicted overflow or overabundance as an indisputably negative phenomenon in *The Theory of the Leisure Class* (1899). This view became well established, and was later linked to economic gains, mass culture, information overflow, and accelerating consumption. The 1950s and the 1960s are particularly fascinating from that point of view, although the debates had different ideological backgrounds and varied in nuances, then as now. The best-known examples are Riesman's *The Lonely Crowd* (1953), Galbraith's *The Affluent Society* (1958), Kerr's *The Decline of Pleasure* (1962), and Burenstam Linder's *The Harried Leisure Class* (1970). Later, for example in many treatises on globalization, overflow has been linked to such notions as excess, gluttony, and corruption. This condemning attitude toward overflow was easily transferred to the issue of information overflow, with Benjamin's famous essay (1935/1999) being the best example. Mechanical reproduction deprived literature and art of "authenticity and aura", and digital reproduction can be said to magnify this process to unheard of proportions.

In the Managing Overflow research program, we intend to free ourselves from the dominant view of overflow as an accelerating contemporary problem. Instead, we are studying the *framing processes* (Callon, 1998), trying to identify the point at which something is "over", and who decides such points or frames. Especially poignant is Callon's observation that it is the very act of framing that produces *over*flow: otherwise, it is merely a flow. Thus, within the program, overflow is seen as being created – and as creating. Both causes and consequences are of interest. An overflow can break down old frames and force the construction of new ones. Faster and more effective communication allows such incredible achievements as organ transplants and space travel, but it also produces an overflow of information for us all. Even so, lonely retirees may welcome such a flow, whereas it can become a real burden for stressed mid-career people. Overflow does not exist as an objective phenomenon; it is always in the eyes of the beholder, as indicated by the specific rules even for what counts as a flood.

Researching how overflows are managed, we need to study and try to explicate such perceptions and such rules, without the necessity of taking a stand. After all, although the consequences of overflow are evaluated in both moral and aesthetic terms, the judgments are not unanimous. Are the contents of a bathroom wastebasket a disgusting spillover of hygienic activities, or is it a work of art? Can its status change by simply placing it in an art gallery?

We intend to rely on the insights of our predecessors, while simultaneously finding new ways of conceptualizing overflow and its management. In constructing our framework, we have been exploiting our transdisciplinary origins, taking economic and managerial perspectives on cultural phenomena and a cultural perspective on economic phenomena, hoping, in this way, to document strong linkages between the two spheres of societal life.

The approach used in this study differs from media studies, which focus on communication processes and the content of the news and from management studies of media resources and owner structures (even if both aspects turn up in my results and in my analysis). As this is not a media study *sensu stricto*, I do not attempt content analysis, although I am trying to direct the readers' attention to what Hayden White (1987) called "the content of the form"; forms, too, are message carriers. Furthermore, I do not offer general observations on the profession of journalism, because journalists at news agencies represent, according to their own admission, a small part of that profession – a part that is distinct, perhaps even atypical. Finally, although it would be perfectly legitimate for an organization scholar, I have little to say about the relatively complicated relationship between "Newsroom" and "Company" – a relationship that representatives of both areas describe with caution. A future study of this relationship could be of interest, although a Wallraff-like methodology would likely be necessary.[1]

Here, the focus is on news *production* in news agencies, and the selection of this focus already contains a premise. I see news agencies not as

---

[1] Günther Walraff became famous for his method of doing investigative journalism, consisting of an undercover study of the phenomena he was interested in. See http://en.wikipedia.org/wiki/Günter_Wallraff; last accessed 29 June 2011.

intermediaries, transferring received information to their clients, but truly as mediators,[2] the *producers of the news*, even if they are merely a link in the production chain. The assumption that the media manufacture and mediate rather than intermediate news extends back to the reasoning of McLuhan (1964), but it needs to be repeated time after time (Esposito, 2004).

The study reported here has been conducted in three news agencies: a national Swedish agency, TT; an Italian international agency, ANSA; and a global agency, Thomson Reuters (UK and US).[3] At the outset, I am framing those sites with the help of a strictly industrial metaphor: as "fact", or rather "news factories" (by their own admission, they produce stories, not facts). The question was: how do they produce their news? The answer required attention to aspects of news production such as suppliers (like the utility in Rome); clients (mostly newspapers, but in case of Reuters, even banks and other actors in finance); but above all, the organization of the throughput.

According to Simon Cottle, "[i]t is disconcerting how many studies of media output are conducted with a complete disregard for the moment of production and the forces enacted or condensed onside the production domain" (2003: 5). Cottle did quote a few exceptions to this state of affairs, however, and I can further add to his list Lars Engwall's (1978) early study of newspapers as organizations, and studies of financial reporting by news agencies conducted by Heath and Nicholls (1997) and Grafström et al. (2006). Studies that addressed the organization of news production (Bantz et al., 1980; Löfgren Nilsson, 1999; Johansson, 2008; Boczkowski, 2009a; 2009b; 2010) have described newspapers or TV news. Among these studies, Boczkowski's studies (2009a; 2009b; 2010) are closest to mine, because they refer to the same period and because he paid attention to the role of technology. In fact, Boczkowski studied the next link in my chain of interest: the newspapers' production and consumption.

I am also aware that "factory" or even "assembly line" (Gans, 1979/2004) has been long used as a metaphor in media studies, and has provoked many debates and protests (see, for example, Löfgren Nilsson, 1999; Nygren, 2008a). I wish to emphasize that this metaphor, or analogy, has a structuring rather than an analytical function in my text, as, for example, in Bantz et al. (1980). I use it to structure my field material because I

---

[2] For the difference between intermediaries and mediators, see Latour (2005).

[3] My study has been financed by the Foundation for Economic Research in Western Sweden, and the writing of this text by Jan Wallanders and Tom Hedelius Foundation, support for which I am extremely grateful. My sincere thanks go to Franck Cochoy, Nina Lee Colwill, Gideon Kunda, GiovanFrancesco Lanzara, Orvar Löfgren, Tony Spybey, David Stark, and all my collaborators at GRI for useful comments and criticisms.

believe that it will be helpful for a reader who is not a journalist or a media researcher; the analytical metaphor of a "cyberfactory" is developed later.

Theoretical Sampling

This study is based on the assumption that a certain phenomenon (overflow) is occurring at certain sites (news agencies). The question guiding the research and, consequently, the sampling (Glaser, 1978) was open: how is overflow managed? "Managing" here is meant as both *coping with* and *controlling*.

The insights collected at the first site – the Swedish agency, TT, which was chosen as an easily accessed site of the occurrence of the phenomenon – appeared to cast doubt on the original assumption. Journalists did not report that they had experienced overflow. But because TT is a local agency, relying primarily on other sources for its international news, there was a possibility that the relatively small size of the agency was the determining factor in the journalists' response.

My interest in "what they actually do" remained, and was not completely satisfied. The first study gave rise to several analytical categories, derived from the field material: a "cyborgization" of the news work, and a noteworthy variation on the global phenomenon of standardization: standardization via product rather than process. Again, it could have been a local phenomenon; Sweden is known for its use of advanced workplace technologies and generally high level of computerization.

The next step would then be to enter the site of a larger agency located in another country – an international agency. ANSA was chosen because I speak Italian. It was there that the possibility of reformulating the initial assumption began to arise; news producers do not experience overflow, they *create it* – and help their clients to manage it, primarily with the aid of coding systems.

This last supposition found its most obvious confirmation in the third study – that of Reuters (now Thomson Reuters), the oldest existing and currently the largest news agency in the world. Furthermore, standardization via product was confirmed and explained in this last study. In contrast to other companies, which tend to imitate each other by gaining insights into others' production processes – directly, by studying available documentation, or with the help of consultants – news agencies do not imitate one another. The denial of such imitation at TT and ANSA could have been explained by local pride, but at Reuters it became evident that each agency develops its own strategies and tactics and its own technologies. The similarity of their production processes can be explained by the similarity of their products, which shapes the production processes backwards, as it were.

They all deliver a *newswire*, a continuous flow of news, and various packages of information. In all of them, the Web is playing an increasing role, as it does for their important clients – the newspapers. Apparently, there are no consultants specializing in news agency operations. This characteristic seems to distinguish news agencies from newspapers (on paper and online), which, according to Boczkowski (2010), do imitate one another.

The studies of TT and ANSA have been reported in their entirety in texts written in Swedish and Italian (Czarniawska, 2009c; 2009d). In composing this text, I chose the parts most relevant to my final analysis. Nevertheless, certain topics are repeated through the chapters, in order to achieve verification – in the spirit of grounded theory – but also in order to highlight local variations.

FIELDWORK

The first step in the design of the study was a guided tour of the agency, aimed at creating a literal map of the premises and conducting an interview with a contact person, who, it was hoped, would provide a general description of the process. The second and third steps were to consist of direct observation of chosen points and complementary interviews with persons working in places or posts that had not been observed. The study in each location was to conclude with several interviews aimed at clarification and corroboration of earlier observations. The actual fieldwork, however, needed to be adapted to circumstances.

TT

My original plan was to conduct a direct observation of the production process itself, either by shadowing persons in key production roles (Czarniawska, 2007) or by using participant observation. (My real goal was to become an apprentice at TT.) I was denied both opportunities, and had to rely on a diary-interview technique, in which the journalists told me what they did the day before, or, if the interview was conducted at the end of their shift, what they had done that day. My questions were simple and open: "Could you please tell me what you did yesterday/today? Was it a typical day?" The interviewees used pages from their diaries to structure their accounts. I also added a question borrowed from the critical incident technique (Flanagan, 1954): "Do you remember any unusual events in your work?" Additionally, I was allowed to make a photo documentation of the agency.

Interviews conducted with the aim of evoking descriptions of everyday life or work can be called "ethnographic", but not in the sense given to the term by US anthropologist James Spradley (1979), who coined the expression. For him, the purpose of such interviews was "to describe a culture". In contrast, Dutch philosopher of science Annemarie Mol suggested in her study of cardiological practices that the term "ethnographic interviews" means that the interviewees become ethnographers (2002: 15). This is also the idea behind the diary-interview technique (Czarniawska, 2007), implying, however, that, as in the case of "professional" ethnographers, some people play this role better than others. This variation became obvious during the interviews as well; some people talked about their jobs in general, abstract terms, whereas others were able to account for the day's events in great detail.

Although I was not allowed to shadow the actual work of the journalists, I could look at their screens and their workplaces. Additionally, the interviews were conducted in the open-plan office of the agency, which gave me an opportunity to make general observations each time I visited the agency.

But not even the most talented ethnographer (which I am not) is able to report everything that is happening in a workplace. As the interviewees revealed, they had not been in the habit of thinking *about* their jobs, especially in the form of chains of events. They thought *within* their jobs – about what should be done and how it should be done, but also in reflections about their profession in general and the agency in particular. Only the beginners and external observers like myself actually attended to what was taken for granted by the experienced news producers.

One thing that is taken for granted, although it is manifestly present at each turn, is the role of machines in the production of news – in this case, computers and telephones. As long as they work as they should, they should not attract attention (Latour, 1998). When they fail to work, there is a level of technical assistance at hand that would provoke the envy of all other professional workers. Malfunctions are resolved in a matter of minutes. Only in a historical perspective – in complementary interviews aimed at evoking the picture of things "as they used to be" – was the change from typewriters and telegraph machines to computers and e-mails cast in relief.

Tacit knowledge – knowledge deposited in muscles and bodies rather than in language or abstract concepts[4] – becomes visible through its absence in the interviews, when compared to observations. Annemarie Mol (2002) used the expression "imbedded knowledge" to denote knowledge

---

[4] Johansson (2008) spoke of knowledge that "sits in the walls" (p. 8). In open-plan offices it sits, rather, in the server.

accumulated in various parts of an action net created by the actions of the producers, their suppliers, and their clients; it is activated by each of them for the purpose at hand without the necessity of anybody mastering the whole of it. Edwin Hutchins (1995), who studied navigation as a cognitive system, followed a similar vein of thought. Navigating a contemporary ship is a cognitive system in itself, of which people are but one part, and in which nobody can or needs to understand the whole of it. Similarly, news producers who sit all day at their computers know the programs they use and can possibly explain what they do, but usually have a vague idea about the functioning of servers (which are central to their work), not to mention the satellites.

It is in this role, perhaps, that external observers can be of use to an internal actor – not because the observers have greater knowledge, but because they can see the job from another perspective. Tacit knowledge, routines that are taken for granted, and mechanical collaborators cannot, by definition, talk themselves, but they can produce visible and observable results. Perhaps it takes two – an actor and an observer – to describe any job.

I was doing my best, therefore, to discover how daily news production looks from my interviewees' detailed descriptions of their daily actions and my visits to the field (12 in all, conducted in November and December, 2007). I also looked systematically for TT news in my local newspaper, *Göteborgs-Posten*, a client of TT, and less systematically in other newspapers. Still, I was greatly relieved when I obtained permission to observe and to shadow the work at the Italian news agency. It must be said that it was only after this happened that I felt that I understood what the TT interviewees were talking about.

ANSA

At the outset I was not quite sure how to shadow people who work primarily at, and through, their computers. In the past, I had frequently shadowed managers who used the computers sporadically (Czarniawska, 2007). True, my colleagues are now developing sets of techniques to be used in creating "virtual ethnographies" (Hine, 2000), that is, research done on the Internet. Ways of studying people working with computers are not yet well-developed, however – apart from computer studies, which have a different purpose.[5]

Much to my relief, my hosts at ANSA easily solved my problems. They simply gave me a place at a computer, such as they were using themselves,

---

[5] Some forays into this domain can be found in Cooper et al. (1995) and in Jemielniak and Kociatkiewicz (2009).

Photo 1.1   Shadowing at work

and though I could not intervene, I could see "the desk" and "the wire" and shadow the news through the production process. When a discussion started in the newsroom concerning any specific piece of news, I could trace it in the database (I had two screens at my disposal) and therefore knew what they were talking about.

Not even my shadowing seemed to be a problem. After all, shadowing consists of watching over people's shoulders as they work, and receiving explanations – and the journalists in the newsroom were certainly used to that process, as can be seen in Photo 1.1. It is common for colleagues – invited or uninvited – to watch over their colleagues' shoulders as they work. It is also common for the person doing the work to explain what is being done and to invite comments and questions. Thus, the journalists saw nothing peculiar about my wanting to observe their work at the computer.

All in all, I visited ANSA three times, each time for a week, between January and March of 2008. I conducted recorded interviews and had a great many non-recorded conversations as well. I took notes during the meetings, and when shadowing – news and people – I asked for permission to print the material that interested me. Additionally, I was reading

La Repubblica systematically during this period and other Italian newspapers less systematically.

Reuters

The biggest difficulty in my study of Reuters was the securing of access. I had the misfortune of making my first contact with a person who, unknown to me, was moving to another location, and naturally had little interest in helping me. It took a year before I finally visited Reuters for the first time, in December, 2008. Once I was there, however, plans were made quickly, and I was able to spend ten days moving among newsrooms at Reuters in February 2009.

My fieldwork at Reuters was similar to my work at ANSA – attending meetings, shadowing people at work, shadowing the news on the screen, and completing interviews. But it was the people at ANSA who were the most generous with their time and attention.

It would be counterproductive to anonymize the agencies, as their identities play a critical role in the production process. In order to protect my interlocutors, however, I quote the interviews by number, and when quoting excerpts from my observations, I use either randomly assigned letters or the functions of the persons involved, most of which are rotating at any rate. I also ascribe gender randomly, hoping in this modest way to contribute to greater equality (many journalists are women but, as in other professional organizations, the proportion of women diminishes at every step up the hierarchy).

THE STRUCTURE OF THE BOOK

In spite of the newsmakers' assertions that the agencies do not imitate one another, one of the most striking impressions I gathered when comparing the production of news in the three agencies was the similarity of the processes. Because the greatest differences were in the agencies' histories, I begin in Chapter 2 by briefly presenting the three histories together – from the longest to the shortest. In the chapters that follow, I begin with a short introduction to the site, then use the site as an illustration of a certain aspect of the production process. The field material from TT is used to describe a typical working day at an agency (Chapter 3); the material from ANSA throws light on the function of meetings in news production (Chapter 4), and the report from Reuters (Chapter 5) scrutinizes the "tooling" of the product. Each chapter ends with a presentation of analytical concepts distilled from the material to be used in the final analysis. Chapter 6 gathers and develops those analytical threads.

Although there were some further differences that could be observed among agencies, the issue of managing overflow acquired an unexpected twist as the fieldwork proceeded. Not only do agencies have no problem with the management of incoming information, they produce an enormous overflow of information in their output, and try to help their clients manage it. I suggest that this is possible because of the increasing *cybernization* (computerized control) of news production, and the *cyborgization* of its producers; two connected processes that may lead to a great many astonishing consequences in the future.

2. Three histories

I begin the story with Reuters, as it is commonly considered to be the oldest news agency in the world still in operation,[1] and I end it with ANSA, the news agency with the shortest history. Although shaped by local circumstances, the construction of the three agencies was linked, directly or indirectly, primarily through new technological inventions, as news production was becoming increasingly global.

In all three cases I attempt to bring the historical account up to the present, focusing especially on the most recent developments that are relevant for descriptions that follow.

REUTERS: HISTORY UP TO THOMSON

Reuters was founded in 1851 by Paul Julius Reuter, born Israel Josaphat – a German who started publishing a newssheet in Paris in 1849 (Read, 1992). When the Paris venture failed, he moved to Aachen, a German city close to the borders of the Netherlands and Belgium. There he opened the Institute for Promotion of Telegraphic Dispatches, and used the newly opened Berlin–Aachen telegraph line to send news to Berlin. The Paris–Brussels news was still sent by train, however, as there was a 122 km gap in the telegraph line between Aachen and Brussels. Reuter saw an opportunity to expedite the news service between Brussels and Berlin by using homing pigeons to bridge that gap, a device that he probably learned about at Agence Havas in Paris in 1848. The French Agence Havas was the first news agency in the world, and for a long time (until it became the government-sponsored Agence France-Presse), served as a model for Reuters.

In 1851, Reuter moved to London. The Submarine Telegraph Company had failed to lay an undersea telegraph cable from Dover to Calais in 1847 and again in 1850, but its 1851 attempt was promising success.

---

[1] At least in the contemporary meaning of the words "news agency". Robert Darnton (2000) and Gabriel Tarde (1901/2003) would probably locate the beginnings of this institution in the seventeenth century.

Reuter established an office called Submarine Telegraph in October 1851, a month before the opening of the Channel cable, and negotiated a contract with the London Stock Exchange to provide stock prices from the continental exchanges in return for access to the London prices, which he then supplied to stockbrokers in Paris. In 1857 he became a British citizen. In the same year the British Foreign Secretary awarded him the privilege of receiving copies of Foreign Office telegrams from India, thus providing Reuter with the opportunity to dispatch non-economic news as well. His first scoop was probably the full text of Napoleon III's speech in Paris – telegraphed to London as it was being delivered (Read, 1992: 25).

Reuter's company was concerned with commercial news service at its inception, and was headquartered in London, serving banks, brokerage houses, and leading business firms. The agency expanded steadily, and in 1858 it obtained its first newspaper client, the *London Morning Advertiser,* and newspapers began to figure ever larger among Reuter's clientele. Nevertheless, the company history is circular in this respect. Especially during the two World Wars, the political and general news dominated the dispatches of Submarine Telegraph. By 1989, however, more than 90 percent of the company's revenues came from products sold to the financial community (Read, 1992).

In 1865, Julius Reuter's private firm was restructured, and became a limited company called the Reuter's Telegram Company. Reuter was early in seeing possibilities for the telegraph in news reporting, and he built an organization that maintained correspondents throughout the world. The agency quickly generated a reputation in Europe as the first to report news scoops from abroad: the news of Abraham Lincoln's assassination, the death of Gandhi, and the capture of Saddam Hussein. Reuters was also the first to report the Berlin Wall going up and first to report it coming down (Reuters Facts, 2009).

The Press Association (PA), an organization representing the provincial press of Great Britain, acquired a majority interest in Reuters in 1925 and full ownership some years later. In 1941 the PA sold half of Reuters to the Newspaper Proprietors' Association, representing Britain's national press, and in 1947 co-ownership was extended to associations representing the daily newspapers of Australia and New Zealand.

Reuters had become one of the world's major news agencies, supplying both text and images to newspapers, other news agencies, and radio and television broadcasters. Directly or through national news agencies, it provided service to most countries, reaching virtually the entire world's leading newspapers and many thousands of smaller ones.

Reuters was always ahead in introducing new technologies. Following

Read (1992), I begin with more recent events and omit pigeons;[2] oversea cables; radio; and a field text writer called the Hell system. In 1960, Reuters began to lease a circuit in a new transatlantic coaxial cable. In 1962, the New York bureau transmitted the first Reuters news to London by satellite. In 1963, the International Financial Printer Company in Brussels started dispatching financial news directly to European subscribers. In 1964, Reuters signed a contract with the US company, Ultronic, to use digital tool company Stockmaster's so-called slave-memory computers, which are unidirectionally controlled by the main computer, to dispatch financial news. "The network was eventually offering over 10,000 stock or commodity prices at push-button command – at first in fifteen seconds, later in only two seconds" (Read, 1992: 298). In 1970, a screen display – a Videomaster from Ultronic – was introduced. In 1973, a new and revolutionary product, Reuter Monitor Money Rates was offered to the clients, allowing foreign exchange traders to insert their rates into the system themselves. From there, it was but one step to allow the actual dealing, which Reuter Monitor Dealing Service offered in 1981. In 1982, a direct satellite delivery by small dishes (SDS) was introduced. No wonder that by 1989 the technical staff reached 4274 persons, compared to 1640 in Editorial.

In 1984, Reuters was floated as a public company on the London Stock Exchange and on the NASDAQ in the US. There were concerns, however, that the company's tradition of objective reporting could be jeopardized if control of the company were to fall into the hands of a single shareholder. To counter that possibility, the constitution of the company at the time of the stock offering included a rule that no individual was allowed to own more than 15 percent of the company (Read, 1992: 358). If this limit were exceeded, the directors could order the shareholder to reduce the holding to less than 15 percent. That rule was applied in 1988 when Rupert Murdoch's News Corporation, which already held around 15 percent of Reuters, bought an Australian news company that also owned stock in Reuters. Murdoch was compelled to reduce its holding by 8 percent in order to stay in line with the rules.

Reuters began to grow rapidly in the 1980s, widening the range of its business products and expanding its global reporting network for media, financial, and economic services. In the mid-1990s, the Reuters company engaged in a brief foray in the radio sector, with London Radio's two

---

[2] Perhaps this omission is premature. As I learned from TT, employees at an IT company in Durban, South Africa, tired of their slow ADSL connection and sent a pigeon carrying a USB stick from a call center in Howick to Durban. The flight took 68 minutes, plus 60 minutes to download the information. During that time, only 4 percent of the same information had been transmitted via the network (*Göteborgs-Posten*, 11 September 2009).

stations: London News 97.3 FM and London News Talk 1152 AM. A Reuters Radio News service was also established to compete with the Independent Radio News.

In 2002, a crisis hit Reuters. Here is the calendar of facts, assembled by the *Financial Times* (17 October 2002). Share price in parentheses is represented in pence, following each step taken by Reuters:

- March 1999: Reuters announces a restructuring plan, saying it will lead to divisional revenues, efficiency savings, and higher margins (830).
- October 1999: Reuters launches its first Internet-based e-commerce product (520).
- March 2000: NASDAQ reaches an all-time high, and the index closes at 5048.62, marking the beginning of the end of the dotcom boom (1590).
- December 2000: Tom Glocer is named head of Reuters, the first North American and non-journalist to run the group. He takes the helm in July 2001 (1150).
- May 2001: The group wins the battle for the assets of Bridge Information Systems, with a bid of £191 (990).
- July 2001: Reuters reports its first underlying loss as a listed firm. On Tom Glocer's first day, he axes 1340 jobs, earning the nickname of "Tom the Knife" (780).
- October 2001: Reuters warns that it will miss second-half sale forecasts for its biggest business. The group eliminates another 500 jobs (610).
- April 2002: Shares in Reuters sink, as the market digests the impact of lower sales at Instinet, its electronic share-trading subsidiary. The company faces shareholder revolt over a share option package for Tom Glocer (500).
- June 2002: Another 650 jobs are cut due to the slump in stock markets, and shares drop to nine-year low (420).
- September 2002: Reuters' terminals shut down temporarily because of a technological problem, enraging the financial community (320).
- October 2002: Moody's places Reuters' long-term debt under review for a downgrade; shares fall to an 11-year low (300).

On 5 November 2002, *Le Monde* diagnosed the company's problems as related to the state of the markets, its organizational structure, and its competition. The dot-com death caused a reduction in subscriptions, and the introduction of the euro cut the electronic courtage (commission) on exchanges, the Reuters cash cow. Poor positioning was also at fault, as Reuters concentrated on high technology rather than service to its clients. This problem opened the gates for its main competitor, the US company, Bloomberg (the *Financial Times* spoke of "terminal war", 17 October 2002). Thus, Glocer undertook a necessary restructuring, and *Le Monde* predicted a friendly merger in the not too distant future. Reed-Elsevier and Thomson Financial were mentioned as two possibilities.

On 15 May 2007, the Canadian firm, The Thomson Corporation, reached an agreement with Reuters to combine the two companies, in a deal valued at US$ 17.2 billion. Thomson now controls about 53 percent of the new company, named Thomson Reuters, the earlier rule of 15 percent ownership having been waived. The chief of Thomson Reuters is Tom Glocer, the former head of Reuters. As Pehr Gyllenhammar, Chairman of the Reuters Founders Share Company, explained, citing the poor financial performance of Reuters: the "future of Reuters takes precedence over the principles. If Reuters were not strong enough to continue on its own, the principles would have no meaning".[3] On 26 March 2008, shareholders of both organizations agreed to the merger, and the acquisition was closed on 17 April 2008. Headquarters are located on Times Square in New York, but unofficially London is still seen as the hub, as there are more journalists located there. "Thomson Reuters merger effective", declared the *Financial Times* on 7 August 2009.

Almost every major news outlet in the world still subscribes to Reuters company services. In the meantime, Bloomberg has become more similar to Reuters, in that it includes general news, and Reuters has become more similar to Bloomberg, even moving from "Lutyens-designed Fleet Street headquarters, with its plush boardrooms and hushed atmosphere" (*Financial Times*, 17 October 2002: 15) to an open-plan newsroom at Canary Wharf. The two companies remain competitors.

TT: A SHORT HISTORY

When TT celebrated its 50th anniversary in 1971, Swedish media scholar Stig Hadenius was asked to write its history. He traced the inception of the agency to a much earlier date, however – back to the first Swedish Telegram Bureau (SvT), created in 1867. "It happened in the same decade as the first train line was opened, four-tiered parliament was abolished, and *Dagens Nyheter* began to produce regular daily issues"[4] (Hadenius,

---

[3] See http://en.wikipedia.org/wiki/Reuters; last accessed 26 June 2011.
[4] Translations from Swedish are by the author.

1971: 16). The sources of inspiration were the German agency, Wolff, in Berlin and the Danish Ritzaus Bureau, the owner of which was also the owner of SvT. But by 1892 the biggest Stockholm newspapers had already decided to create their own agency: Swedish Press Bureau. The syndicate bought SvT in the same year.

During World War I, the distribution of news became a key element of war propaganda, causing many heated debates, emphasizing the need for unbiased news reporting, and leading, in Sweden, to the formation of three competing agencies that then build alliances with and against one another. In 1919 an alliance was constructed between SvT and the Nordic Press Central, which, in turn, comprised two agencies. The alliance took the name Associated Agencies (DFB), and in 1921 was taken over by a syndicate (again consisting primarily of Stockholm newspapers), and received the name Tidningarnas Telegrambyrå (TT, Newspapers' Telegram Bureau). Later the same year it merged with its only remaining competitor and became the sole news agency in Sweden.

The new agency experienced the same problems, and adopted solutions similar to those of many other European agencies. One problem concerned ownership. Should the state or any other individual owner influence the contents of news? Another problem involved the tensions between Stockholm and the rest of the country; between large and small newspapers; between the workers and the bourgeoisie; and, later, between German-friendly and German-hostile newspapers. The decision was to maintain a cooperative ownership, and to aim for objective and unbiased reporting.

In the beginning, TT had three newsrooms – foreign news, Stockholm news, and domestic news – only the latter two of which are of interest to me here.[5] The domestic newsroom collected information with the help of a network of correspondents, and distributed it to the newspapers around the country. The Stockholm newsroom collected information about births, marriages, and deaths, but also monitored the activities of central authorities. As early as 1910, there was a special parliamentary section and a commercial section that distributed information about stock market and foreign exchange.

The year 1924 saw the beginnings of Radio Service (the ancestor of Swedish Radio – SR), and TT's Managing Director was appointed to manage it too, thus starting the long cooperation between TT and SR. Between 1929 and 1938, many experiments were initiated with the use of the teleprinter, which, in the end, became the primary means of news

---

[5] Many others (see, for example, Hannerz, 1996; Boyd-Barrett and Rantanen, 2001) have described the most prestigious part of journalistic activity: the production of foreign news.

distribution. Distribution of the news to the newspapers had previously been accomplished by messengers or through the expensive method of telegraph, and later via telephone (people who read the news on the phone to up to five newspapers at once were called "criers"). As of 1937, TT also began sending foreign news via wireless broadcasting stations that formed part of the so-called Hell system,[6] and by 1938, 77 newspapers were connected to TT's teleprinter (Hadenius, 1971: 33). The agency had the monopoly on news only until 1947, but Swedish Radio did not begin to produce its own news until 1956 (Ewertsson, 2001: 104).

In 1947 TT acquired another newsroom: Sports. Two years later, the agency moved from its original site in the Kungsholmen district of Stockholm to a new skyscraper on Hötorget, in the center of the city. Before the move, TT's journalists were sent to foreign news agencies on reconnaissance, as the move also provided the possibility of restructuring production. Thus, it seems that the agencies did imitate one another early on; Reuters did imitate Agence Havas. A desk[7] system had been introduced, and a decision had been made to design the new office on an open plan, in order to facilitate cooperation. An archive was also created.

In 1970, Central Desk was created and larger sections of the newsroom were to be led by a superior editor (I call this function News Editor in this book) and a deputy. Each editorial office had a Desk Editor (a rotating post), and the Desk Editor of the national office had the last word on whether or not a telegram should be put into the teleprinter. As the material being sent constantly grew, it was soon necessary to open three teleprinter lines to avoid a backlog in the evenings. The first computers appeared, but originally only as an aid in producing teletypes, containing pre-composed telegrams, which the newspapers put directly into their setting machines. But not only technology was changing:

> In 1974 everybody [in the local office] did everything. We had schedules that meant that you could start working in the morning and stop working late at night. We were mostly reactive – we wrote small reportages, phoned the police and fire brigade often. But we tried to show some initiative, looking for exclusive sources, trying to tell the story better than anybody else could, trying to find our own news. It was mainly a school in how to write *a short piece quickly and on time*. . .
>
> I could see the difference when I moved to [local newspaper]. There, I was

---

[6] For more details on the Hell system, see http://www.nonstopsystems.com/radio/ hellschreiber-historyhtm; last accessed 30 June 2011.

[7] News desk refers to such editorial functions as assigning reporters and coordinating news. Originally a physical desk, it now refers to a computer desktop. Desk system means that the assigning and coordinating functions have been divided according to the type of the news, and Central Desk receives a superior coordinating function.

supposed to write a reportage, which was much more difficult than a short news text. Then and there I understood that these were two different ways of doing journalism. . .

So when I returned to TT, I wanted to continue to write longer pieces, to write colorfully, so that the texts should smell and be felt.[8] At that time we had something called "The day's short reportage", and I thought it was great to do it, because I could do what the older guys couldn't – I could go to the field, I could have a dialogue in my texts, I could tell stories about real flesh and blood people. (Int. 3/1)

But this is not how the official historian described TT's task:

As the central news intermediary, TT plays an important role of floodgate for the Swedish media. It is therefore appropriate to have a look at the principles that rule the selection of news at TT. . .

It is taken for granted that TT. . . offer an objective and unbiased news service. . . . These two concepts were the starting point for an investigation into the objectivity of news distribution conducted by Jörgen Westerståhl [a Swedish political scientist]. He divided those further into *truth and relevance* on the one hand and *balance and neutral presentation* on the other. (Hadenius, 1971: 55–7; italics mine)

How was it, then: flesh and blood or balance and relevance? In the sixth edition of *Mass Media* (1999), Hadenius and Weibull noted the "Americanization" of the Swedish news that had evolved over the past decades. One aspect was the "informalization" of the language used: from dry and official to colorful and filled with everyday expressions. The news producers began to heed US journalist Walter Lippmann's advice, formulated in 1922: good news should arouse emotions in its recipients and offer a possibility of identification. But whether this maxim applies even to news agencies, or, to the contrary, should be forbidden there, still remains a debatable point.

The 1999 *Mass Media* also contained the thesis that the new information technology was going to revolutionize news production. The authors also mentioned a new trend: attempts by various actors, both micro and macro, to influence the societal agenda through active participation in the news production. Furthermore, the news grew exponentially, and the news agencies had to reconsider both selection and presentation criteria. Hadenius and Weibull still called the people responsible for selection "gatekeepers", the term they applied to Desk Editors or News Editors. Nevertheless, they did notice that not even the news agencies were passively receiving information to be selected into news, but actively created

---

[8] Reuters' guide for journalists says that the texts should "sing" (see Chapter 5).

the news themselves. In addition, the term was not felicitous, as it gave an exaggerated weight to the role of one person. As to presentation, the number of news items and of competitors made the attractiveness of presentation important as never before. The role of pictures became greater.

The new information technology also meant that the newspapers, especially the large newspapers, seemed to be less dependent on TT. In the autumn of 1998, the large newspapers group questioned the ownership structure behind TT, and together with some provincial newspapers, formed an association, TT Intressenter, with the intention of taking over the cooperative. The same year, the long-existing Associated Province Newspapers (Förenade Landsortstidningar, or FLT) built a new news agency that was to service the non-socialist and the independent newspapers, including some of TT's owners.[9] As Hadenius and Weibull (1999: 332) commented on this turn of events: "Competition between the agencies at the end of the 1990s has many similarities with that of the 1920s; then as now both agencies are suffering losses".

A new version of the mass media textbook (Hadenius et al.) was released in 2008. It addressed many of the issues suggested in its predecessor, but also raised many new questions. TT won "the war" with FLT, which ceased to exist in 2000 (many of its employees moved to TT). The growing importance of pictures must have weighed in the decision to purchase Avisa (now TT Spektra) and the photo company Scanpix. The new textbook also contains a section on the Internet, dedicated largely to the phenomenon of blogging.

The authors note that commercialization continues (visible both in a greater adaptation to the demands of clients and in scarcer resources); news agencies become more like their clients, and the role of the gatekeeper diminished in importance. Another new section in Hadenius et al. (2008) is called "Feminine and masculine in the news flow"; clearly, gender has entered the news world (see also Chambers et al., 2004; Djerf-Pierre, 2005). The authors' observations are in tune with the public debate taking place within journalism, with the US at its center (see, for example, Epstein, 2000 or Darnton, 2008).

Many trends repeat themselves in new forms, or old tendencies coexist with new ones. The most visible changes concern technology. True, TT, like all other news agencies, was, from its very inception, dependent upon and followed developments in communication technology, but computerization and the emergence of the Internet gave it a new twist. I call it the *cybernization* of news production. To understand its range, one can

---

[9] The association was created in 1932, but was originally complementary to TT.

refer to a 30-year-old study by Lars Engwall, who studied "newspapers as organizations" and concluded that, with the exception of the presses, the automatization of newspaper work was low. At the time there was only one computer at the newspaper he investigated (1978: 65). What does the change consist of, apart from the exchange of artifacts – computers instead of typewriters?

> Now everybody is very fast all the time: all newspapers, Sweden's Radio, Sweden's Television, TV 4. We continue to try to be the fastest, but nobody used to be able to say how fast we were, because we were the only ones who sent directly. So now the pressure on us has increased enormously, as *we need to be revolver-quick. It's important to draw out and shoot, not so important to hit the target.* Some news distributors follow this principle, whereas we have to maintain our credibility, show that we are correct. . . But as speed is to be our trademark, one of our cornerstones, we have to work on the speed without uprooting the other cornerstones, which are credibility, correctness, impartiality. (Int. 3/2)

The Wild West metaphor that I italicized here alludes to the "Americanization" of the Swedish media, and creates an ironic distance to it. But the "revolver speed" image returned in many interviews, and it also became clear that information overload is not (any longer?) a problem or a challenge for the news producers. Speed is.

ANSA: A SHORT HISTORY AND RECENT DEVELOPMENTS[10]

The first news agency in Italy was called Stefani. It was created in 1853 at the request of Count Camillo Benso di Cavour, generally considered the founder of modern Italy; his goal was to match the popularity of other European news agencies such as Agence Havas in France, Reuters in the UK, and Wolff in Germany. In 1862, Reuters actually attempted to buy Stefani, but the bid was rejected as too low (Read, 1992: 54).

Stefani had a glorious history until the beginning of the twentieth century, when, after the birth of fascism, it was submitted to the requirements of the ruling regime. The end of fascism was the end of Stefani, and a new agency, Agenzia Nazionale Stampa Associata (ANSA) was created after World War II. ANSA was expected to act as one of the tokens of the renaissance of democracy in Italy. This new, post-war Italy had free

---

[10] The complete history of ANSA, also short but much more detailed, can be found in Protetti and Polli (2007). There is also a video by Francesco Siliato and Marco Dolcetta, *50 years of ANSA* (1995). Translations from Italian are by the author.

elections, a democratically elected parliament, and free newspapers –
and it needed a news agency that conformed to this set of institutions.
The agency was created on the model of Associated Press, with the help
and supervision of the Allied Forces. It presented its first news, distributed by a messenger boy, on 15 January 1945. Changes continued at an
amazing speed. I have divided them into changes concerning technology,
organizational structures, and the profession of journalism, although they
are, of course, closely interrelated.

Technology Runs Ahead

Changes in technology were especially visible in the change of speed in the
transmission of news:

> Once upon a time, the transmission of a photo required such a long time – ten
> minutes or more – that the prime minister's picture would appear at least an
> hour after he delivered his speech. Today, we can send a picture from the very
> site where the event is taking place. . . . Until 1970, the newswire could transmit
> at a velocity of 50 baud;[11] in 1980 we attained 300 baud. Previously, there was
> always a queuing of news items, sometimes for hours. Also, it was necessary to
> have a central unit that could decide the order of news. If there was an espe-
> cially important news item, it was sent ahead of the others. The news items were
> on perforated tapes that had to be exchanged. Now the system allows us to dif-
> ferentiate among items that are Urgent, Rapid, Flash, and Bulletin, *and it is the
> computer itself that sends the most important first.* (Int. 4/6)

As late as 1984, there were still typewriters in use, and the teleprinters
made a constant, terrific noise (Int. 4/3).

> Once upon a time we needed polygraphists who served the teleprinters, and
> ushers who delivered the mail, and criers. These jobs don't exist anymore;
> there's no use for them. . . . The largest developments are in the sales and tech-
> nology departments. We have a large technical staff, because they're needed to
> serve this complex machinery, which has diversified its products, which does so
> many different things. (Int. 4/8)

Like everywhere, it has been the Internet that introduced a true revolution:

> The Internet has changed our jobs enormously, and mostly for the better,
> especially via e-mail; faxes had to be completely rewritten, whereas e-mails can
> be copied. The problem, as I see it, is that it also limited the range of choices.
> Previously, because the faxes had to be written anew, only the most important

---

[11] The measure of the velocity of transmission. The name comes from Jean Maurice Emile
Baudot (1845–1903), who constructed the first multiple teletypewriter in 1874.

issues were quoted in full. Now, as you do copy and paste, many uninteresting things go in, on the principle that *given that we have it, we'll send it*. ANSA news items used to be limited to the quintessential, to a synthesis. Now we have fewer journalists, but the job has been augmented enormously. Because there are websites, because there's e-mail, because a flood of mail arrives every day – actually, checking mails is the most tiring job in Editorial. Then shortening items is even more tiring, because you have to read all of it. The end result is that many things are unnecessarily long, but it takes too much effort to do something about it . . . that's Internet for you. . . . (Int. 4/3)

Thus, the size of the agency makes a difference. Answering telephones was judged to be the most tiring job at TT as, apparently, it didn't receive as much mail – or else its automatic filter worked better. ANSA still receives paper faxes, while all faxes are converted into e-mail at TT. But the perception that the Internet has its pros and cons was common to all agencies. News producers are rarely blind enthusiasts of all that is digital, a common stance among other people adept in information technology.

Marketization

I prefer to speak of the "marketization" of agencies rather than their commercialization – the term commonly used in media debates – because agencies were always commercial, in the sense of selling their services and earning profits. Marketization has more to do with the assumption that markets offer the best organizing principles, and that a proper organizational form for an actor in the market is a company (Brunsson and Sahlin-Andersson, 2000). This development was as distinct in ANSA as it was in the other two agencies; after all, a cooperative is only a form of ownership – of a company. Still, the developments in ANSA have had their historical specificity:

Until the 1980s, the Italian newspapers weren't managed according to industrial criteria; they all had significant losses. It has been said that the newspapers were "the passive voice of the active companies", because historically the newspapers in Italy belonged to big companies. *La Stampa*, for example, belonged to FIAT, and so on. Thus, the Italians saw daily papers as the instruments of pressure, as representing certain parties. Well, perhaps FIAT was nobler, in that it allowed the newspaper to be run by its editors. But *Corriere della Sera*, the largest bourgeois paper in Italy, was liberal and enlightened; over the years, however, it passed from one owner to another. Now and then real battles occurred, because if you were the owner of *Corriere della Sera*, you obviously couldn't exploit it for your own purposes, but you could get special attention. This is why it's absolutely essential to fight for the freedom of press. Perhaps in other countries both the rules of the market and the journalist tradition are so strong that there's no reason to fight for them; if a newspaper doesn't produce impartial news, it won't sell. With us, there's always a danger that strong owners will censor the news because their interest isn't to sell the newspaper, but to protect their companies or their political parties. . .

The 1980s, however, witnessed several serious reconstructions of large industries, and the conditions for the newspapers changed, too; they began to be run as true companies. Slowly, they have even begun to make money. Nowadays the big newspapers such as *Corriere della Sera* and *La Repubblica* are cash machines; they sell books together with newspapers, and attract a lot of advertising. Thus, the management of a type used in industries became usual even in the world of information. (Int. 4/8)

It may be unexpected that the market is supposed to be saving news producers from partiality, but this opinion was actually not isolated, though expressed much more strongly in the Italian context.[12] That is another reason for my avoiding the label of "commercialization"; it was my impression that all news producers agreed that the news must sell, although they sometimes expressed critical views on the methods of selling suggested by their marketing and sales departments. The specifically Italian paradox is that by becoming "true companies", news producers risk conflicts with the true, well-established companies.

But the "company-ization" of news production proceeds globally (and is harshly criticized in, for example, the US; see Epstein, 2000). One of the elements of the construction of a "proper company" within this industry is the separation of the journalistic side – which ANSA refers to as "Editorial" – from the management or "Company" side, and an introduction of the market logic through and through:

We're now living according to the economic logic whereby the final value is the marginal utility of the product. Thus, multimediality, for instance, has become an important ground for the agency as such, due to the use of images. . . .

Nowadays we're probably better known for our website than for our newswire. At the time of Red Brigades, we were known because Red Brigades chose to send us their communiqués. Now we're known through our website, which is the second, or at least third or fourth most consulted Italian site. Thus, we're an important source of information in Italy. (Int. 4/2)

There are several such sources, as marketization also means exposing oneself to competition. In Sweden there are news agencies other than TT, but either they are small or they are local bureaus of large agencies such as Reuters, with which TT collaborates. As described previously, TT fought a battle in 2000 against a serious competitor – and won (the competitor invested too much money in the battle and went bankrupt). ANSA,

---

[12] A strongly differing view of the US media has been offered by Parenti (1986), who quoted many examples (mostly historical) of owners directly influencing news production.

however, needs to keep an eye on its competitors. One of the measures is for regional bureaus – Milan is doing it already – to send their news directly to the wire, thus gaining speed. But the competitors are not asleep, either:

> In recent years, the news race has intensified. Practically anything is transformed into breaking news, for instance. We try to limit this tendency, but other agencies, which have less potent technological means at their disposal, don't want to take the risk of coming out with their news after us. Thus, they transform everything into breaking news: "B. has started talking in the Chamber". Even a sarcastic joke uttered by political opponents is defined as breaking news. If you look at the screen, you'll see "breaking news" coming all the time. It happens that somebody finishes a speech, having made a rather complex political reasoning, and you get something like 50 "breaking news" items, but not even one article that would make sense of the speech. We try not to do it, but we have to do something, in order to be present. I must say that recent years have stirred the work at the agency. (Int. 4/9)

The race between agencies is one thing, but is it possible to beat the Internet? The future of news agencies can depend upon the credibility of their sources. News agencies can usually invest in new technologies more quickly than most of the newspapers can. After all, it was Reuters that was the first to use computers to transmit financial news abroad (see Chapter 5). The issue of competition remains central, though, and it is related to many other contemporary phenomena.

Dilution of News

It has been claimed that marketization has an especially strong effect on free professions (see, for example Scarbrough et al., 2005), and such is the case in journalism:

> Things changed, not only through technology, but also, and above all, in ways of writing. Earlier on, ANSA published only news that had been accredited, institutionally confirmed, from secure sources. Now we're supposed to check the sources, but we can also publish indiscretions, which was unthinkable a while ago. This has changed after Bribecity [a corruption scandal in Italy in the 1990s]; the scandal changed the way of doing journalism in general, because during that time there was nothing but indiscretions. Thus, at a certain point we stood in front of an alternative: either we publish nothing or we adapt. So we, too, started publishing indiscretions, but always from a secure source that wished to remain anonymous. We don't publish pointless gossip. But this has changed our work a great deal, making it more difficult, because before that, we had institutional sources, accredited, and we only transmitted a message. Not anymore. . . . But if we didn't adapt, we wouldn't remain on the market. (Int. 4/3)

Not only has the treatment of sources changed, but also the content of the news:

> Another problem that we share with other Italian agencies – actually, it has become a key problem in Italy – is that the newswire is less and less legible, as it contains too much noise. There are many reported events that have no political or economic relevance. This *dilution* happened mostly through the Internet and e-mail. . . . They send you statements that are very long, coming from sources that don't have any competence in the matter, have no political weight. Still, it's easier to take them and put them on the wire than to read them all, and either to throw them in the wastebasket than cut and edit them. It has reached the point where all the agencies have to manage it somehow, because the network of agencies becomes like the Internet, where there's everything, but you can't find anything. (Int. 4/9)

This non-management of overflow that is explicitly noticed here and the resulting dilution, have been posited only in ANSA. But there is no doubt that all agencies engage in the invention of new ways of managing overflow, by reorganizing the production of news, for instance. In this, ANSA is no exception:

> Until ten years ago all news was sent on the wire by one desk only. All the information flowed to that desk and the only task was to press the button, checking technical correctness, but not the contents. Now the process has been decentralized to specialized desks. Managing Editor now gives permission to publish directly on the wire even to the regional bureaus, as long as their information doesn't conflict with that sent by the others. This innovation is quite recent and is used very carefully as yet, as many would prefer to avoid the responsibility of direct publishing. But you must remember that Italy, unlike any other country, is full of news agencies, and our competitors publish less than we do, but often have an advantage because they have much slimmer organization structures. Therefore we need to recuperate some of the lost speed.
> When I say that they're slimmer, I mean that there are fewer persons who need to be consulted before you do anything. If I have only one boss, I tell that boss what I want to do, and if the answer is yes, I do it. But now, if I tell my boss that I want to do this or that, the answer is "Wait till I ask X", and X may want to talk to me, and so on and so forth. In the meantime, the competing agency has already sent the news. We must combine speed with accuracy, precision with good timing, and when you're big, this is somewhat difficult to do. (Int. 4/4)

In the case of Reuters (Chapter 5), decentralization seems indeed to be a favored solution to this problem.

Furthermore, like in Sweden, there is also informalization:

> When I arrived at ANSA in 1991, a unit called "trigger control" controlled the output. The staff of trigger control read all the news items incoming from ANSA in Italy or the rest of the world, and translated it into standardized language.

At that time, the official language was the language of ANSA. I remember that during my first year there was a convention of the Christian Democratic Party, and I wrote that the Party Secretary issued a "provocation" towards the president. The trigger control people called me up, and told me: "We must not say 'provocation', because this is already an interpretation. We must say 'statement' or 'utterance', that is, words that are neutral. Furthermore, we must not use adjectives, as adjectives imply a judgment".

Later, Managing Editor changed and the new one said, "No, we must not be so official, so formal, as if our words were cast in plaster, rigid. We have to tell stories, just as the newspapers do. A newspaper must be able to take our news and publish it as is".

Thus, we're not as perfectionistic, and the unit that standardized the news no longer exists. You must remember, however, that there were fewer news items in those days. Since computers came in, and a news item, once written, is immediately on the wire, there's no possibility of such minute control, and thus everybody is responsible for what they write. Still, I wish that somebody corrected my orthography mistakes. Not that I don't know my orthography, but I can make a typing error. . . (Int. 4/10)

In fact, most new software aims at introducing spell checks into the editorial system. As far as informalization is concerned, it has happened everywhere (perhaps with the exception of Reuters, which, from its inception, kept a somewhat irreverent tone), and the reactions vary from celebratory (flesh and blood instead of plaster) to warnings (we lose credibility) (Djerf-Pierre and Weibull, 2001). The reasons for these changes can be located partly in technological developments and partly in societal changes. Among the effects are the dilution of news, the increasing speed of transmission, the toughening competition, and the growing informality of the news. These were the main elements of the landscape in which ANSA functioned while I was doing my study.

COMMON TRENDS

There are at least two trends that are common to all agencies – marketization and cybernization. Later on, after having described the actual production of news in more detail, I will add a third one, connected to the two – cyborgization of the news producers. Here, I will focus on the two that can be deduced from the history of agencies.

Marketization is a trend recognized as characteristic for Western societies since the 1980s and the governments of Margaret Thatcher and Ronald Reagan, and intensified after the fall of Berlin Wall (Lanchester, 2010).

However, the postulate of cybernization, or growing automation of control of news production may go against claims such as those by Herbert Gans who, in the preface to a new edition of his seminal study

(Gans, 1979/2004) said that technological change has not been "as pervasive as often thought, especially by journalists. . . . the computer has altered news organization life less than elsewhere" (p. xv).

Gans is partly right in that computers had already entered news production in the 1970s, earlier than "elsewhere". Nevertheless, "many subtle changes" (p. xvii) are taking place, and technological inventions that were only seen as possible in 2004 have already happened. Additionally, Gans studied TV and newspapers, both still limited in space and time. The limitless newswire is truly an epochal change in the history of news agencies. Furthermore, by "cybernization" I do not mean simply a computerization, but as the term suggest, the growing *control* of production by computers, and especially by software.

Of interest is a development related to cybernization that has not been mentioned, neither by my interlocutors nor in the historical documents: the increased possibilities and, consequently, the intensified activities of monitoring. Yet in Boczkowski's studies, this "intensity and pervasiveness of monitoring" (2010: 62) was one of the central observations. The online producers of "hard news" interviewed by Boczkowski emphasized it; they didn't like it, because it led to a circularity of news production:

> "We all [participate] in a circle: they lift [the story] from there, we do it from here, and everything feeds [into the circle]" (personal communication, October 5, 2005).
>   Online journalists charged with producing hard news do not like this state of affairs because it conflicts with their core occupational values and sense of self. One does not usually go into the field of journalism to replicate someone else's stories. (Boczkowski, 2010: 74)

This difference in perceptions could be partly due to the fact that some of Boczkowski's material was collected in 2005; the news agencies probably had those monitoring opportunities even earlier, and had gotten used to them. Most likely, however, it illuminates an important difference between newspaper journalists and news agency journalists. The news agency journalists take it for granted that their task is, if not to replicate, then to edit someone else's stories: be it their own reporters', or anybody else's.

After these brief histories – partly agency-specific, partly parallel – I shall move to the description of the actual production process.

3. TT, or a day at work[1]

In this chapter I present what I see as a typical workday at a news agency. I have chosen TT as the example, because it is the smallest of the three organizations and therefore the easiest to present. The days at other agencies consisted of a multiplication of the activities described here. Strikingly, although the narrative focuses on single events as recounted by single persons (in interviews), it always depicts actions embedded in a much wider action net. Each action is connected to previous actions, to future actions, and many other contemporary actions.

THE LAYOUT OF THE FACTORY

Ownership and Organizational Structure

TT is a privately owned media syndicate comprising the parent company, Tidningarnas Telegrambyrå AB (TT), and the totally owned subsidiaries, TT Spektra and Scanpix. The owners of TT are the following newspaper companies:[2]

● Aftonbladet Hierta AB	20 percent
● Svenska Dagbladet AB	10 percent
● Stampen AB	10 percent
● AB Kvällstidningen Expressen	10 percent
● AB Dagens Nyheter	10 percent
● Sydsvenska Dagbladets AB	10 percent
● VLT AB	5 percent
● AB Östgöta Correspondenten	5 percent
● Norrköpings Tidningars AB	5 percent
● AB Uppsala Nya Tidning	5 percent

---

[1] I would like to thank all my interlocutors at TT, and my colleagues who found time in their busy schedules to comment on my text: Lennart Weibull, Monica Löfgren Nilsson, and Bengt Johansson. Many thanks to Barbara Covellin who offered me a roof over my head when research money was short. This chapter is based on the book containing a complete study of TT (Czarniawska, 2009c).

[2] See http://www.tt.se/detta/styrelse.asp; last accessed 25 November 2008.

- Pres(s)gruppen TT Intr. AB   5 percent
- MittMedia Förvaltn. AB   5 percent

TT delivers continuous newswire to its clients (the owners and the subscribers, which include other newspapers, but also other companies), offers a service called TT Monitor (covering world news) to many types of clients, and further services called Calendar and News Bank. TT Spektra produces complete websites, covers news concerning culture and entertainment, and a review of the media and TV programs. TT Scanpix sells moving pictures, photographs, and videos. My study focuses only on the newsroom Tidningarnas Telegrambyrå, which comprises:

- Stockholm: TT's telephone exchange and reception;
                Central Desk;
                Domestic News;
                Sports;
                Foreign News;
                Video;
                TT news on the phone;
                Marketing Department;
                Technical Department;
                Administration;
                Web on TT;
- Göteborg: Local bureau, ten persons;
- Malmö: Local bureau, eight persons.

Box 3.1 displays how TT presents itself on the Web. [3]
I focused my attention on Domestic News, but this meant that I also studied Central Desk and the local bureaus, which function slightly differently. The Göteborg bureau covers the geographic region that includes Värmland, Västra Götaland County, Jönköping County, and a northern part of Halland. The southern part of Halland belongs to Malmö, where there is an ongoing experiment – the introduction of Scania Wire, which will be sending independently of the main newswire. Geography, however, is not the main criterion for reporting the news; specialization overrules geography. Göteborg specializes in the car industry, for example, so a reporter from that local bureau will be sent to Frankfurt or Detroit, where the main car fairs are held.

---

[3] See http://www.tt.se/utl/eng.asp; last accessed 21 July 2009. The presentation is in English, but the TT news services are in Swedish only.

BOX 3.1   TT–MULTIMEDIA NEWS PROVIDER

Tidningarnas Telegrambyrå (TT) is the largest news agency in Scandinavia, and the only nationwide Swedish agency with a complete news service. TT provides Swedish news media with fast and accurate news around the clock, every day of the year. Most of Sweden's over 100 newspapers, as well as radio and TV stations, government offices, and private corporations, subscribe to TT's service.

We operate with an effective and very professional staff for news coverage of all sorts: domestic and international; sports, economy, and entertainment; for print media, radio, and TV, and all types of electronic media. . . .

TT employs around 140 people, most of them reporters and editors, and our subsidiary TT Spektra another 40. . . .

Technically advanced
TT prides itself in offering modern, flexible and highly reliable technical solutions for all customers. Two examples: We have been active internationally in developing technical standards for the news industry from the very beginning. And we were the first agency worldwide to offer a news-MMS service.

The Newsroom

Photos 3.1–3.9 introduce the reader to TT's newsroom, beginning with the entrance and ending with several specific details.

Co-workers: Those Who Talk and Those Who are Silent

As I mentioned in Chapter 1, I intended to present the non-human news producers as much as possible, but I was unable to achieve complete symmetry. It is somewhat difficult to interview a computer, although it is possible to interview avatars (see Gustavsson, 2005). I have also realized that, although I did not take the software for granted, I was unable to present its action with the same level of detail that I was able to achieve in a description of the work of human producers of news.

Photo 3.1   Entrance and TT's reception desk

Photo 3.2   Computers and other hardware, but also soft animals

Photo 3.3   People can choose to work standing or sitting

Photo 3.4   Coffee room, empty at that moment

Photo 3.5   Even in an open plan, there is some separation

Photo 3.6   Lots of screens

Photo 3.7   The ubiquitous Reuters

RS232	IP (KenCast)	FTP	NITFIN	Webbnyheter	S
09:58:12	09:58:22	09:58:20	09:57:00	(3170) Flicka vådasköts i huvudet	0
09:57:46	09:58:22	09:57:52	09:56:36	(3168) Polisen kritiseras efter massaker	0
09:57:42	09:58:06	09:57:50	09:56:32	(3169) Banker lyfter börsen	0
09:55:06	09:55:25	09:55:10	09:53:54	(3167) Stormbyar drar in över Sverige	0
09:53:44	09:54:04	09:53:50	09:52:34	(3166) 69 örnhäckningar i Norrbotten	0
09:47:28	09:47:38	09:47:32	09:46:16	(3165) Fogh seglar i medvind	
09:41:40	09:42:00	09:41:46	09:40:28	(3164) Browns "Kiss" fortfarande USA-etta	

Photo 3.8   The newswire documented on a screen

How does one become a news producer?

News producers are, almost without exception, journalists by training (a few have different degrees). What characterizes them all, however, is that they learned their job through practical experience and became more and more specialized in news production over time.

Photo 3.9   A bit of everything, only the human being is missing

As I wanted to learn more about recruitment and selection, I asked if they would think of employing me at TT:

> Well, you could be employed if we had reason to believe that you're able to grasp what we're doing here, that you're able to ask the right questions. It isn't very likely that you could get the job just because you happened to have a fresh degree in journalism – you would have to have apprenticed somewhere before. Then I would probably know the News Editor at that place, and I would call and ask him or her. If the answer were, "This is a very good candidate", then perhaps we would risk employing you. But that would be a stand-in job at first. To get properly employed you would have to have a solid job experience. (Int. 3/2)

Such a procedure is not a sign of favoritism, but of a deeply grounded belief that practical skills are critical. No CV, no interview, can guarantee that a person knows or can learn this job. There are certain elements of formal training, but even those are meant to complement knowledge and skills already possessed:

> We have an introduction for the newcomers. But even this aims mostly at checking whether or not they have an idea how we work, that we look for big news, and that we send out a small piece first, because *it is speed that matters*. So if you're going to cover a press conference, you need to know that they'll give you a press release ten minutes before, and then you need to take a look and decide what could be the most important thing in it. So then you call here and tell this to your News Editor or somebody at Central Desk. . . .

And then the editor will say, for example: "OK, write a piece, it seems like it is worth 1200 characters, and put this and that angle on it". And then you do it and we can see whether it is good or not.

This is how it usually begins. If what you have written has inspired confidence, you'll get another, more difficult task. If you can't manage it, you may get something simpler, or else quit. (Int. 3/2)

Apart from one of many confirmations that speed is central, this explanation shows that the job itself is both a test and a training opportunity. One shows one's talent by performing a task, but the performance is also a way of learning how to perform this task. This seemed to me to be a bit too complicated. How can one know how to do something one has never done? By watching others doing it, of course. But is that even possible?

BC: How can you learn what to do if you can't see what your colleagues are doing?
3/2: But you *see the results* all the time! Besides, we're very open with and helpful to each other. You can turn to somebody sitting next to you and say, "Listen, this is what the News Editor told me, but I'm not sure what she meant. What do you think?" Hopefully, your neighbor will be in a good mood – most of us are, most of the time – and will say, "Try to do it this way".

Thus, the product shapes the process, not the other way around. This happens not only at the person-to-person level, but also at the agency-to-agency level: the flow of production is deduced from the characteristics of the product.

Observe also: "most of us are in a good mood" – a remark that will return many a time. And the explanation continued thus:

Of course, one has learned this and that at the school of journalism. But one continues to learn from one task to another. So you have written your piece and say to your colleague: "Have a minute to take a look?" And she does and says: "I don't see what's supposed to be so interesting about it". . . . "I see, you're right. I'll re-write it'. And when the text is ready, you send it for editing to the Central Desk. There sit people who have done nothing but read news all day long for many years, and they can tell you if it's good or not – even if they're very kind to you who are new. (Int. 3/2)

I had some problems with this description. Not for the first time, I seemed to detect some circularity in the process:

BC: Does it not imply some kind of conservatism: the old hands teach the new ones, whereas the language changes all the time. . . .?
3/2: Well, yes, there is some risk of that, but we try not to be set in our ways. It's the gut feeling, you know, that tells you, "This here is done in a completely new

way, but it seems good, we should keep it!". . . . We have several templates that mostly point out the things to bear in mind, but no booklet called "This is how one writes a TT article".

Here is the first mention of the non-human collaborators ("several templates"), but there are more human co-workers and some quite formalized teaching occasions:

> It's often H, the veteran on the desk, who teaches the newcomers. She's very good at all the details, especially language details. She has worked as an editor for a long time. (Int. 3/11)

The preference for this type of learning process naturally creates many opportunities for trial-and-error:

> We [the two new editors] came together during the reorganization at TT. We were actually allowed a free hand to decide how we want to work. There was no one who told us, "This is the way to do it!" Management simply told us that they want it to be done well, smoothly, and quickly, so we did as we thought best.
>
> We tried various ways, until we could see which way worked best – that is, we learned who had the best insight into what, who was the most experienced in what, what times were best, etc. So our way of working developed over time. (Int. 3/4)

Up to that point I was attending to how TT chooses its collaborators, but there is another side of the coin. How do people decide to work for a news agency? By choosing to study journalism, they have already demonstrated their interest in the news, but there are newspapers, radio, TV, and the Web – why TT? Here is a typical answer:

> The reason I landed here is that when I was working as a stand-in I decided that this was a great place to work . . . good atmosphere, job that is fun, good co-workers – to make it short. (Int. 3/7)

I try to demonstrate in this text that this is not merely a workplace that happens to have a good organizational climate, but that this is a workplace that *must have a good climate* in order to function. Most of the people working here actually *are* usually in a good mood.

Newsrooms at news agencies are good representations of what Bastin (2003) called "worlds of production"[4] – sites that can be distinguished by the dominant activity and its product, and not by actors that can be

---

[4] A concept close to my "action net" (Czarniawska, 2002).

identified a priori. Specific positions and roles do exist, but they are largely exchangeable. This is also in contrast to Gans's (1979/2004) description of the near-military hierarchy of news production in newspapers and TV, as I will describe in the next section.

Positions and roles

General Manager/Editor-in-Chief is rarely involved in the daily production of news. A person in this position manages TT as any other company would be managed: taking legal responsibility and being in contact with the owners and the environment in general. The highest position within the news production is that of Managing Editor.

News Editors are sometimes called *assigning editors*; they decide who is going to do what and what should be done, who is to have contact with the correspondents in this role, and who are to coach the correspondents. News Editor and his or her deputy have similar roles – in fact, they often work in shifts. They are supposed to lead their desks, to take initiatives, and distribute tasks. They also have personnel and administrative responsibility for the people working at and for their desks.

Then there are *publishing editors* – those who say, "'Yes, this is ready for publishing', or 'No, we need to work more with this', or 'We should pay more attention to this issue and less to that one'"(Int. 3/3). The person in charge of Central Desk, where all the news is eventually sent, also has a coordinating role:

> I need to see that we don't miss important things . . . and that we set the right priorities. Theoretically, I approve all that is going to be published, but naturally, I have no time to see everything, so I delegate it to my collaborators, who would raise the alarm if something were doubtful, or at any rate if they think I should check it in person. It can happen that I take really sensitive issues to our Managing Editor who may take them up to Editor-in-Chief. (Int. 3/3)

News Editors in local bureaus are both News Editors and Managing Editors; their budgets, however, are decided in Stockholm. Once a month local News Editors leave their assigning duties to somebody else and undertake administrative duties.

In fact, although there are stable positions, most roles rotate most of the time. So, each desk has a rotating position of Desk Editor, who checks all the incoming news and sees to it that nothing gets lost.

Morning Editor has a morning shift at Central Desk before the rest of the editors come in. He or she assigns tasks to Morning Reporter, a generalist who can work with a variety of tasks that can be done quickly (in contrast to News Desk reporters who may be involved in long-term projects).

Evening Editor has a similar function, but in the evening, after most of the editors and reporters have left. He or she collaborates with Evening Reporter. Evening Editors work five days and are free for the next four. Night Editor keeps the watch during the night.

Gate-and-Diary person[5] checks TT's general mailbox and either sends the items that seem interesting to the basket of Desk Editor or deletes them. The main task associated with that position is "to raise the alarm when something important comes across, then shout: 'Check this! Check what has happened! We've received this press release that's clearly very important. Did we know that?'" (Int. 3/5). (It needs to be added that "shouting" here is mostly metaphorical: I haven't heard a voice raised in the newsroom.) The same person keeps the schedule of coming events, which is the basis for the work of Planning Editor. Planning Editor – and there is one for the entire TT – plans for the future and ensures that all important events are covered.

Reporters, editors, and Web editors are specialized, but they can also rotate their tasks, especially at Central Desk. "As it is now, most of the people working at Central Desk work on a rotating scheme, so that one is a reporter one week and a Web editor next" (Int. 3/11). Indeed, one of the most striking aspects of news production is its seemingly perfect interchangeability of tasks. This also means that anyone promoted to a managerial position has likely worked several times in the role of News Editor when the actual NE was absent or otherwise occupied. There are, however, some persons who specialize in only one type of job and are left to it – simply because they are exceptionally good at it.

Silent co-workers
Upon entering TT, I was fully prepared to encounter computers and tele-phones, but what struck me first were the stacks of notepads in the cor-ridor. Everybody I talked to had one, and those I talked to repeatedly had a new one every time we met. These notepads played an important role in memory building:

> I don't remember what we were talking about during yesterday's meeting because I took a new notepad today so I don't have my notes from the meeting. . . (Int. 3/2)

It usually takes me a year to finish a college-type notepad, but, following the lead at TT, I acquired and used several during my project – although

---

[5] Although this is can be seen as a translation of the English "gatekeeper", it has nothing to do with the metaphorical function (usually ascribed to News Editors); my interlocutors used the latter term in English only.

not the big A4 that people at TT used, but the smaller A6 that could be held on my knee. Notepads may seem antiquated in a thoroughly computerized environment, but it needs to be remembered that most people still write more quickly on paper than on a keyboard, as the owners of electronic agendas well know.

Notepads are empty, to be filled, but there were also ready-made texts that had the memory-carrying function:

> Those who are employed full-time write what we call a crib or an instruction for those who come in later. This is the easiest way to transfer information to a stand-in. (Int. 3/3)

Apart from such informal texts, there are more formal ones, such as "TT language", to be found on the Web. There are also aid texts produced each day, but I describe those later under the category of semi-manufactures.

Then, of course, there are machines, but before I move to computers, I need to pay more attention to telephones and mobile telephones. These are seen as essential in the work of traders (Renemark, 2007), but they are at least as important in the work of news producers, whose telephone skills are incredible; they can talk into two phones while exchanging remarks with their colleagues. At the Italian news agency, ANSA, it took me several days to be able to understand who they were actually talking to (it was easier at Reuters, because they were more formal on the phone). The much-discussed "multitasking" acquires a new meaning in this context – or perhaps a new term, something like "multiconversation" is required to cover the use of phones at news agencies.

As for computers, they were countless: big and small, visible and hidden – 35 percent Macs, used especially by picture people, and 65 percent PCs. As the photos already revealed, screens covered the walls: TV screens, Bloomberg screens, Reuters screens, TT screens, and so on. And at each writing desk there were at least two computer screens:

> I have three screens on my writing desk: one Reuters screen, and the two I'm working on. My computer has two screens, so on one I can check various websites and on the other I have my own work list. It isn't my main task to watch Reuters, but I do it because it's such fun to see their flow and see what's happening. . . . You may think that we publish lots of things, but Reuters publishing is grotesquely big. They send hundreds of news items every minute. It just rattles on this screen. And it could be about anything. It is incredibly fascinating to watch this screen. (Int. 3/5)

Just keep in mind that this person watched but one window; when at Reuters, I had at least four windows open on the same screen, and that was few compared with the number I could have had. But what can be seen on TT screens?

> We obviously have one program that we use to work with the texts, to edit the texts, and to publish the texts. Within this program there is quite a lot of room to set it up and adapt to one's own needs and preferences. Apart from this program that we all use to be able to work together, we're free to use any other software that we find helpful. (Int. 3/5)

"Publishing" means "sending to the newswire". Quite a few terms from the past were still used – the conventional meaning of this particular term has changed at present, although it still signifies "make public", albeit not by printing. In fact, people at TT still spoke of the "telegrams" they were receiving, meaning e-mails.

The common program mentioned by my interlocutor can be found on the Intranet, together with internal telephone lists and various kinds of templates. Some templates are technical and are arranged according to their contents: how to write a New Version, Afternoon Version, Corrections. The Intranet also contains a personnel handbook with TT's main policies concerning such issues as equality, journalistic strategy, drug-and-alcohol policy, and so on. There is also a link to TT's archive – in other words, "all that one needs to manage one's job at TT".

The editorial program used at TT when I studied it was called DEWAR; the software originated from Dell, but was adapted to TT's needs. Soon, however, it was to be exchanged:

> The present system is old fashioned and lacks the necessary functions for working rationally with texts and pictures. The new system will improve efficiency and will allow different types of materials – texts, pictures, sound, and video – to be incorporated into the same news. (Int. 3/2)

An editorial program contains certain templates, and the wish was that the new one would contain even more:

> The eternal problem with all kinds of writing is that those who write will write more than the reader is prepared to read. I'd like to see stricter controls on the size of the texts. Today we have oral instructions, but I'd like to see them mechanically enforced. We have that in part: the leads mustn't be longer than a given number of characters. If they're longer, the letters become red, and it isn't possible to publish the text. I'd like to see more of this. (Int. 3/3)

The exchange of the editorial system was an operation taking place in all three agencies. The old systems were similar, too. On DEWAR, one could see the texts coming in to be edited; texts being edited; texts sent between different desks; and of course texts that were sent to the newswire. Texts are sitting in "Baskets".

Last but not least is the Internet. It is used to view the websites of all the main newspapers, to access search engines, and for various services of special use in news production. The most common is the RSS reader,[6] a program that signals updates of selected websites.

TT subscribes to the news service, WIGHS, as well. WIGHS is offered by a company situated in Norrköping; its employees listen to the police radio and inform subscribers when something newsworthy is happening. "When we receive the information, we immediately call the police or SOS in order to learn how big it is" (Int. 3/7).

Anybody can subscribe to such services, so in principle anyone could start a news agency. But when one of the main newspapers, *Dagens Nyheter*, tried to do just this, it soon became obvious that it was an extremely trying, effort- and money-consuming activity. It is, of course, a matter of size – big Italian and UK newspapers do have their own news agencies, but also subscribe to ANSA and to Reuters.

Measured in time, most of the news production is accomplished with the help of DEWAR and telephones. They are the actual collaborators. A technology that plays a smaller role (compared with the newsrooms in newspapers) is the recorder. It is used mostly by reporters who have one or another type of MP3 player. The favorite is Olympus LS-10, which handles even Waveform Audio File Format (WAV) and Windows Media Audio (WMA) files.

The most valuable machine, however, is invisible (at least, I haven't seen it): Dell's server WIN2003 – not to forget the satellites, but I set the limit to my study before those.

THE PRODUCTION OF NEWS

Input–Output

To begin, I describe the production process in terms borrowed from open system theory. Lars Engwall (1978) used a similar model to describe newspapers as organizations, but in contrast to his study, I use the terms as a structuring rather than an analytical device. Thus, any production can be described as a process in which things that enter the system (input) become transformed – indeed, processed (throughput) into products that

---

[6] RSS actually stands for "RDF Site Summary", but is commonly called "Really Simple Syndication".

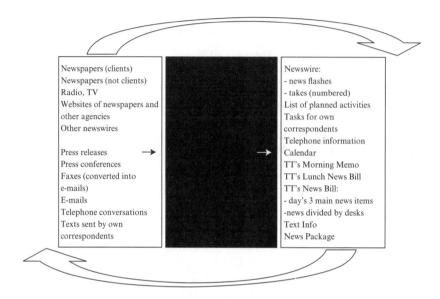

Figure 3.1   TT's inputs and outputs

then exit the system (output). In the next section, throughput remains a black box, which I open in the section that follows it. Nevertheless, it is already possible to glimpse the circularity of the news production, an observation that will be corroborated in all three studies. The TT journalists receive inspiration from the texts produced by their customers, and, far from merely sorting out the incoming overflow of information, they actively order and produce even more information for themselves.

The contents of TT's main product – the newswire that is sent to the clients via the satellite – can be seen as a semi-manufacture, in that the client newspapers are free to rewrite and reformulate the news. An interviewee from one of the client newspapers estimated that they produce about 300 000 characters a day; they produce 200 000 themselves and obtain 100 000 from TT.

Figure 3.1 is a schematic picture of TT's production process, which, although simpler than those of ANSA and Reuters, contains all the main elements of news production.

Throughput: Looking into the Black Box

What follows is a fictive day at TT – fictive in the sense that it comprises many days and many narratives. It is a weekday, as weekends are less intensive at TT. Most events take place at TT's head office in Stockholm, but I also report events at a local bureau. The narrative is woven from many voices that report on their own and their colleagues' work, with my own voice added now and then.

23.00–07.00

Night Editors' shift. The morning papers are delivered to TT the previous evening, so if one of the main newspapers has interesting news, Night Editor makes a so-called clip, which means that the news is re-written and the source is quoted.

This is what happens at the local bureau, which is also open during the night:

> The person who sits here calls all the newspapers in our geographical region. It's part of their contract to send us their best news, so they send an e-mail, or some of them still send a fax – and Night Editor writes it, so it can be put on the 01.30 newswire. Those newspapers see it not only as a service to us, but also a service to themselves: most of them are very keen on having their clip on TT, as the source can be seen. We write "TT" first, but then we add *"Halland News"*, and they see it as an advertisement. Naturally, they have a better idea about what happens in their part of the country. So that at 01.30 one can hear bump! on the TT's newswire and out come lots of such night clips. (Int. 3/9)

Night Editors at Central also phone the communication centrals of every county, according to a special schedule: 01.00 to Southern Sweden, 02.00 to Central Sweden, and so on.

06.00

The local bureaus open for the day. One reporter comes in, together with an apprentice.

Morning Editor and Morning Reporter come to the Central Desk in Stockholm. The Editor meets Night Editor who is still there, and asks if there is anything that requires immediate attention. Then Morning Editor and Morning Reporter listen to the radio news, and watch the TV news. If something "big" happens, they start working with it immediately – it's important to be first. Thus, they check the availability of local reporters, or activate their own. "Our main journalistic strategy is to be first" (Int. 3/5).

Morning Editor opens a computer and DEWAR, the shared platform with texts to be edited, and also the newswire and the website. The Editor's view of the wire and the website differs from what the clients see: it shows times, priorities, and other internal information. TT Archive serves as a backup, as one can check whether or not a news item has already been sent there. Morning Editor also reads Evening Editor's "Testament".

The Testament contains a list of things done – and not done – during the previous evening, together with Evening Editor's commentary:

> Evening Editor accounts for what has been done and for thoughts about it, so that continuity is maintained. After all, we are all individuals, and can have differing opinions about many things. Evening Editor could have written: "We didn't make a clip of the debate reported by *Dagens Nyheter* because the investigation it's based upon isn't well described. We don't know how it was done, how many people were asked, when, where, how. Somebody must call them during the day and ask". But perhaps I read the same article and notice that all this is in fact explained. Then there is nothing to prevent me from saying: "No, we *are* going to report this". Still, it's good to know my predecessor's reasoning. (Int. 3/8)

Next, Morning Editor starts preparing the coverage list, a Morning Memo that will be sent to the clients at 08.00. Even the memo was started the evening before, but under the heading: "Good morning! Today we expect to be able to offer following texts:. . . ." There is only empty space as yet. But there is a list (composed on the basis of the Calendar) under the next heading: "We plan to cover the following press conferences and other events and will write about them if we deem them newsworthy:. . .". Morning Editor can remove some points from the list if he or she thinks they are not interesting enough. Thus, while the list under the first heading grows, the list under the second shrinks. An additional help is a work list, also prepared the previous day, which shows who is available and who is not.

06.30
Web Editor (who works at Central Desk) comes in.

06.45
News Editor 1 comes in. She has already read three main newspapers and listened to the radio news at home. Once in the office, she reads Evening Editor's Testament and checks her e-mail. Then she looks at the websites of her choice, on TT's newswire, and at what the local newspapers have sent (their "best service"). Next, she checks Reuters economic news (the period of my study coincided with the beginning of the financial crisis in the US). After that, she takes a look at the evening papers (which arrive in the morning nowadays), and at the *Financial Times* and *New York Times*. Then she talks to Morning Editor about what has happened during the previous couple of hours.

7.00
A Text Editor who works at Central Desk comes in.

Local News Editor comes in and checks what happened during the evening and the night before, as well as previous plans for the day. After that, he sends a memo that would be included in the general Morning Memo from TT. He also sends a work list internally, showing who should be doing what during the day. The recipients of the work list include two freelance photographers who work for Scanpix and a locally based graphic artist from a company in Stockholm.

07.45

Central Desk Editor comes in. She has already listened to the news on radio and TV, and now she talks to the other editors about the events of the previous evening and night. Morning Editor presents Morning Memo for discussion to Central Desk Editors, News Editors and Local News Editors.

This description led me to conclude that the same topics, the same discussions, are repeated several times:

> Absolutely, in this way we can check everything several times. There are themes that are literally repeated, but very often something is added or subtracted. I see it as an advantage; this way we are sure that we don't miss anything. It happens that when News Editor comes in, she says, "I've listened to the radio news at 06.00 and they were talking about X. . . Why didn't you guys do anything? This is very interesting, because. . . etc". So then we can change our previous judgment. It's an activity that rolls on, it goes on continuously, and yes, there are repetitions, but these are not static repetitions; they constantly develop, move this way or that way, are filled with details and drained of others. And what I thought very interesting in the morning, what I believed we needed to put forward, can be of no importance later on. Perhaps News Editor, who just came in, points out that this topic has been already addressed three weeks ago, but I haven't noticed. We constantly discuss what we should do and what we must not do, and I think this is fun. I wouldn't want to work in a place where there were no such discussions or they were suppressed. (Int. 3/7)

08.00

A TV reporter and a photographer come to the local bureau (the deadline for the TV feature is at 13.00).

Morning Editor at Central Desk sends Morning Memo, containing the list of articles that are to be written that day, and the list of events that are to be covered. The memo ends with a following sentence: "Questions concerning Morning's Memo will be answered by Morning Editor NN, phone:. . . Newsroom's e-mail address is redaktionen@tt.se". The memo is usually exactly on time, so it arrives before the morning meeting at the newspapers.

Between 08.00 and 09.00, economic news flows into TT. In comes the information from the Financial Supervisory Authority (FSA), for example, telling that the investor popularly called "the king of porno" has bought shares in the football league, AIK:

> He himself has been claiming this, but there was no evidence. But today FSA confirmed it, so we immediately started calling round. It's a sensitive matter – AIK does not want him as a big shareholder. There was a lot of writing around the matter before it became known that he really bought a block of shares that makes him the biggest shareholder in AIK. There were a great many protests from, for example, AIK's women's team. But he did it.
>
> In such a situation, News Editor must immediately find somebody to start calling people who might say something interesting. . . They literally need to hunt, because at that time a great many people are not in their offices yet, or one does not have their mobile numbers, although nowadays it's easy to find people's home numbers.
>
> The point is to insist and find as much as possible, as many comments as possible, as many new facts as possible – no matter what we write about – and keep trying, because the situation changes and thus the story can go on. But it must also happen as quickly and as smoothly as possible. It must be quick, but it must be correct. This is what is most important early in the morning. (Int. 3/5)

Observe that the problem here is not an overflow of information, but an "underflow": the agency needs to create more information at the input.

After having seen to the problem, Morning Editor can take a breather and do something else: check other websites, edit texts, check the Central Desk Baskets, answer the phone, take a look at RSS, see if there is a text that has been forgotten.

08.30
News Editor 2 comes in. He logs in, reads his mail and evening newspapers that have already arrived (he reads the morning newspapers at home), and tries to figure out how the day will be. He or News Editor 1 calls the local bureau in Northern Sweden: "sometimes they have their own agenda . . . pay attention to things that are relevant only over there. But it also happens that I assign them some tasks from here, tasks that have a local connection" (Int. 3/5).

Reporters come in. Those who will not be engaged in the "porno king" story will take care of other matters. One receives a task to check stock markets in the US and Asia on Bloomberg, in order to compare them to the Stockholm Exchange, which just opened.

08.45
Managing Editor comes in. She has already checked her e-mail before going to bed, and listened to the radio, watched TV, and read the main newspapers in the morning. Now she reads what has been put on the wire

when she was still at home and forms an opinion on what was good and what was bad (or less good):

> We're bad when we're slow, when it's badly written, when our clients have big news that we haven't written about. . . The opposite is good: we have good texts; we contributed to the fact that certain news became widespread; we've been very quick; we've had good interviews; we've been informative in the material attached to the news; and our clients were pleased with us when they were working on their news page last evening. (Int. 3/2)

09.00

Yet another Text Editor comes to Central Desk. News Editors meet "their" reporters. They discuss "what the previous day was like, what we did and what we didn't do, what we could've done better, and what we did well" (Int. 3/4). They already have a work list that they started to write the day before and update in the morning. If this is a "thin news day", reporters share their ideas about what they could work with in the future.

A meeting at the local bureau takes place when one or two more reporters come in. The meeting is dedicated to evaluating the previous day and planning the next one.

09.30

Morning meeting in Stockholm: Central Desk Editor meets all News Editors and Local News Editors via teleconference, as well as the representatives of Scanpix, TT TV and Graphics. Managing Editor listens.[7] It begins with the evaluation of the previous day, and I ask once more what "good" and "bad" means:

> It could be very different things, depending on the context. It can mean that we were slow; somebody was quicker; we were too late to notice that some news items were going to be important. We've perhaps underestimated the power of a given story, which means that we did not do enough of it. And good is exactly the opposite: we were quick; we saw the power of the story immediately; we called and talked to the right people; we sent a reporter to the place immediately; and it resulted in good, well-written texts. (Int. 3/7)

The criteria seem to be interconnected, yet the speed dominates – an excellent text delivered late loses its impact by the delay.

Then the News Editors present what they believe will be the most important news of the day. But, "when nothing special happens, the answer to the question 'What is the day's best news?' will be 'Hard to say'"

---

[7] At ANSA it is Managing Editor who usually chairs the meeting.

(Int. 3/8). Central Desk Editor and Managing Editor check that nothing is missing, and express opinions on how things should be written, and on what is more and what is less important. How is this decided?

> It depends completely on what it is. After all, we are sitting – all day long – in *a fusillade of information and events*. But somehow one develops this sense for. . . one feels directly [snaps fingers] that this is nothing to write about – and this is obviously something to write about.
> Some things are already known, these are important events that just acquire new details; others are new but easy to judge. But there are a great many in between – on the one hand, perhaps we should write about it; on the other hand, perhaps not. (Int. 3/2)

The importance of tacit knowledge is, in fact, more likely to be acknowledged than is the role of the machines in the news production. "Gut feeling" seems to be a major mechanism of overflow management at the input.

In the meantime, News Editor 2, who does not participate in the meeting, follows the reporters, checking if they know what to do, if they can access background material, if they have telephone numbers of the people they should call.

09.50
News Editors and Local News Editors return to their groups and inform reporters and editors of the meeting's results.

10.00
A small meeting at Central Desk, now fully staffed. Central Desk Editor reports the 09.30 meeting:

> He goes through all that we need to discuss, reports what was judged good and what bad, what we missed, what we could have done better, what are the lessons to learn. He reminds us that, for example, the court will hand down a noteworthy sentence at 11.00 or that there is a significant press conference that we need to cover, so that all collaborators have complete knowledge of what is going on. Are there any important or sensitive journalistic issues that we need to discuss before a text is published? After all, Central Desk is the last instance where the news from TT is inspected. (Int. 3/7)

Reporters go to press conferences, or start calling people or begin to write their texts.

10.00 (Mondays only)
TV meeting: Managing Editor meets TV group.

10.00 (Thursdays only)

Business meeting (for managers only).

10.15

Central Desk Editor checks other media websites and asks News Editors if they are planning to make use of any news there.

10.30

News Editors begin to work with Lunch News Bill:

> After we've had our morning meeting, after we've assigned all the jobs and checked what should be done, and inspected all the flow that came in, it's time to sit down and write the texts we'll write today. I make a list, a short list of all the news that we know will be written today. We don't put short news items on the list, only those that will become texts, and they need to be ordered according to their importance. Those that have been flashed[8] are on the top, and the rest follows. Domestic News Editor does it first, then come Foreign News, and local bureaus send theirs. Central Desk puts them all together and sends on the wire as TT's Lunch News Bill.
>
> The purpose is to let the clients know what they can expect. If it's a day when counties and municipalities present their economic prognoses, all municipal newspapers will publish a story "How are we doing in our municipality?". But they also want to have a national situation from TT. Thus, they learn from the Lunch News Bill that we are going to do it, and what angle we are proposing to take.
>
> It also gives an opportunity for our clients to say if something is missing or something else they want. Unfortunately, they seldom do it. I don't know whether it means that they are satisfied or that they are despondent. At any rate, this is a pointer for them, so that they know what we're doing. It often happens that the smaller newspapers don't do anything themselves, as they know they'll get a text from TT. (Int. 3/4)

11.00

Morning Editor goes systematically through what came to Central Desk. It is between 11.00 and 11.30 that many texts come in:

> On the one hand, there are those texts coming from the reporters that I and other editors at Central Desk read; we decide if something should be done to them before they are put on the wire; on the other hand I need to keep an eye on other news sites – is there something reported there that we don't have? The phone rings: people come with various tips. We have the same telephone number, all of us at Central Desk, so there's always somebody who answers. It could be the clients on the other end, or other subscribers who want to know exactly when some text or another will arrive, if we are going to write about this

---

[8] A one-line news report, called "Alert" at Reuters.

or that detail, if there'll be enough background so the readers can understand the whole thing. So there are quite a lot of things to do.

The main part of the work consists of work with the computer – at least five hours. But we talk to one another as well. If you sat with us at Central Desk you would notice that there is actually a continuous discussion about what we should write, how we should write, and how we should deal with this or that issue. There's a journalistic debate that goes on without interruption.[9] (Int. 3/7)

Local bureaus deliver their News Bills to Central Desk.

11.15–11.50
Central Desk Editor sends out Lunch News Bill. News Editors in Stockholm and in local bureaus see to it that the work "rolls on":

Sitting here, I feel like a *dispatcher* in a truck centre; there's one reporter here and another there, and then there's the TV photographer over there, and another photographer over here, and all this must be planned and coordinated, while I must be monitoring the inflow – is there something coming in that we need to attend to immediately, or can it wait? Or can we even ignore it? I'm making such decisions every minute, because it's every minute that new mails arrive. And if that wasn't enough, I also need to think about what will happen tomorrow. See that we are properly staffed even in the days to come. . . . So it's a continuous flow, with a multitude of – often very small – but still very many decisions. And a lot to take away. (Int. 3/9)

A flow, but not an overflow, at least not openly admitted. Apparently, it is well managed, even if it is a hectic job.

11.30 (every other Monday)
Company managers meet Editor-in-Chief.

12.00–14.00 (every other Monday)
Corporate meeting: strategic and general issues, finances, and technology. General Manager (Editor-in-Chief) chairs the meeting, and participants, apart from TT's managers, are Managing Directors of Scanpix and TT Spektra.

13.00
Central Desk Editor prepares a general schedule, filling in collaborators, times, and tasks. News Editors start working with the Afternoon News Bill:

---

[9] I have witnessed it at ANSA and Reuters. Heath and Nicholls (1997) documented it in their study of Reuters economic news, pointing out the incorrectness of a popular belief that journalists' work is individualistic.

This time around it's: "Now we know how it has become. This is the most important, and this is what we're going to focus on, what we believe is big news". It's News Editor who comes later that does this. And that's the real thing. Lunch News Bill is more wishful thinking. Now it is bare facts: "About 3000 characters with Factbox at 17.30". So that the editors in the provincial newspapers know how much space to reserve in their paper. (Int. 3/4)

13.30

News Editor comes back from lunch and finds the newsroom in agitation. A school principal in Kungsängen has been stabbed with a knife:

> We didn't know whether he'd been murdered or not, we weren't sure whether to flash it or not. We decided not to do it yet: if he dies, we do it. Or if a pupil stabbed him, then we do it. It was obvious that we needed more information. Coordination was necessary. Who will ring the police? Do we need to send a reporter to Kungsängen? Do we send a Web-TV reporter there? (Int. 3/8)

As before, the list of activities here concerns not dealing with overflow, but intensifying the flow of information:

> Also, this story had so many different takes [paragraphs], so we needed one person who would edit it. [Central Desk Editor] told K to do it. My task was to see that we don't miss anything. "K, a new piece has come, take it". "*Svenska Dagbladet* wrote that it was a principal, do we have it?" "No, we wrote that it was an employee". "But has it been confirmed that it was the principal?" "No, it hasn't". "Well, then we must get it".
>
> After that I was supposed to call a union meeting, but I postponed it. There were a great many people involved in covering this stabbing, so there was nobody to negotiate with. If everybody who ought to went to the meeting, the workforce would abandon your news factory![10] (Int. 3/8)

One could say that in a conflict between profession and management, the profession wins.[11] Box 3.2 shows how the news looked at the end, composed of five takes.

14.00

Managing Editor makes a list of things that she must do during the day, and goes around to talk to those News Editors whose desks will be involved in tasks on that list.

---

[10] The interviewee is playing with my factory metaphor, which was generally accepted without protest. They only pointed out to me that TT's output consists of semi-manufactures rather than finished products.

[11] At least in this instance. More on this type of conflict in Raviola (2010).

BOX 3.2   BREAKING NEWS IN FIVE TAKES

Principal stabbed – a 22-year-old detained
STOCKHOLM: Earlier this week he threatened the principal. The school did not report it to the police. Yesterday the 22-year-old boy came and stabbed the principal. Now he is accused of attempted murder.

At 12.47 there was an alarm about a knife stabbing in Käll School in Kungsängen, north of Stockholm. A young man entered the teachers' room and in front of several people attacked the school's principal. The doctors at the hospital established that the principal did not suffer serious wounds, in spite of seven or eight stabbings at his back and his face.

After an intense chase, the police detained the 22-year-old man at Stockholm Central Station.

The young man did not attend the school himself, but knew another pupil who had gone to that school and quit.

The threat was known; the man had come there earlier in the week and uttered threats, said the deputy principal. (TT)

Evening Editor and Evening Reporter come in. Evening Editor reads the TT's newswire and checks on what has been done in the newsroom in the morning and early afternoon. She also talks to her colleagues who worked the previous shift and those who came at the same time as she did. It could have been that a News Editor has already decided what the Evening Reporter should do. It could also be that there is a press conference or a shareholders' general meeting in the evening. Thus, the Evening Editor must know what people are doing before she assigns new jobs to them.

14.30
Local bureaus deliver information that will go into the Afternoon News Bill.

15.00–15.30
Reporters return to the newsroom or send their texts via e-mail. Texts to be edited flow into the Central Desk's e-Basket.

15.00–15.15
Local News Editor leaves the office and transfers his responsibilities to Desk Editor who starts her shift.

15.20–16.00

Central Desk Editor sends out TT's News Bill:

> News Bill is divided according to different desks that more or less correspond to sections of the newspaper. It also conveys our estimation of the importance of each news item for the day, though this is, of course, a very subjective judgment. We usually have a lot of discussion about it; it's hard to call it right or wrong, as it's the impression of the moment. A couple of hours later everything can change. . . . But we do this estimate at any rate, and give it to our clients. The bill is otherwise very detailed; it says what the news is about, whether or not there are Factboxes, how long the text is, if the text has been edited compared to the original, if there are pictures, or videos, etc. It also contains the names of reporters who are responsible for the final version. But this information is for internal use, so we write it by hand on a paper version of the bill. (Int. 3/3)

There are usually three "best" news items of the day. If Lunch News Bill tells the clients *what* TT is going to write about, Afternoon News Bill says *how* and *when* it is going to be written. For example, TT managed to get an exclusive interview with two doctors who were accused of murder by dismemberment some time ago (Box 3.3).

News Editor 2 prepares work list for the next day:

> I do it while checking my mailboxes, answering my calls, and reading reporters' texts. Sometimes it's so that, in order to do things properly tomorrow, one has to start calling today. . . .
>
> Sometimes it's extremely busy. Sometimes it's impossible to plan the next day until it's too late. But then it's possible to form some general impression at least, so that one won't be surprised. Besides, we're two News Editors and we sit close to one another, so we often say: "Can you check the mail box while I do the list for tomorrow?" (Int. 3/4)

15.30

Consigning meeting at TT. Central Desk Editor chairs it, and tells those who have just arrived at work what has been done during the day. Together, they all go through the News Bill and discuss the day's most significant articles. Evening Editor tries to understand the reasoning behind the list: how these news items have been selected, which reporters are responsible for which jobs, and which parts of the articles are not ready yet. Some such parts must be completed, either by additional interviews or by rewriting.

16.00

Central Desk Editor leaves Testament for Evening Editor.

17.00

There are only four people left at Central Desk now: Evening Editor, one Text Editor, a person responsible for publishing on the Web, and a

---

BOX 3.3   AN EXCLUSIVE INTERVIEW

DAY'S MAIN NEWS
Murder by dismemberment
Acquitted of murder by dismemberment, but still pointed out as
corpse dismemberers. Now they sue the State for 40 million
kronor. First time ever, the pathologist and general practitioner are
interviewed together.
Read more under DOMESTIC.

. . .

DOMESTIC
Murder by dismemberment
Acquitted from murder by dismemberment, but still pointed out as
corpse dismemberers. Now they sue the State for 40 million
kronor. First time ever, the pathologist and general practitioner are
interviewed together. "My whole life has been taken away from me.
What angers me most is that nobody says 'Sorry, we were wrong'",
says the pathologist to TT. Tomorrow negotiations begin in Attunda
District Court.

About 3300 characters, background and facts at 17.30.

---

person responsible for Day's Package (short summary of the day's most
important news), who also starts working with night clips.

Most of TT's texts are published between 16.00 and 20.00, both on the
newswire and (partly) on the Web. They are often rewritten, and come as
New Versions, which contain new information or are complemented by
side texts. Evening Editor has the mandate to "rehash and turn", but the
changes are usually not significant:

> 3/10: We aim at reaching an agreement with those who had responsibility for
> the day during the consigning meeting. We need to agree on what is to be on
> the top of News Bill – which articles are most important, how they should be
> formatted, what should be emphasized, and what angle they should they take.
> It's not usual for a reporter to deliver an article, and then discover
> that a completely different text has been published. It has happened,
> but most often the reporter delivers the article to her or his immediate
> superior – News Editor – and they discuss it together. If the News Editor
> thinks that it should be written differently, or from a different angle, then the
> changes are made.

BC: But if you at Central Desk change a word or something that the reporter does not like?

3/10: This happens daily and we hear the reporters' reactions. But our responsibility is to make texts as understandable as possible. It does happen that our opinions clash with those of the reporters, but this is an eternal source of tension between writers and editors, not only in journalism.

BC: Do they make a fuss the next day, then?

3/10: It varies. It varies from one reporter to another. Some of them don't give a damn if we rewrite or edit or rehash their texts, and others are extremely sensitive – each comma counts.

18.00

Evening Editor sends Text Info – a supplement to News Bill – in case there are some newsworthy items that were not included in the bill.

19.00

First News Package is being sent. It consists of the day's two Top News items: the best one consists of 2000 characters, and the second best exactly 1700. The remaining news is in the form of News Items, which consist of approximately 500 characters.

19.30

Somebody in the evening group watches one of the three main TV news programs: *Rapport* on SvT1.

20.00

Many desks are closed, but the "blue light news" (police and emergency – from the blue lights on their vehicles) comes from WIGHS. Editing continues, as does the checking of other people's news items via RSS. Evening Editor begins to work on Morning Memo.

21.00

Somebody in the evening group watches the other significant TV news program, *Aktuellt* on SvT2.

22.00

Somebody in the group watches yet another TV news program: TV4's *Nyheterna*. News items that were announced in Text Info are being sent, together with a new News Package, again with the best and the second best news. It can happen, however, that the Top News has changed, and another news item tops the list now:

> What is special about a news agency such as TT is that news can change form during the day. A reporter can write an article that is ready at 14.00, but then,

during the evening, we may decide that it would be good to seek somebody else's opinion – perhaps ask a responsible minister. So we do that, and the minister says: "Yes, all this is going to change, as I am going to present a proposal next week". Then it's necessary to rewrite the text, and this can happen two or more times before a text is published. At the end several reporters can be involved, and an editor or two, so the final text hardly resembles the original. This is how it differs from a newspaper where a reporter writes his or her text and it's published as is. Here it can change; also our estimate of importance can change – in both directions. It could improve during the day: what was moderately interesting news during the day can become Top News in the evening. (Int. 3/11)

23.00
Night Editors begin their shift. The newspapers *Dagens Industri*, *Svenska Dagbladet*, and *Dagens Nyheter* come out. Night Editors begin doing clips and rewrites.

23.30
Evening Editor leaves Central Desk to Night Editors, telling them what to clip and what has to be monitored during the night, and starts writing Testament. At this point, it contains mostly events known from Calendar, but which will, during the day, become filled with the news in other big media. Testament is accessible to everybody at TT, as it lies on the Intranet.

24.00
The evening group goes home.

One aspect that perhaps is not clear enough in this account of "A day at TT" is the *pace of work*: even if deadlines are not always kept to the minute, all activities during the day must keep up a steady speed. The pace can become somewhat slower after 20.00, but the state of preparedness is maintained in case unforeseen things happen. A speedy product requires speedy work.

FILTERING, ACCREDITATION, EDITING . . . AND OTHER THINGS

It is obvious that people working at TT receive an enormous amount of information, so although they do not define it as "overflow", it is still legitimate to ask how they manage it all. Yochai Benkler (2006), a theoretician of "networked societies", has noted that the central operations required to handle the overflow of information on the Web are filtering and accreditation. They are part of the traditional repertoire of the journalism profession, albeit under a variety of names. I review them here, beginning with filtering, because filtering is traditionally seen as central, not least in the gatekeeper metaphor.

Filtering

For Benkler (2006: 68), filtering means selecting pieces of information on the grounds of their relevance, which is correct in relation to the Web. But in the case of news agencies, the criteria are more complex. For example, they want to avoid repetitions, and wish to have "a good mix" of news.

The main entry for information to TT is e-mail. There are several mail boxes; one common to all is called Editorial. What arrives in it is then moved to boxes of the different desks – "Unread Domestic" or "Economy TT", for example – and from there, of course, to individual mail boxes. Unread Domestic has no more than 100 messages per day, whereas Economy TT may have 300 to 400:

> Editorial Box is emptied by the person whose task is to empty it, sending anything that seems of the slightest interest to a News Editor. It contains a great many different things, and the person in charge of it is expected to be generous . . . as soon as there is anything that *smells of news,* it should go to an appropriate desk box and the editors there will check it . . . it does happen though that that person stands up and hollers. . . (Int. 3/2)

I have italicized "smells of news" because this metaphor was so frequent that for a while I had been thinking of an unflattering analogy between the news producers and truffle dogs. But truffle dogs, which also have to have "a good nose", search for something that may not be there, whereas news producers sniff at a huge amount of information. Perhaps a more appropriate analogy would be with a job that is called "pickers" in Norway – people who decide the quality of dried cod by sniffing the fish (Korneliussen and Panozzo, 2005). A journalist at ANSA suggested that a fish market would be a better metaphor than a factory for a news agency. Gaye Tuchman (1978) talked about "newsnet" using a similar fish-related metaphor.

As with dried cod, even if a good nose is of utmost importance, there are other, more explicit criteria:

> As far as opinion polls are concerned, we've established a kind of a criterion that they must be well done, have a solid statistical base.[12] So it mustn't be "47

---

[12] As US economist William Easterly observed recently, "The press shows certain reverence for social science work with statistics. . . The paradox is that many social scientists familiar with this kind of analysis do not share the press's reverence" (2008: 52). This observation was already made in 1970 by Tunstall, but the reverence remains.

persons answered the question", but it must be properly done. Furthermore, the issue must be noteworthy, and the study must not be ordered by an interested party. If a company Nappies & Diapers[13] orders an opinion poll around the question "Do young parents use nappies?" we are not going to write about it. But if a poll is well done and News Editor thinks it's of general interest, we will. . . Then there are reports, a great many of them, somebody has mapped this and that, somebody else has an observation, somebody else has gathered some statistics – once again, the question is, "Will anybody bother to read about it?". But also, "Who did it?". The sender of the message is also important. (Int. 3/4)

If in doubt, ask somebody else:

> Sometimes I feel that I'm not particularly interested in this kind of thing myself, but perhaps somebody else is . . . then I can bounce the question around the desk. "What do you think about this study? Is it of interest to anybody? To whom?" When in doubt, I look around and ask for another opinion. That's how it is all the time. It happens that one throws away something, and the next day it turns into a big thing. In that case, either you were wrong or the others were wrong, but it turned out as it did. (Int. 3/4)

There is this idea of "general interest" that can be discovered by sounding out colleagues. Clearly, news producers cannot have eccentric tastes.

But how to weed out this multitude of e-mails that come everyday? Even this task is often done together:

> It's not exactly that we carefully study each piece of mail that comes in; rather we try to decide quickly. Often a consultation with a specialized reporter is of great help. Recently I've received a tip that the Defense helicopter training will be shut down in Jönköping and moved to Germany. I really didn't know if this was news for us. I forwarded the mail to our defense reporter to decide. Were it urgent, I'd phone him. He sits only 10 meters away, but I phone him so I don't have to shout in the newsroom. . . . we shout only when it's extremely urgent. (Int. 3/4)

For this reason I compared TT in my Swedish report (Czarniawska, 2009c) to "a quiet factory". And asking questions is not intended to elicit opinions; it is an appeal to shared memory. The reporter is expected to remember or to check Archive:

> News Editors cannot know everything that happened and they are not always here and they cannot have read everything . . . it's completely impossible. It happens that a News Editor says, "Oh, this is good!" and a reporter comes and says "Yes, very good. Only I just wrote about it three weeks ago". News Editor makes the first estimate: is it true? is it correct? is it interesting? (Int. 3/4)

---

[13] An invented name.

Interesting for whom was my repeated question:

> The guiding star in all this is that it must be interesting to many people. Or else, that we can develop it so that it will become interesting to many. It must be of nationwide interest, either because it's big or because it's interesting in principle – because it influences household economy or because it make readers feel pain in their guts. . . There are a lot of criteria for what is good news and what isn't. I take away all that is local and local only. I take away all that I know we won't be able to cover, because we won't have enough resources. One day things can fall apart because there are too many good things, so news can be rejected one day that on another day would make everybody keen.
> And then there are those things in the middle, on the verge of being interesting, but – do we have the resources? How does the mix look? One cannot write only about cars or only about finances; there must be a mix that is useful for the newspapers. (Int. 3/9)

Unless there is a financial crisis and the car industry crashes, one could add with hindsight, but even then other news must be addressed, too.

One change has taken place in TT, compared with its early years: it is no longer only "serious" news that is considered for publication; funny news is also good news nowadays:

> There are some news items that don't exactly constitute big news items, but they are fun to write because they have *high reading value*. Yesterday I got a call from a freelance photographer from Northern Sweden who wanted to know if we want pictures of Swedish elks that are going to be transported to Scotland to reproduce there. They raise elks there and sell them abroad, especially to Germany, because Germans love elks. Thus, a plane is expected to come and take a pair of elks to Scotland. I told him to contact our company, Scanpix, because he wanted to sell his pictures, but then I remembered that we wrote about it some time ago. So I called our reporter in Luleå and asked him if he could call this elk farm because it's such nice story. (Int. 3/4)

Sure enough, not long afterwards I saw pictures of elks on their way to the plane in my local newspaper.

Apart from shared mail boxes there are also individual ones. Their use varies from one person to another, but the aim always seems to be to minimize the time needed to manage them:

> I don't check the quarantine. I trust that it works. If I look at "subject", half of it says Viagra. At any rate, I don't check the quarantine because it runs to several thousands in less than a couple of days, so that it's much too much. The days are not long enough to take care of everything. The risk is that one can forget something important. . . . In what remains, I create thematic folders and then drag mail into them. I also do a lot of deleting, because otherwise it fills up

very quickly. We have default settings that activate "delete" after a certain time, and which can be changed to a manual setting so that a message will never be deleted, but this we can do only telegram by telegram.[14] We reached the decision together about the working of the system. (Int. 3/2)

So here are several automatic ways of managing overflow: quarantine, automatic delete, and some manual: sorting by a theme, saving some messages. But, as many interviewees pointed out, managing telephone calls usually takes more time than the e-mail box:

> Telephone is more difficult, because you can't just put the receiver down. E-mail you can simply delete. Telephone takes more time, because, if you're a nice person [laughs], you don't want to dismiss people even if you already understand that they have nothing interesting to offer. They ring to offer tips or to sell things. They want to sell events: "Will you cover this conference?" "Will you write about this award?" (Int. 3/4)

It is not only that unexpected telephone calls take time. The telephone is a valuable means of creating information:

> As we have a local bureau in Northern Sweden, we have a lot of telephone contact with them. Then there are reporters who sit in the House of Parliament, and I can only contact them by phone during the day. They come to the morning meeting, but then go to Parliament and sit there, and work there. It's a small tight group that works with similar topics and sits in beautiful premises, so I don't think they suffer much. They are specialized political reporters.[15] (Int. 3/5)

Yet another source of information is the longer texts that are attached to e-mails or sent by snail mail to the newsroom. These were a sensitive topic for me. Researchers always feel unhappy because journalists do not want to read their reports – just ask for a one-sentence summary. Still, to be fair, I believe that such a complaint can be launched only against the newspapers' journalists. Can people at TT possibly have time to read long texts?

> 3/11: Another type of news that we knew about in advance, and planned for reporting it, was the report from Defense Working Committee, which was presented on Tuesday.
> BC: But such a report is 70 pages long, if not 200. Will somebody really read it?
> 3/11: It varies. One example of an incredibly large material is the Spring State Budget, but then there are several reporters who work with it. Also, there is

---

[14] The word "telegram" is used quite often, even by the youngest journalists.
[15] I was able to observe exactly such a group in Rome just before the elections in Italy.

always a press conference where they summarize it, so we send a reporter there, and then there are reporters who work with their special areas. Also, a reporter who went to the press conference might come back and write the first take, but then he or she has more time back in the newsroom. Perhaps not enough time to read the whole thing, but at least to skim through it, which may lead to a discovery of important news that was not obvious during the conference. So the final version can be very different than the first take, a completely different angle or a different story.

As I analyzed my first interviews, I noticed that while my questions focused on "filtering", my respondents as often as not told me about various ways of *creating* information. I confronted the next interviewee with this observation and received a following answer:

> *Lack of information is always a bigger problem than an overflow of information.* As for filtering, it's totally based on having a clear idea about what is the core of our news production. And this is perhaps the most difficult, because it's impossible to put in words. You can't draw a diagram where there will be public interest on the one axis and the importance of the news on the other so that you then can know what is news and what isn't news. It would be great to have such a diagram, but, alas. . . You apply a series of rules of thumb but when all is said and done, it's the responsible person's discrimination and judgment that decides. The most often-heard sentence is "Oh, this thing is good, we have to have it". Deeper than that, the analysis does not go. (Int. 3/3)

Does it mean that the news producers do not experience overflow at all, and that they somewhat blindly sail through the flow of incoming information? Not exactly. To begin with, "lack of information" is not the same as "too few news items". Here is a further explanation:

> . . . We talk about a *bad news day* when different media focus on different news, and where there is no obvious, true top news. Then the radio tells one story and *Dagens Nyheter* writes about another and *Svenska Dagbladet* about a third and we have something else yet again. . . Obviously, the probability of finding good news is higher when there are many news items, but the connection is far from guaranteed. Thus you cannot say that there are too few news items, either. . . (Int. 3/5)

Many a time my interlocutors in all three agencies explained what they saw as the difference between *news* and *information*. Incoming information can contain news or not. In the latter case, it is useless. On the other hand, one can have news, but not enough information; it must be found or created. One can also *create news* by provoking a specific input of information – thus, I saw the need to add a new analytical category to those suggested by Benkler. But before I move in that direction, I report on the other traditional professional operation: accreditation.

Accreditation

Like Benkler (2006), I put more than the conventional source analysis into this concept. Accreditation may mean that one news item is compared to another, that a common sense judgment is applied, but also a great deal of detective work on the Web may be required to locate the sources. How does one know what is credible?

> No matter what function one has at TT, the linchpin is that we check that the statements we make are correct. That we check twice or thrice, that we see to it that sources are trustworthy. My first judgment, when I see something – be it a mail or a telephone call – is about the source. Can I trust it?. . . If I think so, I call Morning Reporter, for example, and say, "This seems interesting, we should write about it. But, just to be on the safe side, call and check". Morning Reporter does that and sends the text back to Central Desk.
>   The same questions are asked by a person who sits there and is about to decide whether it should be published or not. Is it plausible? Have we enough grounds to write this way? Are there any doubts about the material? How good was this opinion poll they are referring to? So this source-critical attitude must be in all phases – from the assigning editor to the reporter to the editor who will publish it. It's of vital importance, so that there is no one person responsible for it – we all are. (Int. 3/7)

Three concepts can summarize the contents of the comments above: *plausibility*, *source analysis,* and *collective responsibility*. As these are abstract concepts, I wanted to know in greater detail how accreditation is being done:

> As far as foreign news is concerned, we take the material from Reuters or AFP [Agence France-Presse], and we can't check the credibility of their news. But we *buy the trustworthiness of the trademarks* Reuters and AFP, just like Swedish newspapers buy the trustworthiness incorporated in the name TT.
>   It's different with domestic news. For example, we hear that there were four police helicopters in Göteborg that were shot at. We ring the police and ask what has happened. They say: "No comments right now; we'll issue a press release at 10.00 and will mail it to you". So if there is a mail at 10.00 with the subject matter "The information unit of Göteborg police informs of the night events", we don't check again. We don't ask, "Is it really you who sent this?" Still, if the contents are rather bizarre – I am extemporizing right now – "The shooting took place during the police staff party", we do call and ask "Was it really so? Do you really mean that the police shot at their own helicopters?" – and they confirm or explain. So the first judgment is whether the news is plausible or not, whether it holds within normal variation so to speak. They speak of damages to four helicopters, so it means that they have technical evidence. They say that police went to look for the armed men. It sounds credible, so we don't check it further. But we add, "state the police in their press release". *Thus, the more remarkable the news, the greater the propensity to check.* (Int. 3/2)

Thus, trustworthiness can be "bought" together with the trademark, whether it be Reuters or the police. TT's clients treat it the same way: "TT's telegrams are seen as legitimate news from the public sphere of Sweden" (Johansson, 2008: 43) – although perhaps not necessarily so when it comes to private interests. The plausibility of the news (or rather lack of plausibility) can overcome the reputation of the source. Still, how does one decide what is plausible and what is not? Which news is treated with suspicion? To begin, there are those items that are "too big":

> It was 2001, and the atmosphere after 9/11 was still excited when our Göteborg bureau received a press release saying that men dressed in camouflage shot and killed guards at the Ringhals nuclear plant and ran toward the reactor. This news came on my screen, and we had to decide whether to flash it or not. My knee-jerk reaction was: "No, wait! We must check it further". Because it was too big. . . . I was right – it was an exercise run by the county police. This could have been a serious mishap. Yet we could have pressed the button in the sheer excitement of this amazing news. And the feeling of urgency is always present. (Int. 3/3)

Not surprisingly, speed may collide with credibility, when the news items are not so big:

> We did publish some urban legends, amusing but without any relation to reality. It does happen. Control of credibility can be looser when it concerns something relatively unimportant. There is no systematic difference in how we treat such news, but a person's attention can be lower when it comes to small news items. (Int. 3/3)

The news producers have confidence in their own judgment when it comes to plausibility, and put most of their efforts into checking sources – if they need checking:

> 3/3: Trust in sources is incredibly important. A statement from the Government Office is always trustworthy, but a communiqué from an unknown company must be checked. The best source is always somebody that you have talked to, the most relevant person in the context, or the documents to which you can have access.
> BC: In my job we almost never take oral information literally.
> 3/3: *The difference lies in speed.* Your project is very long, our projects are very short. This forces us to live with uncertainty. What we can do, however, is point out those uncertainties to our readers. We say "These are the results of the opinion poll, but the statistical relationships haven't been established yet". Thus, we create an opportunity for readers to arrive at their own judgments.

Although the responsibility for accreditation is collective, there is a certain division of labor involved:

> It's the reporters' job to check the statements they hear. Most journalists who are working here have worked in their profession several years and know how to do it. Of course we sometimes step on a mine, but as a reporter you must really know what you're talking about and check it thoroughly. . . . We, News Editors, cannot do that. We cannot check everything. We can ponder over plausibility, but it's assumed that the reporter checks the facts. (Int. 3/4)

At this point I should add something that was not mentioned, because it is utterly obvious: telephones are the accreditation instruments par excellence. The appearance of cell phones has made the procedure easier and quicker.

I return to the ways of deciding plausibility, but during this interview I also asked what happens if there is an error. Of course, typing errors can occur, and are easily corrected, but what about substantial errors?

> We've published things that didn't contain grave errors, but still some things that we needed to correct. Usually, I go back to the reporters and ask: "How could it have happened? Why was it wrong?" Still, considering how much we publish, I think that there are very few errors. Typing errors, yes, but not sub-stantial errors.
>
> Our reporters are usually right in what they publish, but it happens that somebody thinks that they were not allowed to finish their reasoning, or that the nuances were lost. I seldom agree with them. Yes, it can happen that some nuances were lost, but the usual problem is that they are not used to formu-lating their thoughts in a concise way, and then they are shocked when they see themselves in print. It can happen that the reporter has misunderstood something, but mostly I believe that they don't realize what they are saying. . . . And then it depends on who is talking. The [Prime Minister] must just accept anything that he has said wrongly, but if you're speaking to somebody who's a victim of a bus accident, you must be careful. But we treat people in power positions in a tougher way. (Int. 3/4)

Creating News

As the notion of overflow was my starting point, for a good while I had not noticed that the news producers not only manage the inflow of infor-mation, but actively contribute to it: they are literally "making news" (Johansson, 2008):

> BC: "Blue light" news – how does that come in?
> 3/5: Most often it's we who ring. We make calls at regular intervals to police in different parts of the country and ask them if something has happened. They also send press releases here.

This is not a mechanical task, but one requiring many skills. One could also say that the news producers work hard at converting news to "good news":

One way of converting a news item to a good news item is to find an honest critic – somebody who is external to the situation and yet can say, for example, that this is intolerable. An easy way to create news is to take a look at a phenomenon and then find somebody who is critical of that phenomenon – then the news is that that person is critical. The phenomenon itself may be not that important; the strong reaction to it is. This is one way of creating news. (Int. 3/5)

My surprise over such a procedure was counteracted in another comment:

If we did not do it, we would be a rather boring news agency. If we did not create news – if we acted only as gatekeepers. If you take a look at what is coming in to us, via telephone calls, fax, and e-mail, you would see that it's a rather small part of it that results in text. Most of it ends up in the wastebasket. (Int. 3/7)

So there is an overflow, in the sense that much more information comes in than is used, but this is not perceived as a problem.

I now summarize what I have learned about the work of news producers at TT.

TALENTS AND SKILLS: OLD AND NEW METAPHORS

Gatekeepers

The old gatekeepers are still here. Perhaps they have become more numerous, in light of the fact that the information flow has increased, and the opportunities to publish have multiplied. There are more media and there is more information about more things. Thus, you need experts to make selections, but how do we do it. . . I don't know. This is the most concrete thing in my job, and yet I don't know how to explain it. It's my job to select it, but how I do it, and how I do it right, it's very difficult to explain. (Int. 3/1)

Several of my respondents used the term "gatekeeper" – in English – which made me curious, as I could not see much basis for it in their accounts of their daily work. The metaphor alludes to the Middle Age cities that had guards at their gates. Their task was to keep away from the city the sick (to protect cities from epidemics) and the potential enemies of the power holders – from foreigners to revolutionaries. In other words, gatekeepers protected cities from external threats.

German social psychologist Kurt Lewin, who emigrated to the US, became involved in a project aimed at convincing US families to change their eating habits during World War II. Beef should be replaced with cheaper food, offal for example. Lewin noticed that it was housewives who decided what the family ate – exactly like the medieval gatekeepers they protected the family from what could be dangerous.

Kurt Lewin died in February 1947, but one article from a manuscript that described the results of his experiments was published after his death (Lewin, 1947). In this text he suggested that gatekeepers could be found even in other social contexts – during recruitment, for instance – when those in power tried directly or indirectly to influence who or what was permitted to enter. The article contained the following formulation:

> the constellation of the forces before and after the gate region is decisively different in such a way that passing or not passing of the unit through the whole channel depends to a high degree upon what happens in the gate region. This holds not only for food channels but also for travelling of a news item through certain communication channels in a group. . . . (Lewin, 1947: 145)

David Manning White (1950) used this formulation as a basis for transferring the metaphor to journalism and the mass media. But whereas Lewin described group dynamics (one can claim that parents act as gatekeepers for what children read), White used the term "gate" to mean "floodgate" rather than "doors". While the doors are literally a passage point that demarcates the difference between "inside" and "outside", water can pass through several floodgates (even if it becomes regulated in the process, and perhaps cleaned of certain substances). "Thus a story is transmitted from one 'gate keeper' after another in the chain of communications" (White, 1950: 384). "Inside" for White meant inside the newsroom and the "gate keeper" that was central for him was the "wire editor" on a newspaper – the person who chose news from telegrams coming from three news agencies (AP, UP, and INS). His study led him to conclude that the selection criteria were highly subjective and depended on the gatekeeper's personal experience.

White's article, which has become a classic in journalism studies, started an almost 60-year debate (for a recent summary, see Shoemaker and Vos, 2008, who make a plea to have "the agency" returned to the gatekeeper). Naturally, there were critical voices. Walter Gieber (1956) observed that the editors he studied were extremely dependent upon technology in their workplace (even if his main conclusion was only that one needs to study "societal forces" behind the gatekeepers). Hadenius and Weibull (1999) criticized the individualization of news work in White's version: his "Mr. Gate" seemed to work all alone. Still, one could defend White by pointing out that gatekeeper was actually not a metaphor but an analogy – in a newspaper, which, unlike newswire, has physical limits, and in times when the capacity of telegraphy decided the speed and the number of published news items.

But times have changed. Clay Shirky (2008) claims that one of the effects of the accessibility of the web is a *mass amateurization* of the media. Another and related effect is the transfer of the gatekeeping function to technology, where it can operate with little notice.

One can also speculate that there is a relationship between the relevance of gatekeepers and the emergence of many different *obligatory passage points* (Callon, 1986). Until 1947 – as long as TT had a monopoly on the news – it could act as gatekeeper for the others. Until 1989, as long as the telecom company in Sweden had a monopoly on the satellite, it could play such a role (Ewertsson, 2001). Now everybody who has means can produce news and even have their own satellites.

Thus, even if the quote from the interview placed at the beginning of this section were to confirm the usefulness of the gatekeeper metaphor today, it still says that the number of gatekeepers has increased. The quote also seems to corroborate White's conviction that selection is highly subjective. Yet an alternative interpretation could be that it is not individual at all, but highly institutionalized – taken for granted and *therefore* beyond reflection.

Other respondents suggested other metaphors, and I coined one, too.

Dispatchers

Some scholars claim that the core of all organizing rests in the function of a dispatcher, a person or machine that can send the right objects and the right people to the right places at the right time to do the right things (Latour, 1998). Respondents at TT compared themselves to "dispatchers at a truck centre", and the person who sat in a "slot position" at Reuters (see Chapter 5) was named "traffic officer". Much comes in, and much goes out. Things, texts, and machines must be at the right place at the right time:

> [Central Desk Editor's] job is perhaps most stressful at TT, because it is so much . . . there are so many who want to talk to me all the time. The phone rings, and when I put down the receiver I see three people standing behind the desk, a queue of those who want to tell me something or to ask me something. But for the most part, I think it is positive stress – not precisely the ringing phones, that's not fun – but it is fun when many things happen, when so many things are going on, when we do a lot of things and big events take place. . . . then it's stressful, because the point is to be out as fast as possible with all the important information as correct as possible. So, yes, I can be very tired when I go back home in the evening, but still I feel that I've had a fantastic day at work. (Int. 3/5)

There are as yet no algorithms that can prescribe correct actions and action sequences, but there are a great many routines. Improvisation completes routines, and the other way around:

Much is routinized. There are routines; there are templates; there are programs; there are checks – all this is 90 percent routine. And then there are such things that are 90 percent dependent on you being able to make an entertaining thing out of them. It varies greatly, but the routines are of utmost importance. We call all the police districts in the country. We do it in the morning; we do it at lunchtime; we do it during the night; and we do it during the day. There is a *rhythm, like a pulse that beats all the time.* You check websites; your RSS is on so you don't miss anything. In that sense, it's very routinized. We have to do those things because that means that somebody else doesn't need to do them. It's the whole point: that others can rely on what we do. (Int. 3/9)

That news production is routinized work has been shown in many studies (for a review, see Johansson, 2008). Therefore, it must be added – and emphasized – that the pace, and the rhythm, are important in this work – for its results, but also for job satisfaction:

I would think it very frustrating to stick to the same project for four months, not to mention five years. Most of the fun comes from big events, when *this large machine called TT jumpstarts.* Lots of things need to be coordinated, the ongoing news flow to be taken care of, when there is much to do. TT becomes a large, organized chaos. The pitch is raised, and so is the pulse of everybody who works then. Everything else is put aside, everything becomes reorganized. We have to send reporters to right places; we immediately call the right people, and so on and so forth. We have to organize our work so that the news flows. What background material can we deliver? What side texts should we write? Do we have moving pictures to add? In short, so that everything starts rolling as soon as possible and as effectively as possible. (Int. 3/7)

This is in contrast to the experience of Boczkowski's producers of "hard news" online. Their work is similar to that of news agency employees, but they reported "significant levels of stress" (2010: 42). The crucial difference may be that of ambient noise. It was high in the Argentinian newspaper that Boczkowski studied, but kept at practically zero level at TT.

Even if normal days can be slower, the news machine has to roll on, the pulse has to beat, and the news has to flow, if in waves. It is important to maintain the rhythm. And though the speed requirements in the journalism profession grow all the time (Nygren, 2008a), in contrast with Nygren's study, my interlocutors did not report any negative stress.

What they did not say in so many words, but what I have learned first through observations at ANSA was that it's not only News Editors who play the dispatchers' role. There are a great many internal documents that play a similar role: schedules, work lists and News Bills (the latter expedite even the clients to places and times). This is not to diminish the role played by the human beings, but to emphasize the role of objects and quasi-objects. I return to this, but stay with the human news producers for a while.

Gut Feelings

A great many things are expected of a News Editor: exactitude and speed among them:

> You have to be precise, and you have to be fast. You can allow yourself about three minutes for any one thing. There is always something going on. There is also a certain type of person who can handle it. You have to be able to make a decision about the way a text needs be changed, and be able to explain it to a reporter. . . You must know how to discuss form and content. And, last but not least, you must be able to judge the news: what is and what isn't news. (Int. 3/8)

Back to the puzzle that White (1950) also wanted to solve: how does one know? It has often been repeated that one must know about the public interest. As Walter Lippmann had already claimed provocatively in 1925, however, there is no "public", but possibly several "publics".[16] Perhaps that is true for the US, but not for much smaller Sweden? I suspect that if I selected what interests me, it would be of interest to hardly anybody else. TT really deals with an anonymous "public" as well, because it cannot identify its readers. The journalists at the daily newspaper can – and must:

> If I get a tip that "There's a lot of police at Stockholm's central subway station", I need to decide whether it's news or not. For an evening paper, it's news that somebody saw Paris Hilton in Stockholm, but not for us. We see the news in a special way. We have something called a "Flash" that we send when something big happens in the world or in Sweden and we think that the newspapers' newsrooms should get interested in. . . . But you need to make a judgment. Is it a Flash or not? Shall we send it or not? And as I see it, I have qualities that make me suitable for this job. (Int. 3/8)

What qualities are those? Can any journalist be trained to become a News Editor at a news agency?

> You can be trained, certainly, but you have to have the capacity to make an overview of a situation quickly and make a quick judgment. Not everybody makes quick judgments – some people want to go deeper, dig into the material. You can't do it when you must quickly form an opinion. But most journalists working at TT could be trained to become News Editors; most of them know how to make judgments.

---

[16] Gabriel Tarde (1901/2003) claimed that the public is a virtual crowd (his adjective!); the main point of the news is that it is shared simultaneously by many.

It does not mean that the judgments are idiosyncratic (this is probably what White meant by "subjective" – otherwise all judgments made by living persons are subjective). Those who are new at TT receive a set of criteria from those who are more experienced:

> If you don't have your own routine, you must rely on certain given criteria. Who is the sender? How important and topical is the theme? And a kind of ranking scheme of things to think about in order not to make a mistake. Things coming from government are interesting on principle, so you must read those. You needn't write about everything, but read everything you must. Then there are some big parties that are interesting, certain large companies, certain authorities . . . but then you need to rely on your gut feelings – what you believe the readers will have, what is important. *Gut feelings and routines.* (Int. 3/4)

It is not difficult to establish who has experience and to set up a series of routines, but how does one diagnose the presence of gut feelings? Others – bosses and colleagues, judge them:

> You go to the press conference about the condition of children's teeth. You read the press release that will have been given to you ten minutes earlier, and after the conference you ring Central Desk or the News Editor to say what you think is most important. . . . And the News Editor can ask: "Did they say how much the condition has worsened? Do children have more cavities than before? Does the care cost more money, or in what way has it become worse?" And if you answer, "I don't know, I didn't get it", then we are worried, you don't seem to have this gut feeling that is necessary. But if you say: "You know, they were very unclear on all that, but I went and talked to the guy afterwards, and then he spilled the beans", then we know that you have a very good gut feeling. . . . (Int. 3/2)

This emphasis on gut feelings may place in doubt the analogy between news production and navigation that I intend to develop in the next section – at least according to British anthropologist Tim Ingold, who contrasted navigation with another way of traveling, wayfaring:

> In brief, the navigator has before him [sic] a complete representation of the territory, in the form of the cartographic map, upon which he can plot a course even before setting out. The journey is then no more than an explication of the plot. In wayfaring, by contrast, one follows a path that one has previously travelled in the company of others, or in their footsteps, reconstructing the itinerary as one goes along. Only upon reaching this destination, in this case, can the traveller truly be said to have found his way. (2007: 16)

But already in this quote it can be seen that news production resembles navigation more than it resembles wayfaring: if "destination" is the way the news has been received by the client newspapers, it is too late for a

TT journalist to change direction. Furthermore, my analogy is based not on the similarity between news production and traveling, but between the cognitive operations involved. Ingold (2008) introduced another contrast between wayfaring, which is based on stories, and navigation, which is based on classification. Like navigators, news producers calculate their way (calculations are made not only with numbers; see Callon and Muniesa, 2005). The necessary knowledge is also imbedded (Mol, 2002) in machines and routines, so that it can happen without much awareness. There is no doubt, however, that better and worse navigators do exist; thus, "gut feelings" can simply stand for a talent that is difficult to describe in words.

My own metaphor for the news producers is that of cyborgs, but as I intend to use it on all three agencies, I am saving it until the last chapter.

COLLECTIVE COGNITION

> Humans create their cognitive powers by creating environments in which they
> exercise those powers.
> Hutchins, 1995: xvi

The picture of the news production at the news agency that I assembled during my fieldwork resembled that painted by US anthropologist Edwin Hutchins in his *Cognition in the Wild* (1995), a close-up study of navigation practices. He used the term "distributed cognition", however, which I abandoned as it seems to suggest an existence of some kind of a whole that is then distributed among people and machines.[17] I prefer to speak of *collective cognition* in order to emphasize that people and machines at TT are connected to one another, and in this way they can better perceive the world.[18]

To be able to do that, they need to speak the same language (which, increasingly, is English), as it is difficult to imagine a news agency where people speak different jargons or use distinctly different vocabularies. They may publish news in different languages, as international and global agencies do, but they must speak the same language to one another.

---

[17] It is possible that his starting point was Alfred Schütz's well-known statement: "Knowledge is socially distributed" (1953/1973: 14), but he did not quote it. Philip E. Agre (1998) has used the term "collective cognition" in relation to virtual communities in general. He pointed out that such communities create (by design and by default) a specific genre of communication. John Swales (1990) saw it as typical for all communities. In the case of news agencies, however, the professional community is created around an existing genre, although this genre is constantly changing through contact with clients.

[18] Beunza and Stark (2010) speak in a similar vein of the "cognitive interdependence" of the traders they studied.

Otherwise, speed would be lost in continuous translations. A standardization of the language used – which is not without a price – is, in my opinion, as necessary in a news factory as it is on a big ship. In order to communicate effectively with everybody, it is necessary to use words and expressions that are simple and understood by all. Even if, in fact, there are at least two languages in operation – the language (or languages) of the product and the language of production – they share many commonalities. The product language must be simple, so everybody can understand it. The production language must be simple so the producers can communicate quickly and without ambiguity.

A collective cognition has several aspects: a collective attention, a collective monitoring, and a collective memory:

> There is such an enormous flow of telephone conversations, faxes, mails, radio broadcasts, newspaper articles – that it would be impossible not to miss something in this flood. But this is exactly why those steps – those repeated discussions between News Editors and the Central Desk – are safety measures. If I missed something in the morning, it does not take long before somebody else notices it . . . and then it's done, even if a bit later. . . . (Int. 3/7)

There is no need for a master plan in order to activate the collective production. Like on a ship, it is enough that everybody in the crew know what to do when a certain situation arises:

> An interlocking set of partial procedures can produce an overall observed pattern without there being a representation of that overall pattern anywhere in the system.
> Each participant knows how to coordinate his activities with the technologies and persons he interacts with. . . . The whole cycle emerges from the interactions of the individuals with one another and with the tools of the space. The structure of the activities of the group is determined by a set of local computations rather than by an implementation of a global plan. (Hutchins, 1995: 200)

This is easy to understand in relation to parallel procedures that can be accomplished without one disturbing another. But if there is no "global plan", how can sequential tasks be accomplished?[19] Here the software steps in. It is impossible to send a message that has not been finished. The editorial program asks: "Do you really want to send this message now?"

Thus, there are two types of organizing involved in the production of news: organizing of texts and organizing of production processes. The first

---

[19] Sequential tasks are tasks that must be accomplished in a given order. For instance, it is impossible to put on socks after one puts on shoes.

is organized with the help of written rules (language rules, for example) and with help of software. The second is organized primarily with the help of routines – for people and machines.

The feeling of collective work pervades everything. "We" is constantly used, which sometimes becomes a problem for the interviewer:

> 3/7: . . . we decided that we were ready when we read the sentence carefully, when we have talked to the prosecutor . . .
> BC: We?
> 3/7: Oh, the reporter, obviously. The reporter in Göteborg . . .

I almost fell into that "we" trap when I was in Rome and spoke to News Editor in the courtyard of Parliament. The famous Antonio Di Pietro, lawyer and party leader, came out into the yard to enjoy his cigar. "We must talk to him", said News Editor and I followed, a bit surprised but very happy to have such an unexpected opportunity. Luckily, I quickly understood that he did not mean me, but one of his reporters who stood nearby smoking. The reporter took out his notepad and approached Di Pietro. "We" remained in our place.

One of the consequences is that most jobs can be rotated (which also helps in the case of unexpected absences, caused by illness and such):

> 3/8: It happens that Central Desk Editor has something else to do, and then leaves the meeting for me to lead, as happened yesterday. Then it is me who prints out the work list and assigns tasks.
> BC: But it's Editor who makes the list?
> 3/8: Sometimes I do it as well.

To make rotation possible, a flexible staffing is necessary. Everybody could be replaced when needed. The connections can be loose, but they must be stable; each agency has a reserve aggregate, but stability is also achieved via *redundancy*:

> Evening Editor writes what he or she decided in Testament. It can also happen that Editor writes a Testament but also sends an e-mail: "Remember to do this today!" So that there are several communication systems. (Int. 3/4)

Connections must be also oiled if they are to work well. This is solved partly by recruiting people who are easy-going and work well with others:

> One way in which TT differs from other places where I used to work is that people here are very good at cooperating. It's easy to work with people here. There is very little elbowing and such things that are common in other places. It feels natural to help one another and to pull in the same direction. . . . It's usual

that one works on the same story, and the reason is that TT is a news factory. As reporters, we are more anonymous at TT than are people in newspapers. If you work here, you don't strive to have a story with your own byline. It has its pros and cons, but mostly pros.

Some people wouldn't want to work here exactly for this reason. They think that TT is something gray and boring. You cannot work on your own profile. There are people who like to work individually, want to be seen and heard, and there is nothing wrong with it – only that TT is not a place for them. It doesn't mean that individuals don't have any room for their own initiative. They do. Individual reporters do fantastic texts, or reportages that become a great success. So there is room in this factory even for individuals who want to make difference. (Int. 3/7)

It can be seen that the TT's personnel do not need a researcher to tell them that they work collectively and that they work in a news factory. But they do tend to forget that they do not cooperate only with their colleagues. This is not necessarily a problem, however. They forget their computers and their telephones as long as they function well, and that frees their thoughts for the contents of their job. (By the same token they do not have to think much about their colleagues if the work proceeds smoothly.) As for machines, they operate more forcefully if their users do not need to know *how* they work, because many more users can utilize them (Hutchins, 1995: 174). Navigators require little knowledge about modern navigation techniques, in contrast to their predecessors in Micronesia, who needed all the knowledge in their heads.[20] The news producers know that someplace there is a satellite and a server (this one somewhat closer) and that somebody takes care of them – that is enough.

As long as they work properly, of course. One of the critical incidents at the Italian news agency, ANSA, was related to the dramatic blackout that struck Switzerland and its neighbors in 2003. ANSA functioned longer than most, because the journalists went to gas stations to buy oil for their diesel generator. TT also has such a generator, but has not yet been forced to use it. "Our history saved us from serious breakdowns. Once we had a computer breakdown on the evening of elections. We stood still for five or six hours. It wasn't fun, but it was long ago" said TT's information officer to an interviewer from the Board for Psychological Defense (Ekdahl and Wigstrand, 2006: 33).

It is not only the presence of diesel generators that makes for the similarity between a news agency and a modern ship. This is how Hutchins described the collective knowledge on a ship:

[20] Or at least in their collective memory, Ingold (2007).

If one human component fails for the lack of knowledge, the whole system does not grind to a halt. If the task becomes difficult or communications break down, the navigation team does not have the option of stopping work. The task is driven by events and must be performed as long as the ship is underway. In response to a breakdown, the system adapts by changing the nominal division of labor. . . .if [one member] is unable to do so, some other member of the team will contribute whatever is required to ensure [that the task is done]. . . . This robustness is possible by the redundant distribution of knowledge among the members of the team, the access of members to one another's activities, and the fact that the individual workloads are light enough to permit mutual monitoring and occasional assistance. Both the knowledge required to do the task and the responsibility for keeping the system working are distributed across the members of the navigation team. (Hutchins, 1995: 223–4)

N. Katherine Hayles (2007) quoted several Artificial Intelligence and cognition researchers who believe that this model applies not only to navigation or to collective cognition, but to individual cognitions as well. In this view, the brain does not require total representation of the world, or "a global plan", in order to act upon it. It is a collection of semi-autonomous programs that map the pieces of the world while acting upon it. If correct, this insight would explain mysterious "gut feelings" as one of such programs, operating beyond consciousness. Also, navigation and news production may be more typical than it may seem at the first glance. Thus, further glances are required, and in the next chapter I present a study of the next news agency.

4.   ANSA, or meetings and teamwork[1]

Even if narrated by individual persons, the collective character of the news production team became obvious in the previous chapter. In this chapter, I report my direct observation of various types of collective actions. Perhaps not surprisingly, my observations show that a collective cognition is both guided by, and results in, common sense – in the positive meaning of the word.

WHAT IS ANSA?

TT is a national agency, dependent upon other news agencies for its international news. ANSA, on the other hand, is an international agency, with correspondents in many countries. In order to cover countries where there are no ANSA correspondents, the Italian agency has a collaboration contract with Agence France-Presse and Reuters (ANSA receives the Reuters newswire) and a contract with Sky. There are also some less formalized contacts with Associated Press.

ANSA is a cooperative of 36 members – mostly the main national newspapers – and has 22 bureaus in Italy and 79 in 74 other countries. Box 4.1 displays ANSA's website presentation[2].

As my research focused on ANSA's headquarters in Rome and one local bureau, I mention other parts of the company only briefly. Apart from newswires in Italian (general newswire, regional, and specialized newswires), ANSA publishes ANSA English Corporate Service, ANSA English Media Service, Spanish Newswire, and Portuguese Newswire. There is also a new wire called ANSAMed (Mediterranean) that transmits in Italian, English, and Arabic. This newswire was originally situated in

[1] Many thanks to all my interlocutors at ANSA, and to the people who made my study possible: Ania Biedzińska and Gianluca Loni. Separate thanks to Claudio Coletta and Gianni Monaco, who corrected my Italian; and to my colleagues, Giampietro Gobo, Marco Marzano, and Elena Raviola, who have kindly read my Italian manuscript (Czarniawska, 2009d).
[2] See www.ansa.it; last accessed 10 August 2009. During the six months since this research was conducted, the number of daily news items has apparently increased from 2000 to 3000.

BOX 4.1   ABOUT ANSA – AN INTERNATIONAL AGENCY

ANSA is Italy's leading news agency and among the top in the world. It is a cooperative of 36 members comprising publishers and major national newspapers, and was established to publish and distribute news.

For over 60 years, ANSA has been providing comprehensive coverage of events in Italy and abroad through 22 offices at home and in over 79 locations in 74 countries. It covers events as and where they happen.

ANSA provides over 3000 daily news items and more than 700 photos a day via many transmission platforms (Web, satellite, mobile phones) able to meet any format requirements or specific requests made by the market. This is complemented by services tailored to respond to the requirements of an ever more demanding public.

Reliability, comprehensiveness and independence have always been and remain values that confirm ANSA's leadership at home and on the international scene, making it the choice of more than 1400 clients (companies, public administration, media). Its continual pursuit of excellence is rewarded by the judgment of customers: more than 90 percent of its clients recommend ANSA products.

---

the Naples Bureau, but during the time of my study it was being moved to Rome.

There is also ANSA PHOTO, ANSALive (video news) and ANSALive Headlines (video news in real time), ANSA Outdoor TV, ANSA by mobile phone, and a website, ANSA.it. The owners of connected sites can use ANSA Web News and ANSA Web News Plus, Multimedia News Browser, and MultiMedia Information Distributed Access (MIDA). These latter four services are seen as the future of ANSA; the activities that I observed, however, are more firmly situated in its past.

Units and Desks

ANSA works under the supervision of the Board of Directors, which includes President (Chairman of the Board), CEO, and 23 councilors.

*Photo 4.1   The frescos in the corridor in the front of Italian News
Desk (Chronicles)*

Ten councilors form the Executive Committee. There is also the Board
of Statutory Auditors, consisting of a chairperson, two auditors, and two
replacements. There is also a supervisory body, controlling adherence to
the statute and the ethical code.

A group consisting of President, CEO, Deputy CEO, Editor-in-Chief,
and Deputy Editor-in-Chief exercise the operational management.[3]
General Manager, Editor-in-Chief and their deputies meet every two
weeks, as the top managers responsible for commercial, personnel, and
legal aspects of the operations, in order to confront arising legal and personnel problems, but also to discuss new initiatives and products.

ANSA headquarters is located in beautiful old buildings that are
not particularly adapted to serve as premises for an office that relies on
modern technology. Nevertheless, as Photo 4.1 illustrates, the premises
are gorgeous indeed.

At the time of my study, ANSA's Editorial in Rome had 15 desks (apart
from their official names on ANSA's English website, I quote in parentheses their short names as used daily, which I use in the text. I have also
italicized the news desks that I studied):

● Editor's Desk (*Central Desk*)
● International News Desk (Foreign Affairs)

---

[3] ANSA has undergone a change in its management group and a reorganization since I
conducted my study. The change took place in June 2009.

- Cultural News Desk (Culture)
- Italian News Desk (*Chronicles*)
- Economic/Financial News Desk (*Economy*)
- DEA News Archive (Archive)
- Foreign News Desk (Foreign News)
- Photo Desk (Photo)
- Internet Desk (Internet)
- Multimedia Desk (Multimedia)
- Network Desk (Network)
- Political/Parliamentary News Desk (*Politics*)
- Sports News Desk (Sports)
- Science/Health News Desk (Science)
- State Property Projects (Demanio)

As at TT, Central Desk was the main point where all activities converged. This office employed five editors, and functioned as a coordination structure, linking the specialized desks with Editor-in-Chief and Deputy Editor-in-Chief. Central Desk in the main newsroom also coordinated the activities of regional and foreign bureaus, hence, the importance of Central Desk, which is not visible to the clients, however:

> The function of Central Desk is to organize, to coordinate, and then to monitor and control, because overlaps among the specialized desks happen often. So we try to plug the holes, to prevent possible errors or lack of coverage. Every time a news item arrives, we must estimate how big it will become: big, small, or medium. Of course, this estimate may change during the day. Another function is to prepare the News Bills that we call "Facts of the Day"[4] intended for a certain type of medium, which is a summary of main news that comes regularly at certain hours. This is a suggestion for Front Page that we sent to the newspapers, to the radio, to the TV, containing the topics that, in our judgment, should be in relief. But the readers aren't aware of our work. (Int. 4/6)

Near the door to the Central Desk office was an armchair where I often sat waiting for my next interlocutor or the person I was to shadow that day. I could therefore witness a continuous line of people who went in and out:

> We make our interventions with the use of the telephone, but when matters are more serious, we go directly to a given newsroom, talk to the journalists there, and discuss together the problems when they arrive. There's much movement in our office; it's certainly not a quiet place. People come and

---

[4] At Reuters they are called Top News.

Photo 4.2   A newsroom

go at all times, because the other desks feel a need to contact us as well. They call us often, especially when they aren't certain what choice to make. "Look, I'm going to send this Bulletin. Do you agree? Is it right to do so, or do you think that it can be remade as Urgent?" Thus, the contact is continuous. (Int. 4/6)

The following is a brief description of the newsrooms where I observed work (one of them is shown on Photo 4.2):

● Economy & Finance: a News Editor, a Deputy News Editor and four Coverage Editors;[5] Desk Editors working in three shifts; and 30 editors-cum-correspondents.[6] Desk duty rotates, and it can be performed, when needed, by more than one person. Not all Coverage Editors are present all the time.

---

[5] I am Anglicizing the titles.
[6] These data can change and are quoted only to create a general impression of the size of the newsroom.

- Politics & Parliament: one News Editor, three deputies, six Coverage Editors, and 25 editors-cum-correspondents. Everybody takes turns at being Desk Editor – sometimes three persons at the same time.
- Italian Chronicles: one News Editor, three deputies, seven Coverage Editors, and 24 editors-cum-correspondents.
- Regional Bureau: may employ only five journalists, but also use stringers (freelance journalists used more or less systematically by an agency) and other external collaborators.

ANSA in Rome also contains a unit that consists of only one position: Editorial Secretary (a position on the same level as News Editor):

> [A] linking pin between the two spirits of the agency [i.e., between the journalistic Editorial and the managerial Company]; a journalist who answers directly to Editor-in-Chief. . . Obviously, Editor-in-Chief also conducts a direct dialogue with Company, but otherwise it is only Editorial Secretary who talks to Company. (Int. 4/8)

Editorial Secretary is a mediator and a translator who presents to Company the suggestions coming from Editorial, returns with the answers, listens to demands from Company, and presents them to Editorial. Communications concern anything having to do with matters of organization, resources, personnel, and industrial relations. The need for such a position has arisen, I have been told, because of a visible separation between Company and Editorial, caused in part by the fact that the journalists felt a need to protect the autonomy of their profession and the confidentiality of the information they possess. The tasks of Editorial Secretary seem to be similar to those of the mythological Mercury, the messenger responsible for communication between gods and human beings (as to which group is which, opinions differ).

One important group in the past was the polygraphists, who took the news typed by the journalists on their typewriters, and converted it into a form that could be used on a teleprinter (and before the days of the teleprinter, on a telegraph machine). Polygraphists have vanished. A few stenographers are left,[7] now called *dimafonisti* (singular = *dimafonista*: a person who writes down what is dictated on the phone, now directly onto a computer). A correspondent in the field who does not have access to the Internet would call a *dimafonista*, who, working with the editorial

---

[7] Nevertheless, the journalists at Reuters still have to take an obligatory course in stenography (see Chapter 5).

system, would transcribe the conversation and send it to the appropriate News Editor. The *dimafonisti* are only in Rome. Some of the previous polygraphists found work in the regional bureaus: they convert various e-mails into a format that can be entered into ANSA's editorial system, do the accountancy, or simply take care of computers and copying machines.

The Non-humans that Work

The infrastructure of ANSA is extremely complicated; there are many services connected to the editorial system: operating systems, networks, security, and assistance. The latter is incomparable to any other offices, certainly to mine. As soon as the smallest problem arises, a technician arrives (assuming that one was not already present). The cables can be hanging loosely around, and putting a computer on may require special knowledge; it may even require moving to another computer if one does not work. But in the end, everything works. The systems are many and diverse. The old ones are called *legacy* (like many other things, the English word), which need to be compatible with the new ones, however, in order to allow *migrations*. Before a new system can be introduced, it is necessary to prepare application *gateways* (still in English) – the elements that allow a passage from the old to the new system, guaranteeing continuation, assuring that the migration does not create problems for either ANSA or the clients.

The SEAN Editorial system and the news browser Telepress belong to old systems. The new ones, developed by the agency, are AWES (Ansa Wide Editorial System), MNB (Multimedia News Browser), and NEMO (NEws MOnitor). AWES is used only in local bureaus and in some bureaus abroad, as it requires an interface with Apple's browser, Safari, which is not used at headquarters in Rome. Its latest version, which can be used everywhere, is called X-AWES (Extensive Ansa Wide Editorial System):

[W]e do use external IT consultants to make it, but *design and development are both done here*. The layout is similar to the old systems; we wanted to maintain continuity. A journalist will find a control panel where he or she can undertake appropriate operations, where the news items can be sifted, seen, worked upon and transmitted. *We're trying to replicate the same work organization as before*, in order to avoid creating difficulties for the journalists. The journalist who will use the new program will find it different, more up-to-date, with a different graphic interface, with new functions; but the working model, the model of operation, is the same. There's an operative panel to the right, where the journalist can see what is to be done, see the news awaiting elaboration, and then send it. Here, a pull-down menu with the familiar commands, etc. So it looks familiar, but, being a new system, it has the capacity to manage texts, and also photos, videos, audio, and general material. (Int. 4/11)

ANSA does its own design and development, just as TT and Reuters do. What they do at ANSA is similar, but they do not have contact with other agencies. And, like their colleagues at TT and Reuters, the journalists at ANSA are completely dependent on technology, but exactly because of that dependency, their IT people try to make the systems practically invisible. Like the ideal servants, the systems should serve their masters without distracting them from their main activity – news production. This ambition creates a firmly embedded paradox: efficiency, speed, and comfort require the black boxing of technology (especially of software), making reflection difficult, if not impossible.

The cooperation proceeds as follows:

All journalists create their own environment, but there's also an environment common to the whole newsroom. An individual reporter and an individual editor contribute their news items to the appropriate desk. Everybody can see which items others are taking, and what finally arrives at Central Desk. But as long as the reporter and the editor work with their news items, nobody can see what they are doing until the items are sent to Central Desk.

As you can see, here are various lists of news items: those that I'm working with, those that I deleted, those that I sent to the desk. Also, our network permits us to send news items between desks – something that we call "message switching" [in English]. Somebody from Economy can send a news item to Sports; Sports can send something to Chronicles, and Milan Bureau can send something to Naples.

If I'm an editor at any of the desks, I take a news item from those "to be dealt with". Right now there's nothing, but I have a function that permits me to create a news item. So I choose "create", and it asks me: "What kind of news do you want to create?" Here I can choose one of the suggested categories, or name it myself. I write "testing", and then I can choose a subtitle, enter my initials, indicate the city from which I'm sending, and then I enter a full stop. I close the item, choose F6, the system tells me that the news items isn't changeable anymore, and I add "(ANSA)", which opens and closes an item. This is a safety measure so the journalists can't add anything after they enter their initials. If I don't remove the last "(ANSA)", the system won't allow me to write. Later, I can also do a series of things: attach photos, etc. Now I can send this news item to the desk. If I now go back to the desk, I can see that where there was nothing to deal with, there's an item called "testing". Somebody at the desk will take it up, will look at it, edit it, decide to add something, and will send it to the Central Desk. (Int. 4/11)

In order to make it possible for the journalists to use the new system, however, it is necessary to exchange the server and the operating system. Whereas this exchange was relatively easy at local bureaus, it is going to be a major operation at headquarters in Rome. The active participation of the users is absolutely necessary:

> To do it here, we must all work together. We have to upset work in the agency, turn 20 newsrooms upside down, and we need to do it over one night. It's a large operation, important but invasive, which is expected but also feared, so it must be well organized, well done. We must be sure that the system functions well, that it fulfills all the demands of the journalists. In order to achieve this, we have working groups in which we share with the journalists the choices we make, so that at the end they'll be working with a system that they already know. Similar to the one before, one that doesn't upset their daily work, but which has a whole series of new things, new functions to offer.
>
> This kind of operation is usually done first in a pilot newsroom, but it also means that we have to activate a whole series of new communication mechanisms. Because the agency needs to work incessantly, it's like a car that is running and that must be modified while it's running. We need to change the steering wheel, and we need to change the motor, without the car ever coming to a halt. (Int. 4/11)

This image of the machine that runs continuously, a flux that must not be stopped, a flow that must continue, returns in many descriptions provided by the news producers.

Then there are machines and systems that are less specialized: Outlook for e-mails, the Intranet, Internet portals, fax machines (even though ANSA asks its correspondents to use e-mail whenever possible), printers, and copiers (Photo 4.3). Laptops are often leased, usually for three years.

The continuity of the flow depends in the first instance on the current. This aspect of the work at ANSA does not usually interest the journalists, yet it is of utmost importance:

> We have a continuity system that is new and very powerful. It consists of batteries that are incredibly expensive. The Quality Unit prepared a very big room where the batteries lie on specially made shelves that maintain the life of the agency, permitting the systems to work for a long while when there's no current. The systems must not be switched off suddenly; any type of a system, and especially computers, need to be switched off and closed in a proper way. A sudden switch off can cause damage.
>
> After a while, a generator is turned on. We have an enormous generator running on diesel oil, which stands in our courtyard. During the famous black-out in Switzerland in 2003, ANSA was one of the few agencies that was able to maintain continuous productivity. We received many congratulations. ANSA continued to distribute the news and function in spite of the fact that most of Italy was without electricity. When diesel oil was almost used up, one of the managers went to the Civil Defense unit and returned with a can of diesel, and the generator continued to work. (Int. 4/11)

Photo 4.3   The collaborators

I have also heard this story in a more dramatic version, in which the journalists went to petrol stations to fetch diesel oil – whichever way it was, the machine continued running (Photo 4.4).

There is also one room at headquarters where all the modems, and therefore all connections with external networks are collected. It must be remembered that all this takes place in a building from the 1500s, with a meter-thick walls. Therefore the cables usually run outside, and are visible everywhere.

There are safety systems: firewalls, access protocols, routers, reserve networks, all of which are necessary in order to protect the agency from hackers, who have attacked ANSA several times:

Photo 4.4   The generator, the heart of ANSA

We've suffered through attempts to saturate our access band, and therefore
our connection to the Internet, with software called zombies. Once installed
in the system, they remain there until they become activated, creating traffic –
URL-spoofing [in English] – by moving toward the same address. Obviously
such traffic doesn't enter, because it's stopped by the firewall, but it saturates
the access line, especially access provided by COLT, a European provider. We
suffered such an attack during the World Water Forum in New Delhi in 2004.
For a short time there was intense traffic toward the addresses in our network,
endangering the COLT router. It was forced to black out our address to stop
the traffic. For a quarter of an hour, it was impossible to reach any of our
addresses. In cases of such attacks, the victims have no means of defense – only
the provider can intervene. (Int. 4/11)

A zombie attack is particularly dangerous, but does not happen often.
More frequent are viral infections, probably brought in via laptops. "If

*Photo 4.5   Altogether now. The photo also shows my vantage point:
I was sitting behind the two screens on the right*

somebody arrives with an infected laptop and connects it to the network,
not even armed guards can stop it" (Int. 4/11). There are also two different anti-SPAM systems, because ANSA's mail is organized in two layers.
Thus, one system controls the SPAM created internally, and the other
SPAM coming from outside. The two systems are independent, and they
create both false positives and false negatives, but the idea of having a
generic SPAM system has been rejected as inefficient and problematic,
in that it can eliminate important messages. About 50 persons work with
information technology at ANSA.

Last but not least, there are many non-mechanical collaborators. Paper
is everywhere: newspapers, notebooks, books, folders, pictures. . . (Photo
4.5).

The People

About 400 journalists work for ANSA. Who are they? In the Swedish TT
they were persons with degrees from schools of journalism at various universities, but the career road in Italy is more complicated:

> There are short degrees, of two or three years, in information technology or
> journalism. Recently a school of journalism also emerged, and one enters that
> with a completed university degree, usually in languages or political sciences,
> after which one can take the state exam. Until recently, one could only take the

state exam[8] if one was already employed by a journalist company as an apprentice. Since the appearance of the school of journalism it's possible to take the
exam directly after graduating from the school, but there's no guarantee of a
job. (Int. 4/7)

There is a well-entrenched conviction that journalism is a job that one
can learn only by doing it. The graduates of schools of journalism may
find jobs in such areas as press offices and information units, but the road
to true journalism is through apprenticeship:

> An apprentice is a person who does 18 months of apprenticeship,[9] dedicated to
> learning the basic notions of the journalist profession, the basic activities, after
> which comes the state exam that certifies one as a professional journalist. Then
> you can become a junior editor, then an ordinary editor, then a correspondent,
> then a Deputy News Editor, and in the end the News Editor. There's also a
> career within Company, where you can become a Deputy Managing Editor,
> Managing Editor, etc. (Int. 4/8)

The challenge, therefore, is not to pass the exam, but to find a place to
apprentice:

> If you fail the exam, you can repeat it, no big deal. The big deal, the threshold,
> is to find a place for apprenticeship . . . it could take up to ten years to find one
> . . . there's usually one place for ten waiting journalists. (Int. 4/8)

There are also young people trying to acquire practical knowledge of their
discipline by doing a three-month internship; this period is regulated by
law, and is unpaid.

The Company

ANSA's Company employs 250 non-journalists and uses other systems
and other software that Editorial does not: System Management
Resolving Tool (SMART), for example, which helps solve the administrative issues. As I have not studied Company, I cannot say more about
its activities. In what follows, I concentrate on Editorial. As the working
day is organized almost identically to a day at TT, my focus here is on the
central activities within ANSA – which, this time, I was able to observe
closely. Usually, I shadowed a News Editor, a Deputy News Editor or a

---

[8] To become a professional journalist in Italy, one must pass the state exam, consisting of
a written test; this passed, one can take the oral test. The committees that evaluate the
candidates are composed of lawyers and journalists.

[9] A condition introduced by a law decree from 1963.

Desk Editor, which means that I also went to meetings in which the first two participated. The observation took place during the period from January to May 2008.

ACTIVITIES

I have selected the activities that I saw as central in the production of the news (apart from reporting, which is beyond the scope of this study). In ANSA, these were:

- the general meeting at 10.30, chaired by Editor-in-Chief, his deputy or one of the Central Desk Editors, in which all the desks participate, represented by News Editors or their deputies;
- the newsroom meetings, held after the general meeting, which I describe under "A day in the newsroom";
- the collective work within the newsroom; this, too, is described in "A day in the newsroom";
- the work of Desk Editors.

The meetings and the days are fictive, in the sense that they are composed of observations conducted at different times, but they are factual in the sense that they actually took place. As descriptions are made on the basis of my field notes, there can be errors due to misperception, therefore I also quote fragments of actual conversations, which were recorded incidentally during the interviews. As in the previous chapter, I attribute gender randomly and identify the persons only via their functions as currently fulfilled, as most functions rotate. Italic small capital letters indicate News Editors whose turn it is to speak.

The Meeting at 10.30

The representatives of Central Desk meet Editor-in-Chief (or his deputy) and all the News Editors during the two daily meetings. There are four screens in the conference room (Photo 4.6), two with the Italian news, a third showing BBC, CNN, or Sky, and the fourth showing the participant from Milan Bureau.

It is not unusual for a mobile phone or the telephone on the table to ring during the meetings. A participant answers the call, but talks covering the mouth.

> CHAIR [often, but not always, Editor-in-Chief]: First some general matters, some of them quite important. Tonight Sports has an emergency situation; therefore

Photo 4.6   Meeting room. Milan Bureau participates via videoconference

they'll close at 21.30 and will switch with Foreign News. This switch from Sports to Foreign News is a legacy of old times, when Sports at closing didn't switch to Night because Night was afraid of being flooded by sports news from the US. Because space is no longer a problem, this problem no longer exists. So sooner or later we need to do something about the direction of the switch.

SPORTS: At any rate, we'll make a round to see if there's anything of special interest before we close.

CHAIR: I'd also to remind you that every destruction of a news item, but also every substantial change made by Desk Editor, needs to be confirmed by a colleague.

Not for the first time, I could notice a similarity between the news production and financial institutions: in a bank, each check to be cashed needs to be confirmed by a colleague.

CHAIR: Then, and I must add, at last, after the visit of Editor-in-Chief in Naples, it has been decided that ANSAmed will move to Rome in May at the latest. Now, let's talk about yesterday. As usual, we begin with things that went well and with those that didn't go so well.

The news items must be comprehensible in their entirety, even if we're talking about well-known personages. "Hillary" is called Hillary Rodham Clinton. And then, what is she campaigning for?

SPORTS: But at least we've put the US flag in the item!

A critique or a tense situation is often resolved by a joke, mostly relying on word play, and some of them, though not all, are very funny.

CHAIR: Milan, you haven't sent the promised piece of news on time. Also, in the text it should be "connected" not "controlled".
MILAN: I've only heard it about one hundred times by now.

As can be seen here, not everybody tries to relieve tension, but the majority do, which makes the exceptions only too visible.

CHAIR: There were two similar headings in the period of a few minutes [he quotes]. There were also two contradictory items on the same sports league within a few minutes.
    Culture transmitted a piece of news on Michael Jackson under the category "Film".
CULTURE: This is because the correspondent from Los Angeles sends us news forgetting the time difference, and then they may be wrongly classified by Night Desk.

This is one of many times when I witnessed the importance of categories: clients interested in Michael Jackson would not be looking under the "Film" category. The criticism and Culture's defense provoke an animated discussion, which ends with a conclusion that it was Culture's error: "One must control one's own desk!"

CHAIR: Compliments to Economy. All the newspapers have taken up your news item and now everybody is writing about it. Generally speaking, yesterday was quite a good day. Now it's your turn, Central Desk. You checked the newspapers: do we have the same things or not?

Possible answers are: "No, and why not?", "Yes, but we write in a different way", and "Yes".

ECONOMY: I've seen this thing about inspectors who don't control flights properly; we need to follow this.
CENTRAL DESK: There's this story of a mother who killed her daughter because the little one didn't want to eat. We don't have it.
CHAIR: Have we written about Waterloo [see Box 4.2], by the way?
CULTURE: No, actually I don't know why we haven't.
CHAIR: I've heard about it for a few days now, and you do nothing. I also believe that I've already signaled this to you.

Various desks offer various explanations:

NETWORK: Well, poor thing. . . After all, both Austerlitz and Waterloo lie in valleys.
CHAIR: Waterloo lies on a hill. At any rate, I only wanted to know if it's an accident that we don't have it.

BOX 4.2   WATERLOO BLUNDER

Luca Luciani, a manager at Telecom has been rendered immortal on YouTube. . . during a meeting, encouraged "his fabulous team" to imitate Napoleon at Waterloo. . .[10]

As in many similar cases, there is always someone who has almost encyclopedic knowledge of the topic, no matter how obscure. Foreign News ends the discussion of the Waterloo case by saying: "At any rate, now we're doing it".

CENTRAL DESK: *New York Times* has run an article headed "The story of the new barbarians" about Romanies and the homeless in Rome.
CHAIR: And we haven't noticed it? Strange.
CENTRAL DESK: *La Repubblica* says: "Meredith [Kercher, a British student in Perugia] has perhaps been killed with two knives".
CHAIR: The Meredith case teaches us a lesson: we haven't worked enough on the hypothesis of two killers.[11]
CHRONICLES: Our reporter says that there are a great many stories around the Meredith case. Which one should we choose, not having confirmation?
CHAIR: We must await confirmation.

The importance of verification through confirmations is often stressed.

CHAIR: Let's start the usual round.
FOREIGN AFFAIRS: D'Alema is in Israel, after which he goes to Caracas [see Box 4.3].
CHAIR: And what are we doing in Caracas?
ECONOMY: Scaroni [a chief executive officer of Italian energy company Eni SpA] is also in Caracas.
CHAIR: Are they going to be there at the same time? And are we doing something?
FOREIGN AFFAIRS: We had it yesterday.
CHAIR: But are our people in Latin America informed?

---

[10] *La Repubblica*, 7, April 2009. Unless a version already existed in English, I have translated all the Italian texts. For a video on Luca Luciani with English subtitles, see www.youtube.com/watch?v=MbEFmkHW6CQ. See also http://www.italymag.co.uk/italy/society/telecom-manager-red-faced-after-waterloo blunder: both last accessed 1 July 2011.

[11] "Sat Dec 5, 2009. PERUGIA, Italy (Reuters) – An Italian court sentenced American student Amanda Knox to 26 years in prison and jailed her ex-boyfriend for 25 years after they were found guilty of murdering Knox's British roommate during a drunken sex game. . . . The November 2007 murder of Meredith Kercher and the defendant's 11-month trial in the university town of Perugia, drew huge interest around the world. In 2008 a man was sentenced for his part in the murder".

BOX 4.3   MINISTER AND CEO VISIT CARACAS

28 February 2008 – A few minutes ago, Vice Prime Minister and Minister of Foreign Affairs Massimo D'Alema left Roma for Caracas, where he will meet with the Venezuelan authorities tomorrow. There he will also meet Paolo Scaroni, CEO of Eni, who is also in Venezuela to sign some agreements on petroleum in order to end the protracted dispute with the Venezuelan government.

Although my interlocutors often pointed out the difficulties related to the need for coordinating work among the various desks, the fact is that the attempts at coordination are continuous.

FOREIGN NEWS: The Olympic torch arrives at San Francisco, where peaceful protests are expected. The Mayor will hold a speech about peace. We shall see how it will develop. In Peking there will be a meeting that everybody will attend.

SPORTS: The new idea is that the torch should be extinguished. What do you think? Will our politicians go to Peking or not?

CHAIR: We can pose this question to all the candidates for the Prime Minister. What do they think about the torch? Would they go to Peking as the official representatives of the Italian State? We can ask the same question of Ex-Prime Minister Romano Prodi. But going there or not going there has really nothing to do with the Olympics. . . here we have a lot of confusion.

SPORTS: For example, Bush said that he might not go, and after that he said today that he would go.

FOREIGN NEWS: Merkel says, "Let's send the athletes, but let's not go to the opening ceremony".

CENTRAL DESK: Considering that the television and the press simplify everything, it's very easy to confuse the two things.

CHAIR: But the Olympics must not be confused with Tibet.

SPORTS: But all sport pronouncements have a political tinge.

CHAIR: Sheer hypocrisy. It doesn't cost anything not to be at the ceremonies of honor, and China doesn't care.

CENTRAL DESK: We've already seen those who said they wouldn't go and then they all go.

A general discussion follows, ending with a conclusion: "All these guys love making empty gestures, but everybody wants to trade with China, and nobody dares to offend the Chinese".

Such a discussion could have taken place in any cafeteria in any company. The difference is that here there are no expressions indicating strong political preferences. Worth noting is their distancing of themselves from the television and the press. Obviously, ANSA does *not* simplify.

POLITICS: Ballots: reprint them or not? Press conference of Casini [President of Chamber of Deputies] who is for reprinting.
SPORTS: A woman from the US writes that. . .

A general discussion about the ballot papers, which are seen by some as misleading. Since the infamous problems with ballots at the US election in 2000, the issue of legibility of ballots has become pertinent everywhere:

CHRONICLES: I can't see the problem. Why not ask if one is uncertain?
CHAIR: Yes, but the elderly, or the immigrants. . .
CHRONICLES: Well, at least we've explained why there's a problem with the ballots this time around.
POLITICS: It's mostly because there are no coalitions.

There were various coalitions, but not, as many times before, two large coalitions that compete with one another.

CHRONICLES: This means that we have to explain it once more, but also ask Pisanu [Home Office].
POLITICS: Pisanu is going to be together with Berlusconi in Alghero and Cagliari. [Sardinia. He explains how they are going to be interviewed.] At any rate, the ballots are made according to the law that had been passed when there were coalitions. Now there are no coalitions, but the law remains.
CHAIR: Do we have the ballots from previous elections? We can ask the Chair of the Electoral Committee for comments.

Once again everybody joins the conversation. Politics says that they must not complicate matters too much, because the lady – that is, me – will not understand. Chair answers that, compared to politics in Poland, all this is simple enough. True.

CHRONICLES: Two kid brothers from Gravina [found dead in a well] are on all the front pages. Is it possible that they survived for 24 hours? Are there traces of their nails on the wall? Perhaps, perhaps not.
CHAIR: Let us develop two original themes. First, why weren't they found earlier? Who has drawn an arrow on the wall? [Signaling that the well has been controlled.] In America it's obvious who leaves the signs. Another topic: why is the father still in prison?
CHRONICLES: They have controlled the well, but they couldn't see anything from above.

A general discussion on the construction of wells begins. It will continue in the newsroom, where it becomes even more obvious that the specific expertise of the journalists is strongly reinforced by their belief that they represent common sense.

ECONOMY: Everybody is talking about the list of persons who evade taxes by having bank accounts abroad,[12] but no such list has been made public. Everybody knows, though, that there has been a general flight from taxes.

POLITICS: In my opinion, it's all connected to the elections. I've been told . . . [he says what he has been told], but this is worth nothing, just gossip.

CHAIR: But do we have this list or don't we?

ECONOMY: Officially we don't.

POLITICS: Still in my opinion, it will be never made public.

CHAIR: That's a challenge for our investigative journalists. . . We have to find it.

POLITICS: This is truly important.

Chair suggests an action plan:

CHAIR: For the time being we can say, graciously, that we know that such a list exists and that its existence influences elections. Afterwards, you can ask Di Pietro: "What would you do if you received that list?"

POLITICS: Alright.

ECONOMY: If that list came from the political left or the political right, it would have been already accessible to everyone. But behind this there's some joker.

Discussions of this kind illustrate well the tensions between the requirements and acceptable conditions of a news agency and those of the general media. Whoever will find that list (if it exists) will make a sensational scoop. But a news agency cannot be found guessing, and must not quote informal rumors. It can only say what its journalists know, or what they have learned by eliciting responses from the sources.

ECONOMY: The new Chair of Alitalia Board of Directors, Pollice, seems to be very cautious. Tomorrow they'll meet the unions, today they're meeting the government, but it's clear that the problems can't be resolved before the elections. The French [who offered to buy Alitalia but were rejected by the Italian government]. . .

CENTRAL DESK: For Jean-Cyril Spinetta [of Air France] this meant losing face. There's also a technical problem: the lawyers say that Alitalia's books must be balanced before it can be sold. Time and room for the maneuvers are very tight.

CHAIR: What about Alitalia itself — is it looking for some other way out?

ECONOMY: If I've got it right, Alitalia wants to have some more time. . .

CENTRAL DESK: It has wanted more time for a year now.

ECONOMY: Well, but the unions need to understand the situation of the company.

Many comments concern the contents of the news – not only its form. Still, they reveal the line of reasoning – following common sense rather than political attitudes. This is what happened the next day:

---

[12] "Evaders of Lichtenstein", 29 February 2008. Later, the government offered amnesty to tax evaders.

ECONOMY: Alitalia won't meet the union representatives today, probably in order not to irritate them unnecessarily before the meeting with the government, which has been postponed until tomorrow. It's also said that, as it is now, Alitalia can survive for two months: April and May. The French say nothing for the moment. The new government will need at least a month to be able to do something. It will be even worse if there's a break-even in the Senate.[13]

SPORTS: There's this boy who has been hurt ["Collision in the field; 19-year-old footballer at death's door"]. Shall we interview the traumatologist?
CHAIR: It seems that the cause of all this was the fact that they were playing on artificial ground – that is, on the field made of a synthetic material.
SPORTS: Exactly. Synthetics can be dangerous, as the movements become unnatural.

Now, perhaps it is to be expected that Sports News Editor knows such things, but how is it possible that Chair – and almost everybody – possesses this kind of esoteric information? One would assume a specific expertise, but in the group there is always somebody who seems to know what needs to be known. When nobody knows, somebody promises to find the information needed – and it is not necessarily a journalist occupied with this issue:

SCIENCE: There's this story of the day-after contraception pill.
CHAIR: I promise to collect more information on this matter. There's a law that says that even if a physician is a conscientious objector [i.e., opposes the day-after pill] an organization such as a pharmacy or the emergency unit is obliged to provide the pill.
SCIENCE: I don't think there's a possibility of declaring a conscientious objection on this matter. But the Vatican runs a strong campaign against the pill.

REGION LAZIO (i.e. Rome and vicinity): A boy has been reported to the police for erasing Nazi graffiti on the wall of his school and replacing it with the anti-Nazi one.
CHAIR: Has he been suspended?
CHRONICLES: No, not at all, just brought to the police headquarters. He's a son of a well-known journalist, so it has been hushed up.
DEMANIO: Explain?
CHRONICLES: Well, there's a debate on the difference between erasing and writing graffiti. . .
CHAIR: And the difference between defending Auschwitz and writing graffiti?. . . Sorry about this.

---

[13] Alitalia remained under Italian ownership, rescued by 16 private investors and a government crisis package. One of the investors, Roberto Colaninni, became Chair of the Board. Alitalia has also merged with Air One.

CHRONICLES: The police can't see it that way.
CHAIR: But it's a defense against fascism. . .

Here, the usual caution breaks down. Everybody has an opinion on the matter. It could be because the topic is especially sensitive in Italy, or perhaps because the problem is a new one, and common sense cannot provide an easy answer. Is it permissible to write graffiti defending just issues?

Such conversations, almost chats, seem to run counter to the cybernized picture of news production that I am trying to convey. This type of overflow – out of the framing imposed by technology, the requirement of speed and schedules – is typical of all human gatherings (see also the controversy between Latour, 1996 and Dodier, 1997; and between Knorr Cetina and Bruegger, 2002 and Beunza and Stark, 2005). Sooner or later, however, somebody or something will manage the overflow, re-imposing the frame – in this case, the usual speaking order).

Now it is the turn of Milan, Multimedia, and Network, but I haven't found particularly illustrative examples of their conversations. At the end, Central Desk summarizes the round, repeating the news that has been accepted. The list will be mailed to everybody.

A Day in the Newsroom 1

12.50

The News Editor who participated in the morning meeting at 10.30 repeats the conclusions reached and assigns work. The most important is the letter sent by Berlusconi to all the voters, in which he explains his program and his projects and presents his candidates. This will be the work of journalists 1 and 7, with 5 joining in as soon as she can.[14] This article should be ready by 15.30. Are there any questions? And what are the plans for tomorrow?

ADMINISTRATOR (an employee of Company who is visiting): The electoral candidates are in Bari and Torino.
NEWS EDITOR: We can only send one person.
ADMINISTRATOR: The same person who goes to Bari could go to Torino.
NEWS EDITOR: I have nothing against that.

Journalist 2 reminds everybody of the press conferences for tomorrow. Journalist 9 comes in:

---

[14] I am calling everybody but the heads of a desk "journalists", as they can both report and edit.

NEWS EDITOR: Considering that you're here, could you perhaps do a piece on Veltroni's electoral coach? 3, should we give up Milan?
JOURNALIST 3: Great!
NEWS EDITOR: Better to do Naples and . . . no, we won't send two people; Naples is enough. Let the Milan Bureau do Milan, Bologna will do Bologna, and we'll do Rome on Friday.

The logistics of transports and services is important, as it is in any factory. The right people should be in right place at the right time. It is better to send two people rather than no one, but it is best to send one instead of two (especially when an Administrator is listening to the plans, with an eye on expenses).

NEWS EDITOR: Could somebody give me the right numbers? Those I have are all wrong. . .
JOURNALIST 2: Have you read the interview with the economist, Polito? He said that in these elections everybody travels and nobody can understand anything anymore, because it's possible to see two TV programs simultaneously, one showing the same person in the TV studio and another showing him on a city square. . .
NEWS EDITOR: The piece with the right numbers, please, please!

Apart from the virtual memory deposited in Archive, there is also the collective memory. News producers, like everyone else, forget things (to quote witty Journalist 2: " I've just remembered that I forgot. . ."), but there is always somebody else who remembers, or who can find the right numbers.

NEWS EDITOR: Bari has been done already yesterday. Potenza Bureau can do Potenza. 3; you better do the piece on the ballots. I, I know nothing about anything anymore.

Journalists 5 and 9 remind him of a pending press conference, and he sends one of them there:

JOURNALIST 2: We could interview X. . .
NEWS EDITOR: No, no, Culture will do that. Unless even Gianfranco Fini [the Finance Minister] shows up.
JOURNALIST 6: How about this TV duel between Berlusconi and Veltroni on Friday?
NEWS EDITOR: Don't have any information on that yet.

In contrast to a factory, at least a traditional factory, here coordination cannot be planned in advance – that is, it is planned, but is changed and adjusted continually. Perhaps this is why one of my interlocutors suggested to me that, instead of talking of a news factory, I should be using the metaphor of a fish market. News and fish must be caught fresh, and then treated with caution and flexibility. Gaye Tuchman (1978) used this metaphor in describing news production, speaking of a "net of news", and using other fishing metaphors.

Journalist 5 discusses the idea of a text with News Editor:

> It's not a great piece but I could do it.

News Editor calls somebody on the phone:

> Would you be interested in a piece dedicated to what our government thinks of Alitalia? Yes? Great!

The contacts with other desks are frequent, and it is not rare that a journalist from one desk does a piece for another desk, as in the previous case.

> JOURNALIST 6: Gee, I'm tired! I've just put in a wrong name.
> NEWS EDITOR: Blast! I've just sent it to the wire. Help! It's my fault entirely, I should have noticed!

News Editor transmits the corrected version, while Journalist 6 calls Central Desk to explain what has happened. Thus, even corrections are made collectively.

News Editor puts the receiver down and turns to his colleagues:

> It was Central Desk. Attention everybody, if anybody says, "according to the polls", we omit the information.
> JOURNALIST 2: Right! The noun "polls" is prohibited.

A couple of hours later:

> NEWS EDITOR: Candidate Valeria Marini says that the People of Freedom [PdL, the coalition led by Berlusconi] has a 4 percent advantage and the undecided will therefore become the key to the situation. But I've been told, and several times at that, not to quote the polls, not even the old ones . . . [everybody watches him in silence, expecting a decision]. I find it absolutely right but . . . [changes the text so that the reference to the polls is inside a quote from Marini's statement].

This decision actually derives from an iron rule, observed by all news agencies: there is a critical difference between "X says that it is like that" and "It is like that".

Most journalists end their working day at 21.00. News Editor stays on, just in case.

A Day in the Newsroom 2

12.34

Meeting at News Desk: News Editor 3 repeats what has been said at the 10.30 meeting. The most important task for News Desk is to cover a specific event. During the three days before the elections, the parties will be presenting their symbols – identification marks – in Quirinale, the presidential palace. These presentations should be covered, together with a final presentation when all parties have presented theirs, after 16.00 on 2 April. On 9 and 10 April, there will be a presentation of candidates:

> *NEWS EDITOR 1*: Thousands of years ago, it was enough to go and see who arrived first, and then check the rest by the phone. In those days, symbols were just that – symbols. But now. . . At what time does it start? I must know who to send there.

Coverage Editor 1 reminds her that Journalist 1 has changed her working hours, so it's only Journalist 2 who will be here on Saturday and Sunday. And then there is the trainee – from 08.00 to 20.00.

> *NEWS EDITOR 3*: Are there gay candidates in the Democratic Party?
> *JOURNALIST 3*: There are two already.
> *NEWS EDITOR 3*: The little brothers from Gravina. How was the search organized, do we do like in the US where those who searched through a place leave a sign?
> *NEWS EDITOR 1*: Ah, the Chair didn't read his newspapers! Everything has already been explained.
> *NEWS EDITOR 3*: But the father's situation? Also, a lecture on vanished persons. Further: the traces of the nails on the wall. There's a discussion about whether it was a false clue or not.
> *NEWS EDITOR 1*: We've clarified that it wasn't true. They continue to write it, and we continue to deny it.
> *COVERAGE EDITOR 1*: It's not that there's contradictory information. What has happened is that the attorney who defended the father said that.

Here again, the difference between "the attorney has said that there were nail traces" and "there were nail traces" comes to the fore. An utterance must be put in quotation marks, which immediately changes its status.

> *NEWS EDITOR 3*: The same thing in the *Sole 24 Ore* [the Italian equivalent of the *Financial Times*], they write either too much or too little. One of us could speak to this boy who discovered the well while looking for a friend of his who also

vanished. Furthermore, they said during the meeting that we could interview the proprietors of the land on which the well is situated.

News Editor does repeat the conclusions of the 10.30 meeting, but elaborates upon them, translates them for the requirements of this desk, and adapts them if necessary.

> *NEWS EDITOR 3*: The massacre of Erba [a married couple, Olindo and Rosa Romano, have killed the wife and two-year-old son of a Tunisian, Azouz Marzouk]. There will be no cross-examination because the husband and wife admitted their guilt voluntarily.

Then, the idea of a piece on the inheritance of profession was very well received:[15]

> *DESK EDITOR*: Can't somebody else do it?
> *NEWS EDITOR 1*: Sons go to the same university that their fathers do and choose the same profession, says the sociologist Ferrarotti. And on 12 March there's a big meeting between the graduates and the companies. . . .
> *NEWS EDITOR 3*: The newspapers are all talking about the list of people who have accounts abroad. There's a hunt for that list. According to Politics, such a list may or may not exist, or else can be produced in the last moment. Who will have it, in your opinion? The Internal Revenue Service or the Ministry of Foreign Affairs?
> *COVERAGE EDITOR 1*: There will be a press conference at the Ministry of Finance.
> *JOURNALIST 3*: It would be an utter calamity if we didn't get that list.

As during the 10.30 meeting, the topic causes much discussion.

> *NEWS EDITOR 1 TO DESK EDITOR*: The newspapers are talking about abusive fathers. We've used the wrong address and a wrong category.

Desk Editor defends his predecessor:

> But it was all very hypothetical.
> *NEWS EDITOR 1*: If you don't believe it, don't send it.

Here is another iron rule; such rules are more like mantras. I do not think they are repeated for my sake; it's for the sake of the new people and trainees, but also for general memorizing. Also, it becomes clear that every desk counts its successes and errors; its members not limiting themselves to those mentioned during the 10.30 meeting.

---

[15] "Profession? You inherit it from your father," 29 February 2008.

The meeting comes to an end and the work begins. An urgent press release arrives, first noticed by News Editor 3:

> That's a good one! Palermo has released [because the legal time of arrest without accusation has expired] Giuseppe Salvatore Riina, the third-born son of Totò Riina, the Mafia boss from Corleone.

He sends it practically while reading it.

In the case of certain news items, speed is more important than checking the correctness of the text. I managed to get down a conversation in its entirety:

> *NEWS EDITOR 2*: Excuse me 1, have you heard anything yet? Any changes?
> *NEWS EDITOR 1*: No. Only Milan has responded.
> *NEWS EDITOR 2*: Have you read this incredible story?
> *NEWS EDITOR 1*: No.
> *NEWS EDITOR 2*: A man was keeping two corpses in his house, and then he went out and died on the street.
> *NEWS EDITOR 1*: Did he commit suicide?
> *NEWS EDITOR 2*: No, no, at least they don't say that.
> *NEWS EDITOR 1* (controls): Oh yes, they say so in the last version.

And another mystery:

> *NEWS EDITOR 2*: A pupil beaten up by fellow students – have I read it already in the newspapers or am I wrong?

I was posing the same question myself. After all, it is not likely that such things happen twice on the same day. But apparently, as it turned out, they do:

> *COVERAGE EDITOR 1*: Perhaps these are further developments.
> *DESK EDITOR:* No, there are two girls. One went skiing with her classmates, and the other was invited home by her classmates and then beaten up.

News Editor 1 is making a call:

> Is this a new news item or an old? Is this the same case or not? (Turns to News Editor 2.) Let's wait, they'll send us both pieces of news, so we'll see.

The latest version is reproduced in Box 4.4.

ANSA's Archive has done the verification. The very same day, another case needed verification:

NEWS EDITOR 2: A Chinese girl threw herself from the window. We have to check if this was a family problem or another case of bullying.

Ten minutes later, another news item arrives from the same place – this time it is an Ethiopian girl:

NEWS EDITOR 2: Let's put them together, after all, it's the same Scandicci [a town of 5000 inhabitants in Tuscany].

BOX 4.4   VERIFIED BULLYING STORY

No end to bullying? Another girl beaten up by her classmates, this time because of a conflict over a boyfriend

A 15-year-old girl from Mantova, attending the first year of the Technical Institute in Mirandola, Modena, has been beaten up by her classmates (seven or eight girls) when leaving school; the incident was in connection with her boyfriend.

The episode, reported by "Carlino Modena", took place on Tuesday. The 15-year-old was beaten and kicked by the other girls, and was suffering from several contusions.

She went to the emergency unit and had to wear a medical neckband for ten days. The grounds for the conflict were the anonymous compliments to her boyfriend posted on the Internet, which the jealous 15-year-old attributed to one of her older class-mates, who had earlier suggested that she had no chance with the boy. The older classmate first denied it, but then, angry, attacked the 15-year-old outside the school, with help of her friends.

[Follows another take.]

Source: ANSA

It turns out that the Ethiopian girl did not throw herself from the window, but from the stairs, because she did not like her mother's new partner:

NEWS EDITOR 2: The heading is all wrong, "jealous of her mother" sounds as if they had the same boyfriend. "Annoyed with her mother"?

News Editor 1 on the phone:

Do something on those two girls from Scandicci. Urgent – 50 lines.

A new text arrives: the Chinese girl wrote in her diary (not in a letter, as it was said before) that she wants to die, and left her diary on her school desk. At home she slept in a room one-meter by one-meter, without windows.

Another item arrives: the name of the school was wrong in the previous one. A new text arrives: the Chinese girl will live, she only broke a leg. So will the Ethiopian girl.

This case is a good illustration of the "development" of news. The race for speed means that the news is transmitted immediately. In time, other details arrive, and many errors and misunderstandings are explained. When ANSA writes the final piece, though, the news has already been verified.

During my day in Newsroom 2, I also witnessed many examples of the ways in which tensions are resolved:

NEWS EDITOR 2: Trainee, could you do Mantovano [an MP], please?
TRAINEE: Ridiculous, I already did it yesterday.

News Editor 2 does not answer. I'm expecting a serious breakdown in communication, or at least some cooling down, but the trainee returns after a few minutes and the conversation continues as if nothing ever happened.

Another situation: News Editors 1 and 2 do not agree on a certain matter. News Editor 2 apologizes, saying that she did not have bad intentions. News Editor does not answer, which to me signals an interruption in the contact. Later, I learn that, on the contrary, this is one of the typical reactions to what may be a beginning of a conflict: saying nothing dismisses the original situation as if it did not exist. Many small conflicts exist, but are truncated at the start. Apart from that, there are great many jokes, easing possible tensions. Not everybody is very good at this game, but everybody tries.

The newly arrived Desk Editor has a fit of anger, quite unjustified. News Editor 2 attempts to placate him:

NEWS EDITOR 2: Would you like a mint candy?
DESK EDITOR: No, I wouldn't.
NEWS EDITOR 2: Pity because it's truly good.
DESK EDITOR: In such case I repent and take it with thanks.

I am sure that real conflicts exist, deeper and longer (I have eavesdropped on many private conversations around the copying machine), but everybody sees to it that the production of news proceeds smoothly.

The Work of a Desk Editor

Desk Editors work with the program, SEAN Editorial, and what they see after opening the Basket "Texts to be dealt with" is shown in Box 4.5.

When Desk Editor chooses one of these texts to be dealt with, its title appears in red on others' screens. I am observing Desk Editor, who has no text to deal with, so she starts preparing the work schedule for the next day, which will be updated at 13.30. The list is ordered according to the importance of things that need to be done – from the most to the least critical, as decided by News Editors.

A text appears in the basket. Desk Editor does not understand it, so she goes to Archive to see if there is a better one. There is none. She calls the correspondent (who can be identified by initials) demanding improvements. Again, nothing. Desk Editor checks the newswire.

A text arrives, informing that one of the candidates in the elections is a Chinese woman. The text cannot be modified because it ends with ANSA/.

BOX 4.5   THE SEAN EDITORIAL SYSTEM

SEAN Editorial

Heading and subheading
Addresses for transmission:
Priority (for example Urgent), Categories and Addresses for sending (for example ECO FIN, Economy, business and finance)

Initials and Take Number (for example BC 2)

SEAN has a limit of words for a given type of text. If this limit is exceeded, the computer highlights the excess in yellow and asks: YOU HAVE REACHED THE LIMIT OF 16 LINES. DO YOU REALLY WISH TO CONTINUE?

When the text is ready, Desk Editor writes /ANSA or TO BE CONTINUED. After that, there is a choice among the commands: Transmit (to the newswire), Flash, Send (to somebody else within ANSA), Register, Cancel, Filter titles, Update (data).

If there are corrections, "Correct" +++, "Repetition" RPT+++-

But Desk Editor does not like it: she presses F6 to overrule the ending. She then calls the journalist:

> "The first ever Chinese candidate". In Italy or in the Municipality of Campi Bisenzio?
> "Candidate on the civil list". But which one? Perhaps you could interview her?
> [I can hear the answer: the journalist says that she has already talked to the woman.]
> You did? And you have written only four lines? Do cancel and write anew, please.

Desk Editor says to me that she can make a wager that this is the list of the Left. A new text arrives: she was right; the Chinese candidate belongs to the Democratic Party in Campi Bisenzio in the Province of Florence.

News Editor has heard that a rapist has been released from prison. Desk Editor checks the newswire and Archive, I check on Google. We find nothing.

A text arrives, concerning an armed student at the University of Lausanne. The court sentenced him to: "suspension, no need to justify the sentence". Desk Editor finds that curious, and discusses the matter with L, who specializes in legal matters. Texts of this kind are usually sent to him first.

Desk Editor makes a call:

> Those 26 lines on Claudio Fava [an MP from Catania] and the elections are somewhat heavy. I put it in Hold Basket.

Ten minutes later, she asks the journalist (who sits in the other room):

> Is Fava ready?

A text arrives. She sighs. "Still heavy". She transmits it to the wire.

A text called "Against the nouveau poor" (most likely, a reaction to the *New York Times* article on the new barbarians) arrives in the basket. Desk Editor sends it to Politics and Economy, with a comment: "I believe this could be of interest to you".

Desk Editor is not certain what category to ascribe to a text. She confers with L, who says: "Put it in two categories". Desk Editor: "I did actually".

A text on the funeral of the two little brothers from Gravina arrives. It is called "Gravina: The bishop says we should weep over our sins". Desk Editor confers with News Editor and they decide it should contain

---

BOX 4.6   LA REPUBBLICA'S VERSION OF GRAVINA STORY

Gravina: Father, Adieu my little angels

9 April 2008 at 17:48 – Source: repubblica.it

"Adieu my little angels" – with these words, Filippo Pappalardi bid goodbye to his sons, in a message read at the end of the religious service in Cathedral of Gravina. In those few lines read in the church, he mentioned that as nobody heard "their shouts; I am tormented by the cries of pain of Ciccio, by the desperation of the little Salvatore who helplessly watched his brother passing away in the cold darkness of the cistern, praying for help during these long, long hours". These were "the moments of most cruel grief, adieu Ciccio, adieu Salvatore, adieu little angels.". . . He followed the coffins of Ciccio and Tore, the two sons, of whose killing he had been previously accused, in total desperation. . . .

---

four takes, one containing the bishop's entire speech. The last part is the father's letter, who was previously suspected of infanticide. It was read during the funeral by a cousin, as the father was too shaken to read it himself. Desk Editor consults with News Editor and Coverage Editor over the subheading. The choice is between "Adieu my little angels" and "I am tormented by their cries". After a long discussion, Desk Editor chooses the latter. The newspapers, however, decide differently (see Box 4.6 for *La Repubblica*'s online version).

Next Desk Editor arrives; the person I observed says to him: "The desk is spotless".

The Speed

In order to help readers understand the pace of work, I also report fragments of conversations that I recorded during spontaneous breaks in the interviews. They sounded like the conversations of rappers:

> The telephone rings: Yes, . . . A? . . . Ah yes, I do know. C is working on it and sent me a message saying that she's preparing a piece. Talk to her for a while. . . Yes, talk to her. . . talk to her for a second at any rate. OK? Ciao.

As you're here, you can tell me if the piece by X should be sent to somebody else or straight to the wire?
I'd put it on the Internet, and send it to Newsroom Y.
Gotcha.
Put it. . . put it on the net, give it, give it.

D! Our piece is still there because E still doesn't have those five. . .
Then cut this piece . . . cut it inside and give it without this thing here.
But our table is all in negative. Shall I update it all?
The whole thing, quickly. Thanks. . .

Hello? Eh. Yes. Yes. Yes. We want it in Reloc [regional-local wire]. It seems useless to me. . . . Yes, exactly. Well, give it to Reloc considering they've written it. OK. Thanks. Bye.
Turns to another person: G! . . . G!
Yes?
Excuse me. There will be an item arriving to the desk from Y. There's an interception . . . you put it only on Reloc.
Only on Reloc. But it was blocked, wasn't it?
Take it off the block. Thanks.

Hello, M? Hi beautiful[16]. Certainly, certainly, whenever you want . . . even in ten minutes. . . Listen M, how many non-journalists work in ANSA?. . . Then I got it right. (Lifts another receiver). S! Is the boss there? . . . (returns to the previous call) Ah, M, there's the executive committee. When will it end?. . . Ah, at three o'clock? But we start now, no? At quarter to three . . . only recently? (Takes the other receiver.) Ciao S. Thanks. M, we talk later then. Learn how it looks. See when it ends . . . hem . . . keep your ears open no? Eh, because now I'm . . . I'm running the risk of distraction because actually I'm in the middle of a long conversation . . . OK. Ciao.

This is the flow of work. I now concentrate on those elements of the flow that seem to me to be crucial to the production of news.

FILTERING AND CLASSIFICATION

To Select the News

I described filtering processes in the previous chapter, but here I return to the topic, for two reasons: in order to make a comparison possible (how similar or different are the agencies?) and in order to focus on somewhat different aspects of these processes.

---

[16] M is a man, as is the speaker. This is not a homosexual allusion, but the usual way of addressing people one likes in Italian.

The very name of the product – news – suggests the direction of filtering processes. Apparently, the peculiar grammatical usage of news in English (it appears to be a plural noun, but it is actually singular) is because it was originally an acronym for North East West South – information coming from all over the world. The news in Italian is called *notizia* – something to be noticed. The Swedish word is *nyhet*, which offers a good explanation of what the news is. *Nyhet* can be read as a combination of two words: new (*ny*) and hot (*het*). So, the news must be new and hot. Still, these are the generic terms, which cannot guide the practice. New for whom? Hot as judged by whom? Where? When?

> An item of news brings in new information. But there can be too much new information. For example, all stock market companies have to present their accounts, but nowadays there are 400 companies on the stock market. Obviously, the news is the accounts of the biggest ten or 20. (Int. 4/1)

The relevance of the source is one criterion, but not the only one. Equally crucial is the weight or importance of the topic. This, however, is a volatile criterion:

> 4/3: Today we've written about the government crisis because it's the most important topic. This means that coverage that has been promised often hasn't been delivered because the government crisis surpassed any other event. As far as our desk is concerned, the most important topic, which has dominated the news for several days now, is the waste disposal problem in the Campania Region.
>
> *BC*: Does it mean that the government crisis limits the space you can dedicate to the waste disposal problem?
>
> 4/3: No, no. News agencies don't have those kinds of problems. It's the newspapers that have to deal with it, because they have to insert the ads and the news takes the space that remains. Thus, if there's reporting on the government crisis, there's less room for the waste disposal problem. As a news agency, we don't have such problems; *we give all the news that we can give.* The more news we give the better, because then the newspapers have a choice. And as, in our opinion, the question of the waste disposal remains hot, we run it in parallel with the government crisis.

Once again, it becomes clear that the phenomenon of information overflow is not a problem for news agencies. "We give all the news that we can give". One event can surpass another on the priority list, but space is limitless. The resources are not limitless, however; people and machines must be redirected to a new important topic, and some coverage can be delayed.

It may seem that no information is ever thrown away, but this is not the case. It would be more correct to say that the *news produced by the journalists* is almost never thrown away. Filtering of messages that arrive by fax and e-mail occur much earlier, as they arrive. During a day at Newsroom 2, I watched one of the News Editors who was checking the arriving faxes. It looked like a (dis)assembly line. She placed a pile of faxes to the left of her desk and placed a wastebasket on the floor to her right. The transfer from left to right occurred at an amazing speed. I do not believe that she kept any of the faxes, but she certainly scrutinized all of them. These were not news items, but simply messages – the raw material, obviously judged to be inadequate. The product – the news – is treated differently:

> Naturally, before throwing away the result of a person's work, you need to discuss it thoroughly. In 99.9 percent of cases, the news is not thrown away. It'll be discussed and probably changed. That's our job, the job of Central Desk: we watch what arrives, and we do a lot of things with it. We're allowed to do any kind of intervention where the editing of news is concerned. (Int. 4/1)

The regional bureaus send almost everything they receive, because they primarily receive official releases. One reason that I undertook a study of news agencies concerned a local event that I had studied – the introduction of the fast tram in Rome (Czarniawska, 2002). The local bureau, ANSA Lazio, transmitted to the regional wire all the faxes received from ATAC (the company responsible for public transport), from traffic police, from all the trade unions involved, from the Municipality of Rome, and from the political parties. This was because the regional newswire is intended for use by the regional newspapers. When a regional bureau is not certain how to classify a news item, a national code is added to it, and then it is up to the editors at headquarters to decide if the news is of general interest. If not, they remove the national code and the regional code is the only address code that remains. Certainly at the regional level, however, but sometimes also at the national level as well, these procedures lead to the dilution of news:

> We often have a discussion about the dilution problem during the two daily meetings. Additionally, the problem is sometimes discussed in more general terms in the meetings between Editor-in-Chief and the News Editors. This isn't an easy problem, because every time some political release is omitted, we receive ten calls of protest. Thus, our challenge is how to inform everybody that this is how we work, that these are the criteria we use when selecting news. As we started from a situation in which everything used to be transmitted, we cannot cut it down rapidly. This is one of the issues that we reflect much upon at ANSA. The first step was to create distinct reading elements. "The facts of the day", given three times a day, offer a synthetic picture of the principal facts reported. Now we're launching a continuously more rational use of breaking news, the signal to the reader where to focus attention while reading the wire. Then there's an increasing use of Rewrite nowadays done during the day – not merely at the end. (Int. 4/9)

Thus, practices that, especially at Reuters, are taken for granted, turn out to be the result of a historical development. It can be said that these are institutionalized ways of managing the overflow at the point of output. A newer set of managing tools exists, however: classification of news items into categories.

The Importance of Categories

The main categories in use indicate the importance of a news item: Flash (an English word is used, but in Reuters these are called "Alerts"; one line), Super-B (Super-Bulletin, two lines; the heading is surrounded by bars to differentiate it from the rest of the wire), B (Bulletin, eight lines, bars), U (Urgent), and R (Routine). While the news items are being transmitted to the newswire incessantly, once, sometimes twice a day, a Rewrite is transmitted (these are real articles, 70–80 lines). The item ends with "(ANSA)", often with the name of the journalist, but, in contrast to TT's journalists, the names of ANSA journalists are rarely printed in newspapers. Flash means "breaking news"; indeed, it interrupts the transmission of the routine news and acquires a priority. Bulletins do not interrupt the transmission, but acquire a place on the top of the news queue.

There are great many more categories in the system, though:

> Look at this news item that I've just transmitted, observe the codes. R means "Routine", that is, the news item isn't very urgent – otherwise I'd have put a U. Then ENV, which means that the news has to do with the environment; next I should be putting in this new code, introduced only recently – IPTC, subject code [see below], but I can't find it right now, and the most important anyway is R14. R14 means that this is a regional news item. Had it been national, I'd have to put R13 to send it to Chronicles, R15 to Politics, or R10 if it was Economy. At the end I need to insert the output codes, S0A if it's Politics or Economy, S0B if it's a Chronicle. (Int. 4/10)

At the end are the initials of the journalist and Desk Editor. The new system of subject categories is seen as critical, as it allows the clients – and the editors – to browse in Archive:

> All these categories serve to maintain a balance in the newswire – a balance in every sense of the word. It helps the clients to understand and to follow the development of big events; it structures the newswire as such; and it helps the newspapers to make their reporting balanced – not too much of one thing and too little of another. (Int. 4/2)

As in TT, the client newspapers are expecting a balanced mix of the news items: not too much of one thing and too little of another. But what are those "things"? Here, the IPTC categories come into question. IPTC stands for International Press Telecommunication Council, and here is the justification of its existence:

> Metadata Taxonomies for the News Industry
> The IPTC not only provides news exchange formats to the news industry but also creates and maintains sets of concepts to be assigned as metadata values to news objects like text, photographs, graphics, audio- and video-files and streams. This allows for a consistent coding of news metadata over the course of time – thus we call them IPTC NewsCodes.
> The universe of NewsCodes is currently split into many different sets – taxonomies – for increased manageability as topics usually relate to a specific area. A taxonomy is also likely to be used exclusively in a specific metadata property of a news exchange format.[17]

As can be expected, the taxonomy is in English. The Italians resolved this difficulty by maintaining the abbreviations but finding Italian equivalents that are phonetically close enough. This is what it looks like (I am quoting the Italian terms as well):

- ACE – Art, Culture & Entertainment – Arte-cultura, intrattenimento
- CLJ – Crime, Law & Justice – Giustizia, Criminalità
- DIS – Disasters & Accidents – Disastri, Incidenti
- FIN – Economy, Business & Finance – Economía, affari e finanza
- EDU – Education – Istruzione
- ENV – Environmental Issues – Ambiente
- HTH – Health – Salute
- HUM – Human Interest – Storie, Curiosità
- LAB – Labour – Lavoro
- LIF – Lifestyle & Leisure – Tempo libero
- POL – Politics – Política
- REL – Religion & Belief – Religioni, Fedi
- SCI – Science & Technology – Scienza, Tecnología
- SOI – Social Issues – Sociale
- SPO – Sports – Sport
- WAR – Unrest, Conflicts & War – Agitazioni, Conflitti, Guerra
- WEA – Weather – Meteo

These are main categories, but there are also two levels of subcategories, most of which lie within Sports. All of these categories have numbers, but it is improbable that anybody but a computer could remember them:

---

[17] See http:www.iptc.org/site/NewsCodes; last accessed 2 July 2011.

There are hundreds and hundreds and hundreds of categories and subcategories and sub-subcategories. There are three levels of categories, and under those are 17 levels of minor subcategories. Now, we don't have rodeos, but they do in the US, so there's a Rodeo category, instead of, for example, Cricket, which is played in the UK and India.[18] (Int. 4/11)

The new editorial system inserts the codes automatically, but an editor can refuse them and insert another code manually.

These are categories and codes used by news agencies and therefore by ANSA, but classifications are also made by others, and they have to be respected as well:

> The police call us sometimes [like at TT, the normal procedure is that they call the police everyday]. For example, yesterday I was told that in Trento a fifth bag snatch occurred since the beginning of the year [it is now March]. But then they told me that it wasn't a bag snatch, but a "dexterous theft", because the woman whose bag was snatched kept it in the basket of her bicycle. If the thief had pushed the woman, it would become a "robbery" – these are the categories of criminal offences. (Int. 3/10)

Perhaps the police are especially sensitive to proper classifications, because they know that the category of the criminal offence decides the sentence. My interlocutors did not seem to think that the categories and news codes were of great importance (it was very different at Reuters!) – they merely serve to introduce some order – but I, convinced by Bowker and Star (1999), believe that they do much more. Categories not only introduce order into words or news items; they also introduce order into the world. The adoption of the Anglo-Saxon classificatory system contributes to the progressive Anglicization – perhaps inevitable – of the Italian news (Czarniawska, 2004). Furthermore, the order thus introduced, arbitrarily one may think, becomes naturalized over time. The taken-for-granted division of the newspapers into parts dedicated to economy, culture, and sports obscures the fact that sports is central in modern cultures, for example. It is probably more central than art and literature, although this is a point to be decided by future anthropologists. Neither is classification always easy and obvious: should the news concerning Michael Jackson be coded as "Film"? Or, to which newsroom should a given item of news belong?

The growing significance of categories is related to the growing significance of the Internet. Gaye Tuchman (1978) observed in her study 30 years

---

[18] Actually, there is a Cricket category (15017000), but it has no subcategories, whereas Rodeo has several: barrel racing, calf roping, bull riding, bulldogging, saddle bronc, bareback, and goat roping.

ago that journalists used typifications rather than categories. Bowker and Star (1999) would have commented that this observation points toward a difference between the Aristotelian classification, in which all the elements under consideration must be classified under some category or another; and the one based on prototypes (indeed typification), in which the elements are classified on the basis of their similarity to a prototype.[19] The Aristotelian classification is stricter and better serves the present times when the standardization of everything progresses (Brunsson and Jacobsson, 2000). Thus, the emergence and general acceptance of IPTC. Categories and codes acquire a central importance in work at Reuters, described in Chapter 5.

VERIFICATION AND VALUATION

Accreditation

As in TT, the first, and perhaps the most vital aspect of verification is accreditation. This happens in two steps: in the first place, a source must exist; in the second, it needs to be situated:

> We can't do like the newspapers that go after rumors. If we publish a news item, we have to have at least one source. So this is the first thing that separates us from the newspapers. They can also have in-depth examinations, general reflections, evaluations, and simply chat – these are all terrains that we don't enter because they aren't ours. (Int. 4/2)

There is a conventional hierarchy of sources, established through decades of experience. Among those highest accredited are the sources from public administration, and the reliable friends:

> The police, for example, are an official source, communicating through the press office of the Department of Security. Then there are privileged sources, sought after by all the journalists, people who in time become intimate, in the sense that we know them and they know us. These are informal sources, and can't be quoted too often, but these are people who we call when we need to check a doubtful fact. For example, there's somebody who calls, and who sounds quite crazy, and says: "They have found a bomb!" You call the person you trust, who confirms it – or not. Good relationships with police and traffic police are essential. (Int. 4/3)

---

[19] They have borrowed this distinction from philosopher Charles Taylor.

Again, like in TT, certain newspapers have the status of an official source:

> I've done a retake from *Financial Times*. I translated the text, took the parts
> that seemed most important to me, I summarized it, made a heading and put it
> on the desk. Coverage Editor has checked it and then sent it to the wire. (Int.
> 4/5)

When in doubt, it is important to obtain confirmation from a person
at the source, especially when they are quoted verbatim. Seems easy, but
it is not. Among other persons that have the experience of the media, the
politicians are best at playing hide-and-seek:

> I had to meet one of the candidates for the election in person, which was much
> better, because then I can put his words in print with complete confidence –
> with quotation marks. In general, it's easy to find the politicians, and they are
> very happy to be in the published news. But then sometimes, for one reason
> or another, especially when there are complications, there's no way to find
> them. . . (Int. 4/10)

For the news producers at news agencies, the previously mentioned distinction between "this is how it is" and "X says that this is how it is" is
crucial:

> When Ciampi was President of the Republic, and especially during the [previ-
> ous] Berlusconi government there were constant clashes, and sometimes there
> was open conflict, especially considering Berlusconi's personality, who is very
> fond of his point of view and is a skilled communicator. He often offered inter-
> pretations: "This is happening because. . ." and often attributed certain deeds
> and opinions to President Ciampi. Then we've been in a very delicate position,
> because we don't write, "The President of the Republic did this and that" if we
> don't have a direct confirmation. Therefore, each time the Prime Minister said
> that the President did this or that, we had to confirm it with the President, and
> his version was often very different. In such cases, you don't know what is the
> true fact. Our rule is to report what we know. We don't say, "The President
> rejected the Prime Minister's version of the story", unless the refutation was
> official. We could say: "According to the Prime Minister, the President has
> done this. However, the press office of the President claims that. . .". Thus, we
> weren't rejecting one version in favor of the other, but were giving the readers
> the elements, the coordinates, situating those elements. The readers can decide
> which source enjoys better credibility, still knowing that the other versions have
> been accredited by other sources. (Int. 4/9)

Thus, although the "iron rules" are the same in TT and in ANSA, the
practical application can become less or more complicated. The rules
remain untouched, but dictate different practices.

What are they after? The facts, as Italian journalist, Marco Travaglio, would say, complaining that in our times the facts have vanished (Travaglio, 2006). The following is a good representation of the moral and cognitive stance of ANSA journalists, offering a reflection of the state of affairs in the contemporary world:

> The only way is to be honest in saying what you have seen, and you must say it sincerely, forcing yourself to say things as you have really seen them. Because it's obvious that there's no absolute truth, especially not in the face of another absolute truth. It depends on the point of view. You report an accident, and you say: "The guilt lies with the bus, because its driver made a strange maneuver", but somebody else who was standing in another part of the street could see that the bus did this strange maneuver because there was a car pushing it from behind. *Giving information means rendering the complexity of different points of view*. When we fail to do that, we deliver information that can technically be called objective – even true – but it's not enough. Information that contains passion is usually aligned. That's why it's called partial, because it offers a part. If you want to sell your point of view, you cut a part of the perspective, don't you? So, this is what we must not do – cut off anything of relevance. Of course it doesn't always mean shortening information – after all, even filling the news with details can be a way of obscuring the main point, can't it? If we report all the points of view, we may obscure those that are truly relevant. So, it's not easy. This is the complexity of our job. (Int. 4/9).

Errare Humanum Est

> ANSA makes errors. Everybody makes errors . . . thus even ANSA makes errors. We try to make errors as rarely as possible, and when we do, we try to correct them as soon as possible.
>
> There are mechanical errors, but they aren't all the same. If you made the newspaper reprint an error on the sports pages, it has more visibility, even, than the one on the political pages – and we get more protests. Then it may happen that we misunderstood something. In such cases it's usually the source that calls us and says: "Oh, you have me saying something that I never said". Or else we can understand something the other way round. Finally, we can make errors in evaluating information: we believe that a story is very important, and then nobody takes it up. Or else we think that something is of little importance, and the next day it explodes. The last two errors aren't frequent, though. . . . What happens more often is that we give a story 20 lines, then the day after one newspaper makes a page out of it, while everybody else reprints our 20 lines. This is the choice of the newspaper, not our error.
>
> Finally, we have errors consisting of not knowing something. Even here there are two types: if there's only one media type that has a piece of information, and nobody else, including us, has it, this is this medium's scoop, and we take it up next day, acknowledging the source. If we don't have information that many others have, however, then it's our miss. This, too, doesn't happen often. Usually, there's something like ten topics a day that could have been treated better, which in the total of 2500 isn't bad. (Int. 4/4)

These were textual errors – the same that were mentioned by the TT interlocutors; but there are also organization errors:

> 4/3: These start with such trivial matters as errors in the organization of coverage – for example, two colleagues from two different desks go to cover the same event, which means that they both waste time. This happens quite often, as the topic can be halfway between the two desks and everybody thinks this is theirs.
> BC: Couldn't it be clarified during the 10.30 meeting?
> 4/3: Yes, but during the meeting it's impossible to foresee everything that will happen during the day. And then there are very important topics that are discussed and less important topics that aren't mentioned at all; otherwise we'd be sitting in the meeting all day long. Thus, it happens that we overlap.

The overlap is, in a sense, a side-effect of the necessary redundancy. Reuters dedicates its meetings primarily to the issue of coordination, however, as shown in the next chapter. Another problem is the opposite: an event appears only under one category, whereas it could be interesting for many other readers:

> It happens that there are two news items on the same event, or only one in, for example, Economy, whereas it would also be interesting for Foreign News. When Central Desk notices that, we take up the item and repeat it in the other category, so that other clients can find it. There can be a newspaper that prints only economic news. If an item goes to Politics only, the people at that newspaper will never see it. Thus, we take it and send it to Economy newswire as well. (Int. 4/6)

As has been seen in the case of the "little brothers from Gravina", the choice of a heading is critical:

> Quite often it's the headings that are erroneous, in the sense that they don't hit the nail on the head, they aren't forceful enough. Even in this aspect, ANSA has changed a lot. Earlier, we used to have very flat headings, very simple – now we're trying to make headings of the same kind as the newspapers do. This is why there are often errors, though these aren't really errors, just erroneous choices. Still, it's always better if the newspapers repeat our headings. (Int. 4/3)

Errors also exist that are typical for certain desks and not for others. Chronicles depend a great deal on information from police and hospitals. This information may change in time, as could be seen in the case of two girls from Scandicci:

> It happens that we publish a news item because the police told us that a certain event happened in a certain way, and then in the middle of the day the same police source says that in truth it was completely different, and the previous

information was wrong. Then we have to withdraw the previous information, and put out a new news item, under the subheading: "Cancels and replaces the previous one". (Int. 4/3)

Corrections coming from Economy can be highly detailed:

> The most common errors are those caused by a mistake in some statements, when one word is taken for another. Or during a rapid typing, somebody puts in a wrong digit. This is serious in economic information, so we do corrections. It can happen to a Desk Editor that he or she writes the correct number in the text, and puts the wrong one in the headings, simply because of a typing error: there's "sales + 10%" in the heading and in the text "sales + 20%". If neither Desk Editor nor Central Desk notices it, we have to correct and repeat it. It happens often that the company in question notifies us, rings and says, "Look, you've made a mistake".
>
> A correction means that you write: "Attention to the news item sent by X, at Y hour, with the heading Z. Please replace in the fourth line number 10 with number 20", you send this correction, and then you send the news item once more, this time correct.
>
> This is a problem shared by all news agencies: nobody can cancel something that has been already sent to the wire. I've never seen a newspaper print the wrong information, however, if we've corrected it. (Int. 4/5)

So, errors, yes, but nothing serious, and then they are corrected. In fact, as the next quote explains, the errors are banal because work is commonplace. As Niklas Luhmann pointed out, the organization of the news production is the opposite of what the news producers define as newsworthy: "The organization fulfills its social function precisely by working differently" (2000: 35).

There are stories of more dramatic incidents, even if they may be apocryphal:

> Luckily, we're not surgeons, . . . though now and then you say to yourself: "I could have done it better; I could have done it differently". In essence, you make an error if you wrongly evaluate the situation. But normally we don't make errors, not because we're so good, but because it's work like any other, and you don't make errors in your work. Anybody can make an error, but there's nothing dramatic to it, it's not that kind of work.
>
> But then there are errors that are food for stories. There was a Vatican specialist who made an error reporting the death of the Pope in 1950. At that time there were no cell phones, so he made an agreement with a cardinal that when the Pope died, the cardinal would open a certain window. It so happened that a cleaner passed by and opened that window. . . This is a historical anecdote, I even believe it's true, but it's not something that happens normally. Our work is too banal for such incidents to happen. (Int. 4/1)

The iron rule in ANSA, like in all news agencies that care about their reputation, is to check and to control:

We verify carefully, because it often happens that certain persons or press offices call and say: "Ah, you have said this and we haven't said it". Well, there can be some deviations, or else somebody quoted wrongly. . . But in most cases these persons, especially politicians, realized that they were too free with their utterances, that they have said something that can be used against them. Then they call and say: "Ah, no, this isn't what I meant to say". But it's rare that there's a real conflict, you know, with somebody suing and the whole thing ending up in a court of justice. In 90 percent of cases, the issue is resolved on the spot. If we believe we've made an error, we correct it; if not, we don't, and that's that. (Int. 4/2)

Like in Sweden then, the politicians have to "eat up" their words, even if they taste bitter. As there's so much effort put into verification, the process of correcting is mostly initiated internally: in ANSA and by ANSA (this is the role of the Desk Editors and of Central Desk). Only later do the voices from outside arrive, sometimes to correct and sometimes to manipulate. I also asked the same question as at TT: do you have organized feedback from your clients?

BC: Is there something like a daily feedback?
4/3: No, there isn't. Apart from the fact that there are many calls from the daily newspapers to ask: "Will you do a rewrite on this?" "Will you take up this and that topic?" A classic demand on Sundays is that we do a piece on the weather, especially if the weather is bad. A piece of bad weather is well appreciated on Sundays. . . Or about traffic accidents, as there are usually many traffic accidents during the weekend, and we do a rewrite on accidents each weekend, as there are so many young people who die after the disco.

Here local specificity is obvious: in Sweden one does pieces on good weather (a much more rare event), and people are afraid to drink and drive. But though there is no systematic, organized feedback, the newspapers can be in touch in order to protest something or suggest something:

After the notice on Planned Coverage, if the clients have complaints, they call. They usually call a specific desk or Central Desk. . . . There are also some who say, "I'd like to see a piece on. . ." and if we can do it, we do. If there's an inhabitant of Brescia who has been abducted in Venezuela, for example, it's likely that the Brescia newspaper will call us to ask: "Can you give us extended coverage?" Perhaps it would be the only one interested in it – the others will be happy with 20 lines. But if we can do it, we do. Also, some newspapers' Editors-in-Chief write, telling us about problems or difficulties that they experience. And if a local newspaper is going to have important information, they tell us: "Tomorrow we'll have this, do you want to take it up?" There's quite a dialogue with our clients. (Int. 4/4)

This is yet another of few differences between ANSA and TT, where clients seldom intervene. Another difference in climate, this time of another kind?

I return to the similarities and differences among the three agencies in the last chapter.

THE COLLECTIVE COMMON SENSE

The picture of news production at ANSA corroborates the previously coined concepts of collective cognition and memory, of cyborgization, and the importance of connections. Here, I would like to add another concept related to collective cognition: common sense.

David Manning White (1950) in his famous article on "Mr. Gate", arrived at the conclusion that *common values* are a critical factor weighing on the choices that must be made among potential news items. The picture I have assembled from my interviews at TT and my observations and interviews at ANSA led me to conclude that rather than "common values", it is collective *common sense* that plays such a critical role in news production. Now, as this term has a great many interpretations, ranging from positive to negative, I begin by quoting my preferred definition. It has been used in a text describing the attempts to teach computers to use common sense:

> Common sense reasoning is the sort of reasoning we all perform about the everyday world. We can predict that, if a person enters a kitchen, then afterwards the person will be in the kitchen. Or that, if someone who is holding a newspaper walks into a kitchen, then the newspaper will be in the kitchen. Because we make inferences such as these so easily, we might get an impression that common sense reasoning is a simple thing. But it is very complex.
>
> Reasoning about the world requires a large amount of knowledge about the world and the ability to use this knowledge. We know that a person cannot be in two places at once, that a person can move from one location to another by walking, and that an object moves along with a person holding it. We have knowledge about objects, events, space, time, and mental states and can use that knowledge to make predictions, explain what we observe, and plan what to do. (Shanahan, 2005: xix)

Conventionally, common sense has been contrasted with science: first in the eighteenth and the nineteenth centuries during debates between the Scottish school of philosophy and the idealist philosophy (Scots being for common sense, of course), and later in a great many quotes of Einstein, who has allegedly said that "commonsense is a collection of prejudices acquired by the age of 18" (Horgan, 2005). Nevertheless, sociologists, psychologists, and science and technology scholars have long claimed that the difference between common sense and science is grossly exaggerated. Scientists use common sense like everybody else does, and laypersons are able to make surprising and insightful observations (see, for example, Farr, 1993 and Boudon, 1998). Perhaps it would not be wrong to say that the final argument in favor of common sense was exactly the fact that computers were unable to learn it:

> A two-year-old child who finds a chocolate bar hidden in his mother's bag is performing a feat of common sense that our most sophisticated AI systems would be utterly incapable of matching. It is true that we now have programs that can defeat chess masters – but only at chess. To a cognitive scientist, the most remarkable thing about a chess grandmaster is that, having played a great game of chess, she can then go and make a cup of tea. (Shanahan, 2005: xviii)

It needs to be added that common sense does not have to be that common. Listening to the discussions of the well in Gravina or of the use of synthetic material in sports, I was in awe. They all seemed to be extremely knowledgeable, no matter what their specialty. My common sense was certainly not up to engaging in these types of conversations. ANSA's journalists resembled the encyclopedists more than the simple producers of news from material provided them by other people. Perhaps dealing with the news is an education in itself. A young woman in Reuters told me that two months at the Finance Desk felt like doing a degree in finance. The difference between the common sense of the news producers and the opinions of experts did not seem to be great, even if the news producers often relied on expert opinion.

Were there "common values" behind this common sense? Obviously, a collective judgment on what makes more or less sense is, to a certain degree, dependent on some type of common value, but they were the common values of journalism, and especially of news agencies – those that were behind what I called "iron-clad rules". Perhaps there are differences between the European and the US media, or at least have been. Robert Darnton has described his experiences as a young trainee in a newspaper in Newark in 1959. The aspiring journalist quickly understood that a murder connected to a rape is going to be interesting news, but he did not understand that this assumption was not valid if the persons in question were black (Darnton, 2008; see also Gans, 1978/2004). News agencies such as TT and ANSA have explicit policies to avoid stigmatization through the use of stereotypes and generalizations: common sense yes, but not common prejudice. The ideals of the Enlightenment are still alive, in spite of all the laments that they are dead and buried. So perhaps there are some common values, after all.

To return to ANSA, I must add that I was extremely impressed with the ability of ANSA's journalists to separate their private political opinions from the news, in the middle of a tempestuous election campaign. Cool and common sense – these are the attributes of the everyday production of news, although it is not certain that they survive on the other end of the newswire.

5.   Reuters, or tooling of the news[1]

Collective cognition and the common sense of news producers provide a wider frame that organizes the production of news and steers the management of information overflow. In this chapter, I take a closer look at the passage of the product through various phases of production. Such perspective reveals, among other things, the importance of one news producer: the software. The active role of hardware and software does not diminish the intensity of human interaction, however; it increases it by mediation.

THE MATRIX

In this chapter, the term "matrix" is used both literally and figuratively. Although the figurative meaning will enter the text later, I would like to note here that Thomson Reuters is, in fact, a matrix organization. Table 5.1[2] is deceptively simple, as it covers hundreds of units (here is the first hint of the metaphorical use of the term matrix, as it is almost impossible to reconstruct an organization chart at Reuters, in contrast to other agencies that have it on their Web pages).

Media, in turn, comprises two parts: News Agency and Professional Publishing. My focus is on News Agency, which, I have been told, may be the smallest part of Thomson Reuters, but is certainly the best known:

> Thomson Reuters is the world's largest international multimedia news agency, providing investing news, world news, business news, technology news, headline news, small business news, news alerts, personal finance, stock market, and mutual funds information available on Reuters.com, video, mobile, and interactive television platforms. Thomson Reuters journalists are subject to an Editorial Handbook, which requires fair presentation and disclosure of relevant interests. (www.reuters.com)

[1] I would like to thank everybody at Reuters for their patience and generosity with their time. Special thanks go to Anthony's wife for her banana cake. Antonio Cordella, David Knights, and Nigel Thrift helped me to gain access to Reuters, for which I am extremely grateful. Newcastle University Business School and Martyna Sliwa gave me shelter during the writing of this chapter – many thanks!
[2] See www.thomsonreuters.com/aboutus; last accessed 13 July 2011.

Table 5.1   Reuters – A matrix organization

Markets Division	Professional Division
Sales & Trading Information, trading, and post-trade connectivity for buy-side and sell-side customers in foreign exchange, fixed income, equities, and commodities	*Legal* Information, decision support tools and services for legal, intellectual property, compliance, business and government professionals throughout the world
Enterprise Information and software for business automation within the capital market	*Tax & Accounting* Information, decision support tools, and software applications for tax and accounting professionals
Investment & Advisory Information and decision support tools and integration services for portfolio managers, investment bankers, research analysts and executives	*Healthcare & Science* Information and decision support tools for healthcare and information professionals, researchers, and scientists
Media Indispensable news and information for media and business professionals around the world Major services include text newswires, video, pictures, digital syndication, graphics, financial information, International Financing Review (IFR), Project Finance International (PFI), Buyouts, and Reuters.com	

Here are some more facts about Reuters from Reuters Facts (2009):

- Extensive reach: established over 150 years ago, Reuters News is seen by over 1 billion people every day.
- Global and local presence: as the world's largest news agency, Reuters has journalists and photographers on the ground in over 197 bureaus around the world. Reuters recognizes the value of having people from the area covering the story:
  - 2500 journalists including 230 full-time photographers;
  - filed news from 210 countries in 2007 (Reuters News Facts, 2009);
  - 9515 headlines per day, over 3500 in the US;

- 3 million news messages per year;
- 730 000 Alerts per year;
- news in 20 languages;
- 515 000 picture images per year;
- 45 000 video stories per year;
- 23 million people visit Reuters websites every month;
- 4 million stream per month over the Internet.

News Agency is divided into three regions: the US, Asia, and EMEA (Europe, the Middle East & Africa). EMEA, with its central editorial office in London, was the regional office I studied. It comprises seven internal units: Treasury, Corporate, Commodities & Energy, Politics and General, Sports, Life Styles, and Top News, which collaborates with the other six editorial offices. The first three units deal with similar information (finance and economics) and engage in a great deal of cooperation, but were created with different readers in mind. Treasury deals with macroeconomic issues, treasury, and trading, showing how economies are performing and what governments are doing. Corporate deals with micro-economics, following what companies are doing. Commodities & Energy is focused on specific markets, but overlaps in part with both Treasury and Corporate. Politics and General, on the other hand, focuses on non-economic policy-making, which is usually closely related to economic policy-making, however. Sports and Life Styles are also alert to economic and business connections of the events they are reporting. As an example of a local newsroom, I chose UK & Ireland, also located in London.

The newsrooms are supported by a variety of corporate services, from Technology to Marketing to Sales to Public Relations. The matrix organization continues within the units:

Technology as a whole is something of a matrix. In terms of the horizontals, we have a program management team that handles all our project management, an operations team that handles all issues of operation support, ensuring that the right support is there for the journalists and for the technology out in the field – in the bureaus.

We have two development teams. One development team focuses on the actual production applications that the journalists use; the other development team is focused on distribution and aggregation of technology and infrastructure, in terms of the fees that are coming in, and also in terms of our ability to distribute content to businesses or directly to customers.

Then we have two product management teams; one is focused mostly on everything around production and creation, and the other is focused on improvements that need to be made to the speed and automation that we need to build into all tools, and especially in the alerting area. Then on the vertical dimension, people focus on the strategy, issues around speed, issues around the actual customer

Photo 5.1   Reuters building at Canary Wharf

experience of news. All these people are distributed among Boston and New York, Hong Kong, Bangalore, London, Geneva, St. Louis. (Int. 5/4)

In London, the newsrooms (Editorial) are in one gigantic open-plan office, whereas the leadership and the services (Company) sit on other floors in the impressive building at Canary Wharf.

The above and following are pictures of the Reuters building at Canary Wharf and a general picture of the newsroom (Photos 5.1, 5.2).

THE NETWORK

As many details of work in newsrooms have already been highlighted in previous chapters, and they do not vary much across the agencies, I focus in this section on the central part of news production – the tooling of news at Reuters. One of the main points is that, even if tooling can be seen as a linear process – from input to output – it is performed by and within an enormous network, including human and non-human actants. I begin, therefore, by introducing at least some of them (the network seems to be infinite).

Humans: Various Positions

As with the other agencies, there are some positions at Reuters that are stable: EMEA has its Managing Editor and deputies for Europe, the

Photo 5.2   EMEA newsroom

Middle East, and Africa. Each office has its head (whom I call News Editor) and News Editor's deputy; the local bureaus are led by Chief Correspondents. The editors are responsible for strategy, for planning of coverage, for ensuring that all the newsworthy stories and events within their domain are covered, and for directing the coverage: how should an event be covered and who should cover it?

Different offices are organized differently, according to their needs. Treasury, which covers the financial markets, is more centralized than other offices: they have 12 subeditors in London, and 21 reporters, five of whom deal exclusively with emerging markets and investment strategies. This is because London is a financial hub and because Europe now has a common market, so that they are representing the whole of Western Europe. Some specialize in stock markets only. The UK is also treated separately, as it is the biggest market. Government financial reporting is centralized in London because the government is in London, and because government finances are centralized. Eastern Europe and the Middle East have their own reporters, who collect all the economic data and information on policy-making.

Apart from those positions, a great many are rotating, and may vary from one office to another. In all of them, various items of information come into Baskets. A Taster checks the Taste Basket with the incoming items in order to "taste copy", "which means having a quick look at stuff, moving quick, urgent stories to the XMIT (transmit) Basket or into a

Sub-Basket, for longer stories, not so urgent, which need a more detailed editing job" (Int. 5/1). The role of a Taster goes to experienced members of the team. Sometimes, but rarely, they "spike" stories – that is, throw them away. The name comes from the old days when there was actually a metal spike on which the rejected telegrams were placed.[3]

Politics and General have more rotating functions because they receive a great variety of stories. They have 30 editors in London and the correspondents "all over the world". Definite Copy Taster receives all stories and "farms" them out to the subeditors. Duty Editor checks if all stories have been farmed out, and if there are overlaps; also, he or she checks if the lead is right, and if the length is correct. Definite Copy Taster consults with Duty Editor when in doubt. There is also a Deputy Copy Taster.

The London Editorial Office includes, apart from the editors, a TV person, a photo person, and a Web person. Other non-rotating positions are Defence & Military (one person), and Treasury (three people). In the center is a slot position (called "Desk Editor" in TT and ANSA), a "traffic officer" who catches all the media and receives all reports. This person, in consultation with Chief Correspondent, decides what is most urgent. The two of them actually sit across from one another and can shout over the screen tops when necessary.

Last but not least, there are correspondents, some of whom are located at Canary Wharf, but most of them in the local bureaus. The requirements are high:

> [I]f you're a journalist, and especially if you work for Reuters, you have to know what's going on outside of your sector. But I also know that we want to encourage specialism, too. Because that's where we can show a difference from our competitors. (Int. 5/2)

As in TT and ANSA, there is a collective cognition at work, as well as a collective memory; people are constantly consulting with one another. Common sense is constantly applied, often approaching expertise. A woman who moved from Treasury to Commodities & Energy told me that it felt "like doing a degree in two-and-half years, and now starting on another" (Obs. 5/19).

Two elements of the physical environment were striking, and both delivered clear messages to the journalists. One was the importance of time, in at least two senses of the word: differences in global time (Photo 5.3) and the importance of keeping time (Photo 5.4).

---

[3] For the history of the spike, see Stothard (2009).

Photo 5.3   Global times. London (06.00–19.00) shares the main desk with New York (19.00–03.00) and Singapore (24.00–11.00), with necessary overlaps

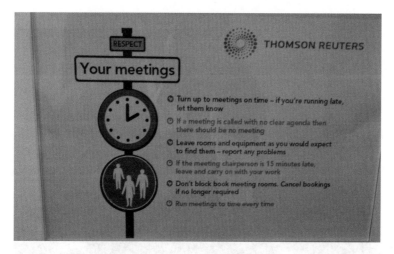

Photo 5.4   Keeping time

The other was the decoration of the walls – both at Canary Wharf and in the UK bureau at Kildare House.[4] They consisted of pictures of competitive sports: a clear message (Photos 5.5–5.7).

---

[4] Located off Fleet Street. 85 Fleet Street, the original home of Reuters, has another owner now, and the Reuters name has been removed.

Photo 5.5   The wall decorations

*Photo 5.6   The ubiquitous sports theme stresses the importance of
achieving*

Photo 5.7   Sports pictures dominate the landscape

Indeed, speed and competition are keywords at Reuters. On the Intranet there is a format called Beats & Exclusives containing claims from correspondents who broke some news. A Beat, for example, is "a first article on a given subject intended to excite further debate, published before everybody else – 'Tiger back to golf'⁵" (Int. 5/2). These claims are approved or rejected by the editors, who then send the accepted items to people in Marketing, so they can tell it to the clients: "So here somebody was on a telephone conference call, heard the news, put on Snaps, and then added Analysis and Comments. Neither Bloomberg nor the Dow Jones had the news, but the shares fell as much as 26 percent" (Int. 5/1).

Here is another Beat, more dramatic:

> I covered a bomb in London near my house. . . we were the first journalists to get there. It was a bomb in the Strand, in Central London, and I lived a ten-minute walk away, and I ran, because I heard the bomb go off. And it was in a bus; it demolished the bus and killed the bomber. I rang the news desk from there with the news. I wanted to make sure that it wasn't fireworks or something, but it wasn't. If you hear a bomb, you know it's a bomb, actually. Then I just interviewed the people around the bus and got the story. . . . The good thing these days with technology is that if you've got your laptop, or even your BlackBerry, you can bring your stories from everywhere. (Int. 5/2)

As computers get smaller and mobile phones acquire more functions, the fusion between people and machines, which I previously called cyborgization, is more and more pervasive. But speed is not everything:

⁵ This was before he concentrated on other activities, as of December 2009.

competition also requires exclusivity. An Exclusive is an interview given to Reuters journalists only:

> The biggest Exclusive we had this year was to name the new Chelsea manager. We learned from the new manager that he'd been given this job, and this was a big story for us. That was about two or three weeks ago, and we only got it because we were the only international news organization that was with him in Turkey. . . And I told the reporter, you must go and talk to him and get the information. . . And he did. (Int. 5/2)

One source of motivation for the journalists is the annual awards: Best Commentator, Best Scoop, Story of the Year, British Press Award, Business Journalist of the Year.

The editors have performance targets, and they are met with varying responses. A poster from the union chapel in Breakout Room announced that the time has come to resist the "pay for performance" trend in the company, reminding its members that it was the union that saved Reuters from reductions. The latest raising of targets provoked reactions such as "People are working hard all the year and just to double it without any rewards for what was earlier doesn't seem fair. It's like being penalized for having done good work" (Obs. 5/23). The News Editors, however, were suggesting that the targets were "aspirational", and that there would be "a good deal of flexibility" in interpreting them.

The "oldies" may stay at the same desk for 20 years, but people under 30 move after two, three years, and also go abroad – although this happens less often now, as it is expensive. Generally, however, rotation and mobility are characteristic traits of Reuters editors.

The Non-human Collaborators

As everywhere, the main collaborators are computers and telephones; TVs, radios, and recorders play second fiddle. Photo 5.8 is a picture of these "silent masses" (which are actually only temporarily silent; when activated, they make a variety of noises).

The next picture (Photo 5.9) presents the complete team: a human, computers, the software being used, telephones (the mobile barely visible to the left), a small radio, and a recorder. To the left, a lunch bag.

I wish to add yet another non-human actor whose presence at Canary Wharf impressed me enormously: the faucet that produced both cold drinking water and boiling water for tea and coffee (Photo 5.10).

But perhaps the most important collaborators, the cyborg-like parts, are the quasi-objects: the software such as Coyote, Kobra, Julius, Microsoft Outlook, Dow Jones Factiva (an archive that used to be a joint venture

Photo 5.8   The non-human actants at rest

Photo 5.9   The complete team

between DJ and Reuters; they sold it to Dow Jones), FAT (actually also a hardware: Fast Alert Terminal), Internet Messaging Program, Firefox, Explorer, Glance, AIM, Hermes, Citrix Program Neighborhood, RSI Guard (for managing and preventing repetitive strain injury – an exercise program), Hot Screen. I shall tackle only the most important among these.

The grandfather of them all is the Coyote, the editorial system, dating back to 1984. As one of my interlocutors said:

*Photo 5.10   Technological wonder in Breakout
Room*

When I started at Reuters, we had a system very similar to this one, it was just a predecessor system. And my editor at the time said: "It's a shame you have to learn this, because we are phasing it out". But it is still here, many years later, and the point is, it does what it needs to do. It's pretty reliable, touch wood. And it is reasonably quick. So to get something better is quite difficult. (Int. 5/1)

Coyote's Menu is simple: File, Edit, Options, Soft-typeset, Window, Help. Coyote has its faults: it does not update by itself, the "refresh" button must be pushed, and it does not have a spell check. Also, one needs to remember the commands – they are not displayed. It fails very rarely though, and when it fails, they use Hermes. However, Hermes was originally Russian, and the issue of copyrights was unclear.

Outlook is used for many internal purposes: news planning is done on Outlook. The journalists do "Outlook" for the day, for the week, and for the month – story plans that they have – and send them to News Editor, who circulates them. Then News Editor does an Outlook and sends it to Top News Editor, who puts them together and circulates them around.

Kobra (Reuters 3000Xtra) is a newswire for rich clients such as investment banks. Apart from the running wire, there is also Archive on Wire, and a picture archive called Reuters Pictures.

Julius, so named after the first name of the company's founder, is an Editorial Intranet, hosted on Explorer. It is broken down into regions, of which EMEA is the largest. Among other things, it contains the *Book of Codes*,[6] and *Handbook of Journalism*.

There is also a chat room with instant messaging – a novelty, which can be used internally, but also by subscribers. It is called Reuters United Communication Centre, and each bureau has its own chat room, as do the desks – EDT_TopNews_Editors, for example. When a message comes in, an icon will flash. The chat room is helpful, but it also multiplies ways of communicating: there is e-mail, and Coyote also has a message function, by which the message shows on the top of the editing screen. Like the rest of Coyote, this screen-top messaging is old-fashioned, but people like it, and want to keep it operating within the new system.

The technology team has been developing a new system, however. Its strategic goals are as follows:

> . . . developing the technology, the systems, and the applications in order to support Editorial in using and producing the news, to enhance its ability to collaborate around creating stories or investigating stories, its ability to create and add more value to the news and stories they create – through packaging the stories or creating multimedia or adding more context and tagging. Also, to ensure that the news produced is valuable and caters to the needs of our customers in different distribution channels. (Int. 5/4)

As in the two other agencies, engaged in the same kind of system change, there is a legacy – even more so, as Reuters is older:

---

[6] Not to be mistaken for the enormous code books used at Reuters at the turn of the previous century (Read, 1992: 62). At that time, codes were used to make telegrams shorter and thus save money, but also to protect the news from the eavesdroppers.

There's a lot of legacy in Editorial staff – people who've been around for 35 years and upward, and many of them for 15 years or more. So there's a lot of experience, but also a lot of people who are comfortable with the way they currently work. And there's a lot of antiquated technology available to the journalists as well – systems that have been around for the past 25 years. . . And when individuals and technologies have been around together for a long time, work patterns become settled, and it's difficult to become agile and flexible, difficult to change, to move in new operational directions. Because you've got both a people issue and a technology issue to resolve. (Int. 5/4)

This legacy problem is partly counterweighed by various "technology freaks" who argue for the new solutions even before they have been properly tested, especially in the image-based units. But the aim is "to change the core technology platform so as to support innovation across the board" (Int. 5/4): not to keep the useless legacies, but not to jump into risky experimenting, either. The new system, called Lynx, is to offer a new editing and packaging platform, combining editorial tools with coordination and communication tools, allowing for multimedia. It is to be delivered in phases over a period of three years, and is seen not as one multi-tool, but as a set of tools integrated in one system.

The previous failures led the present team to emphasize what they call a user-centered design, "which basically means describing what the current system does, conceptualizing what the future system could do, and then working with journalists on mock-ups, warfares and prototypes" (Int. 5/4). About 120 journalists were involved in testing the system. Fully aware, however, that there is always a danger of replicating old routines in new technologies, the team sees to it that the journalists' experiences are well-balanced, with the input of technology-knowledgeable developers. "We have a checkpoint on a regular basis, to ask ourselves: are we replicating, or are we simplifying? Are we replicating because this particular replication has to happen, or are we replicating because this is something that we are used to having?" (Int. 5/4).

[W]e asked Editorial to give us three things that would make the program successful. . . First, keep things simple. They don't want to be thinking about technology; they just want to get on with their job. Second, make sure the system is reliable, so they'll never have to worry about it falling down. The third thing, which was kind of interesting, was that they came up with their favorite communication tool: the screen top. They need to know what's going on, to be in continuous communication . . . and have access to each other as they go about their jobs. (Int. 5/4)

Such systems cannot be bought on the market, although there are many systems that do certain things that need to be done, but not all in the same system. Thus, the team is trying to integrate various technological modules into a whole that makes sense to Reuters. This is the same principle as in each of the agencies – much as their systems are alike and fulfill similar functions, they are nevertheless tailor-made.

The requirements of the journalists, who want a system that permits them to forget about the technology and concentrate on the job at hand are completely consistent with what Clynes and Kline (1960) had in mind when they introduced the idea of cyborgs – a combination of machines and human beings that will relieve the human from tedious work. Does it work that way? I return to this issue in the last chapter.

Another fascinating observation concerning technology is that there are no consultants specializing in news agencies:

> I don't think there has been any real traction from consultancy in this area. . . I think some of them can be like Axentia, Pricewaterhouse, but they weren't trying to get involved with us. So I've got a feeling that maybe our field is where the consultants are focused on the smaller-scale engagements, where they may be working with our customers – newspapers, magazines, TV stations, who feed off the news that we provide. But I'm not so sure that I ever came across a consultancy that has truly positioned itself as understanding a global agency, and is able to provide added value there. (Int. 5/4)

This observation confirms my earlier impression that news agencies standardize their production via their products, rather than imitating procedures and technologies – the latter process usually encouraged and aided by consultants.

In the meantime, the support is highly efficient and also matrix-like. A problem with Top News Packaging had to be reported first to the Technical Desk in London, which told the reporting person to report it to the Help Desk in Bangalore. People in London could not do anything about it, but they would inform the Editorial Development Centre in the UK, which is why it had to be reported there first.

Externals

Reuters makes use of BBC Radio Four, BBC News, newspapers and weeklies, Sky News, CNN, and others. BBC Monitoring send Reuters their stuff, though Reuters usually has 90 percent of it already.

In various places in the newsrooms there are weeklies: *Newsweek, The Economist, Time, Der Spiegel, Le Point, Africa Confidential,* and *Fortune.* The most commonly seen newspapers are the *Financial Times, Herald Tribune* and *Wall Street Journal.*

But "externals" means not only reaching out and securing cooperation, but also protecting Reuters and its journalists from external dangers, whether symbolic or literal. It is Public Relations in Company that takes care of it:

> Let's say government people say that they saw one of our pictures of their Prime Minister, and that it's Photoshopped. They may say: you either depicted somebody in a wrong way, or you're biased. Did you retouch the picture to make it look different, and that's obviously not something we ever do. . . . We adhere to the guidelines, across the board, like Dow Jones and AP [Associated Press] probably do. It's mostly about pictures; there's not much fuss about our texts. Unless, God forbid, we've reported something a bit off, or one of our sources turned out to be not as right as we like them to be. And that happens very, very rarely, but every now and then. We. . . try to correct it, or try to figure out what's going on. . . all the way up till we resolve it somehow. (Int. 5/3)

Then there is the problem of journalists' safety; they do get killed on the job. As Read (1992: 382) wrote in his history, "The general rule everywhere has always been that Reuters correspondents should never risk their lives for the sake of the story. But in practice some stories simply cannot be ignored". Thus, courses on security in demonstrations and security in war have been organized. When a fatal accident happens (Box 5.1), PR makes sure that the family is notified, composes a message to the press, and makes contact with one of the journalists' safety groups, like the Community to Protect Journalists, asking for aid.

BOX 5.1   TRAGIC DEATH OF REUTERS CAMERMAN

17 April, 2008. The editor-in-chief of Reuters demanded that Israel launches a "thorough and immediate investigation" into the killing of one of its cameramen in the Gaza Strip yesterday (David Byers writes).

Footage of Fadel Shana, 23, being killed by a tank shell in the Gaza Strip has been released by the news agency, which said that the cameraman was hit, despite clear markings that showed him to be a journalist.

After medical examinations of Shana's body, Reuters said that Israel had used a controversial type of tank shell which scatters metal darts, or flechettes, around the surrounding area after exploding, risking civilian casualties. Israel refused to comment on the report, but stated that the weapons were not illegal.

> It's always awful when a journalist dies, but this really went into overdrive. Everybody just dropped what they were doing, and got on board and figured some way to help. So there wasn't much chaos; it was just one of the most horrible moments we've had. And it can be very traumatic. (Int. 5/3)

Public Relations acts as a kind of "a shield, so people bounce something off us first and then we either filter it and let it in, and pass it along, or not" (Int. 5/3). I have had the opportunity of personally testing the truth of this sentence, in trying to gain access to Reuters.

Competitors

In Europe, it is Bloomberg that is perceived to be Reuters' main competitor of Reuters ("Bloomberg is excelling in some places, so we are always watching out for them", Int. 5/3), whereas in the US it is the Associated Press, which is much better known in North America, although mostly through its non-financial reporting.

> [W]e do not focus on what other agencies are doing, apart from the timing and the newsbreaks. We have an e-mail that comes from time to time showing how we match up in terms of timing the major stories. I don't really know who sends it. . . I think there's some kind of timing unit and they can tell you the percentage of wins – like we've won 75 percent of timings over Dow Jones, etc. . . . From time to time somebody may look at somebody else's website to see if our story is better than theirs – actually that's not bad, it's a good lead, etc. but to be honest, there's not much emphasis on it, it happens occasionally. We're more focused on getting our story right from our point of view. (Int. 5/1)

I have quoted this at length because it supports two of my observations: that people at Reuters do not have to have a picture of the whole organization (other people knew who did the timings, and that was enough), and that agencies compare themselves to others by results, not by internal organization and the like.

There is another agency in the UK – the Press Agency – and several Reuters journalists have worked there before. In their judgment, the Press Agency does not have as stringent sourcing standards as Reuters does, and often employs inexperienced journalists straight from college or university, at low salaries. At one time, it did compete with Reuters, but recently it cut back on its international coverage. Thus, the Press Agency is domestic, delivering news to local papers, and aimed at a local audience.

Although particular journalists may be checking most or many newspapers, this is not done systematically, because the important newspapers have their own news agencies. *Herald Tribune* actually has four pages called "Business with Reuters" in all editions, but this is a commercial deal.

THE NEWS TOOLS AT WORK

It is possible to distinguish two levels of organizing necessary for the tooling: organizing how a text is to be produced and organizing the text itself. I start by exemplifying the former, then give examples of the latter.

Organizing the Making of a Text

Here is an example of organizing the making of a text:

> *BC*: Can you tell me about the Stanford story: how it develops, and what is being done? [7]
>
> 5/2: . . . we got it very quickly from the States, so the first that I knew of it was when we snapped it up from the US, I think it was snapped up from Washington.
>
> The first thing I did was to get in touch with the Sports News Editor for the Americas, so I spoke to him, and then I spoke to the man who runs the General and Politics wire from the States, and we had a planning call, during which we arranged very quickly how we would cover the story.
>
> As it happens, a large part of the story is in the West Indies – his HQ is in Antigua. We had a reporter in Antigua last week who was covering the cricket, and I got hold of him, and he helped with an overall coverage of the Stanford situation. We know that he has pumped a lot of money into cricket in particular, so we've got quick reactions from the boards of various cricket authorities involved, particularly the English one. We gave Alerts on those, and we did a separate story just on sports, on Stanford's connections with sports. Since then there've been Analyses and so on. And I got one of the reporters to do a question-and-answer Factbox on Stanford's influence in sport. Since then, we've had daily conference calls, usually at 16.00 our time, 11.00 EST, and I talk to the other editors involved with the Stanford situation, and we talk about how we cover the story.

The editors are in touch with the reporters concerning their stories, and the politeness of their conversations is striking. I have witnessed (one-sidedly, but I could guess what the correspondent was saying) a correspondent calling Reuters London and complaining about the lack of clarity in changes and suggestions from the Desk (Obs. 5/18): the complainant threatened recourse to the News Editor, whereas the editor did his outmost to calm the correspondent. This happens rarely; more typical are conversations like the following one: News Editor is speaking on the phone to a journalist in South Africa about an interview with the local authority, and taking notes as she talks:

[7] Stanford is a Texas multi-millionaire with a bank in Antigua, who financed, among other things, the British cricket, and who has been accused by the Feds of fraud.

What did they say? If there's a chance of snapping something up, it's worth it, if we can cross-reference it to the interview Jackie did, because it's quite a tricky time for them to raise the tariff. Did they hint how much?. . . So the hint is that it's not going to be as much as they hinted previously?. . . But surely there'll be a lot of political fall-out and social unrest. People don't have that much disposable income, or have they?. . . Isn't it something worth snapping up if they're considering changing the position?. . . If we say, "consider", pointing out that there's a complete shift of position. . ., we should definitely snap that up, because I'm not sure anybody believes that they could go through with it. . . I think it's worth it, and if we got a broader context, too, it will be great. Lovely! (Obs. 5/17)

As one of my interlocutors put it, an editor must be "painfully polite", avoiding humiliating people at all costs. If something is sensitive, they phone or e-mail, instead of just sending a screen-top message. The rationale is that many correspondents are working in difficult circumstances, and there is no reason to aggravate the situation.

Much of the coordination and preparation takes place in the form of teleconferences. I was allowed to participate in some of them. Here is a telephone meeting on grain in Commodities and Equities:[8]

Grain telephone meeting at 14.00
Participants: News Editor (NE), J from Brussels, M from Germany, T from Moscow, S from Netherlands and France, N from Spain and G from France. Six countries represented at once:

> *NE*: Sorry to have sent you this thing again. (To S:) If you just sent it back saying, "please do not repeat the request". . .
> *S*: I've already forwarded it to N, but somebody has to tell them that it was wrong from start to finish. . . well, just as we speak he has sent a mail.
> *NE*: I have an e-mail from N. Let me see if he can join us. Shall we kick off? N will join us when he can.

An introduction like in any other meeting; they could have been sitting around a table.

> *S*: Grain prices were going down; the market is quite pessimistic, no support, neither from imports nor from the euro. Euro is falling, but it stays definitely pretty strong. Falling will help them. Same in Chicago. We'd need fresh fundamentals to freshen things up.

No comment; apparently this was known or expected.

---

[8] It should be added that the grain market was of special interest to Julius Reuter (Read, 1992: 16).

M: Germany still within the variable range bound, not much goes down, the euro up and down. People were very disappointed with Europe's non-reaction to Egypt . . . and the euro is weak.

NE: What about the Middle East?

M: There's a lot of talk, but when it comes to prices in Chicago, the buyers wait for the prices to go down.

NE: Where do you think something will happen? – we've had Egypt, Syria. . .

M: The Iraqis last week remembered that they were supposed to buy from the US. Georgia is supposed to come up, and [some other country]. . . The Lebanon is in, Israel is on. . . could be that Algeria. . . so there's some good demand in the background. Also, shipping charges are cheap.

Although M is supposed to report on Germany, it is clearly Germany in the context of the rest of the world. This will be repeated in each report: they are not describing a local situation, but the connections between a local situation and the rest of the world.

NE: T? Russia – Brazil?

T: What's bad is that all kinds of news – professional and not – is leaking to the markets. After winter holidays, I've discovered that our Plant and Animal person negotiated with Brazil an export of wheat to Brazil. Apparently he said in Berlin that we could replace wheat that Brazil used to buy from Argentina. I wasn't very excited because our Plant and Animal person is a veterinary. I talked to the expert who says Brazil is too far – they'll buy from the US or somebody closer. . .

NE: But it's worth flagging, because there are weird things coming up. . .

T: Yes, but the official in question isn't available. I suspect a hush-hush deal being done, but they're not talking.

The Brazilian delegation is still here. They say there will be a memorandum tomorrow, but I called the Ministry of Agriculture, and they're not talking.

NE: What about the general mood?

T: It's hard to speak about it because one of the Agriculture ministers was fired was appointed the governor of a province. Of course when Putin put Zubkov in as a Deputy Prime Minister responsible for agriculture, Godejev was in the way.

This time around, a specific connection is focused upon Russia – Brazil, because of the latest event – the visit of the Brazilian delegation to Russia. As I cannot see NE, I constantly wonder if she is writing detailed notes (no time for it), making notes on a list already prepared (very likely), or just has an incredible memory?

NE: N, you're with us? Oh lovely. Spain.

N: Fundamental piece of news is that grain from Ukraine dried up. It was supposed to come in the second part of the month, but nothing. Much to my surprise, I've seen some British wheat shipped together with Bulgarian maize. The market is in the doldrums. If people panic, nobody knows what's going to happen. The demand can be lower because of the livestock diminishing.

One more thing, a story last week. The government asked industrialists and traders and said they were considering a levy on. . . Farmers went against it.

Again, "news from Spain" covers connections with three other countries. Nothing is truly local at Reuters.

J: Nothing interesting as yet. Maize and [something] might be interesting.

At this point, with no visible (audible?) clue, the angle of the reporting is changing. NE kind of summarizes previous comments, and moves to the second item. What were the correspondents doing? And what were the consequences? Most likely, this is the routine agenda of the meeting, so NE does not need to evoke it explicitly.

s: Downward sentiment, prices tending downwards, that's the impression from the last week. Shall I tell you what I was doing?
NE: Yes.
s: Now I have a trainee helping me with the biofuel textbook, and I was planning to talk to the Farmers' Union this week.
NE: Our guy has spoken to British farmers – contact him. Strange that they're not commenting on M's Rotterdam story.

NE is doing linking – and giving and asking for feedback.

M: Very strange. Maybe I went the wrong way.
s: I'll try to reach them.
. . .
M: Several European governments said that they were worried about biofuels because of grain problems – and I remember that UK and Germany were among them. . .
s: The industry is touched by the obligatory blending, but the real problem for the companies are the prices – they have buyers, but they would have to lower the prices to keep them. . .
M: It's a very strange market, almost deregulated. I don't know how they manage to get it through the EU.
s: Yes, the rule says that if you produce up to X, you'll get a tax cut. Of course they can't produce more if they don't have buyers.
NE: Did you do Analysis? It's such an interesting stuff!

NE uses the spontaneous discussion for assigning, or at least a suggestion for assigning, which is received positively, developed, and modified:

s: I've tried, but the length of Analyses is limited. But I tried to put all the EU countries in. Other people can come with specific stories – I think this would be good, as I can't fix everything within 90 lines.
. . .

Now it is time for checking work plans, but it comes like a natural part
of the conversation:

> *NE*: T, what will you do next week?
> *T*: Brazilian delegation, grain exporting company. Let's see who will be Minister
> of Agriculture.
> *NE*: J, you?
> *J*: Greece. France, confirmation from Prague.
> *S*: G and I'll be doing a feature on farmers.
> *G*: We'll try doing it before the Agricultural Show. We'll ask how farmers are
> trying to supplement their incomes, a couple of farmers on the phone.
> *S*: There's a meeting of EC, speaking about moving support from one region to
> another, from rich grain growers to poor breeders. Now things have changed
> and grain growers don't want to pay. The minister doesn't want to have farmers
> in the streets. He'll probably be giving a speech on Thursday. He's inaugurating
> the Agriculture Show. Two weeks. It will keep us busy, but we can't write too
> many stories from it. Some interviews. . .
> *NE*: What people think, how do they feel, will they be adjusting etc.

In principle, NE is giving (most likely repeating) standard instructions on
how to conduct interviews, but these, again, sound like spontaneous reactions during a friendly conversation.

> *N*: As we speak. I got first estimates for the winter cereal campaign, so with your
> permission I'll call off.
> *M*: Daimler and biofuel, this week, and then biopetrol and Rotterdam.
> *NE*: As I told you on e-mail, if you want to ask questions, contact L in Rome.
> She'll be there at the conference that starts tomorrow. (Obs. 5/17)

Several things are achieved smoothly and seamlessly at the conference.
They are doing the planning (and coordinating their plans); they are
selecting what is going to be covered, and they are deciding how it will be
covered. I am unable to reproduce the tones of voice, but my inserted comments suggest that the tone of the meeting is very different from a typical
meeting of a manager with subordinates. There are no changes in intona-
tion, no "Right! Now off to work!" stuff – just a group of people talking
about things that interest them.

Technology is not mentioned – after all, everything is functioning as it
should. It was different during another telephone conference at Treasury
(Obs. 5/16), when some fault or another caused the voices to come through
the participant's loudspeakers rather than his phone. Consequently, everybody sitting around him (myself included) became interested and asked for
explanation. He shrugged his shoulders and said it was some kind of a technical error, and exploited the situation of having free hands to work with
his computer while listening – now and then – to the others. This made me
realize that the telephone conference participants do not behave like I did,

squeezing the receiver in my nervous hand, not to miss a word. Telephone conferences create freedom unknown in face-to-face meetings: neither the facial expression nor the postures nor the use of hands can be observed. As Allucquere Rosanne Stone (2007: 35) has observed, however, in the epoch of virtual reality it is necessary to redefine both "meet" and "face"...

Formal planning is achieved by collecting and coordinating the "Outlooks" that all journalists and editors prepare. The Outlooks are the basis for Skeds, or work schedules. There is a weekly planning meeting on Fridays; its product is an "EMEA Weekahead Newsplanner", with the following structure:

- Top Themes and Stories;
- Treasury Overview;
- Markets;
- Equities;
- Energy;
- Commodities;
- General and political;
- Sport;
- Features;
- TV: Insider.

Under each heading is a list of themes and stories that were deemed most important during the Friday meeting. There are also monthly Newsplanners.

The main purpose of the daily morning meetings is *coordination*, so the various offices know what the others are doing. There are few surprises at such meetings: the News Editors have already sent their planned Top News to the Top News Office, which has already compiled a list. After confirmation, it is sent around as "today's EMEA Newsplanner". The aim is "to keep everybody in the loop" (Obs. 5/23).

Because Reuters is a global agency, and because its main clients are financial actors, its production is "rolling" rather than going from one specific time (the morning meeting) to another (the final – for the day – delivery of stories). Diaries plus individual decisions lead to Outlooks, and Outlooks plus team decisions lead to Skeds. "An awful lot is diarized, but an equal amount is non-diarized – things are rolling on, and decisions on these items are important. They're things that are impossible to predict" (Obs. 5/18). And, one may add, are more likely to lead to breaking news.

Like the other agencies, Reuters needs to make choices, especially as the amount of information received is even larger than it is in other agencies. In its estimation, it picks up five issues out of every 100 coming in. Thus, choices are important. What is also important is the covering of diarized events and the collecting of all the background data. This is somewhat in conflict with the bureaus' constant ambition to try to break news, so they must be controlled and focused by the Editorial Office. But breaking news is the main target for everybody, combined with an ambition to obtain exclusive news – not merely being five minutes earlier on a release.

Another important matter is proper use of the available information. The German Finance Minister gave a long speech, for instance. What should be kept and what should be skipped? Local bureaus are usually the specialists on such matters, but London keeps an eye on it. Thus, the purpose of planning meetings is the sharing of information and the achievement of coordination, rather than decision-making. There are several thousand stories a day on the wire, and there are Top News items every hour. And it is not only the clients who must make sense of the wire, but their analysts as well. Therefore, all these disparate stories must be made into a coherent narrative in which the main operations are what the narratologists call *embedding* and *interlinking* (Todorov, 1971/1977).

Organizing the Text: Making a Coherent Narrative

Tooling of the news is directed by the imperative of making a coherent narrative. A story of an event proceeds from an Alert (a one-line Alert is called a Snap) to a Brief, then to a full story, and finally to a Wrap-up and Top Wrap, which was added since the financial crisis. In the meantime, several Updates may take place, and also some versions may be faulty and therefore have to appear in a Corrected version.

09.52 HEAVY SHOOTING IN EQUATORIAL GUINEA CAPITAL
MALABO IN EARLY HOURS

This is a Snap, that is, a one-line red Alert.

> If you work in this sort of journalism, timing is the definitive thing. To beat the other competitors in breaking some major news, or new date, or some companies' results. The rest is a sort of aside. . . That's why the Alerts, breaking news, is so important. (Int. 5/1)

The timing of Alerts is especially important because of the existence of robo-trading, or automated trading. Financial information is traditionally released daily through a "lock-up": all (legitimate) reporters are locked up in the Statistical Office in the morning for 30 minutes to familiarize themselves with price-sensitive information. They are released after this half-hour, and the markets receive the information simultaneously. Reuters prepares seven versions of the information, the most important of which is an Alert. At 09.30, clients receive the reports.

The last decade witnessed the emergence of algorithmic trading models that are designed to read the data and trade automatically.[9] The competition is then a matter of nanoseconds, or so they say at Reuters. There is a special format for that, called Real Time Economic Data, and a polling unit. The latter is constantly polling financial strategies (Steel Poll) and forecasts formal consensus. The average forecast is plugged into Real Time Economic Data. The trading computers will pick it up and will execute the trade.

The US releases an unemployment report, for example: first, what the forecasters foresaw, then showing that the actual situation is worse. The dollar will go down and bonds will go up, and as the traders compete in speed, the computers beat the humans. The problem is that after an initial violent price move, qualifications may follow; actually, the unemployment data showed the usual seasonal distortion. After 30 seconds or so, the human beings return: the journalists come in with interpretation. As the story builds up, it changes, also because it reaches different clients, finally reaching the "man on the street" as it goes from traders to lay people.

Robo-trading constitutes about 30 percent of foreign exchange trading, and is executed primarily in London, New York City, Singapore, and Hong Kong. Latency is counted in milliseconds (probably called "nanoseconds" for better effect), and trading becomes a technical issue – whose computers are quicker. I've been told that some hedge fund traders realized that physical closeness to the Bank of England increases speed, so they located their offices nearby.

MNSi (Managed Network Systems, Inc.) is a rival of Reuters. As I watch, Reuters delivers an Alert at 09.00.01, MNSi at 09.00.04, which is an important difference for robo-trading (Obs. 5/18). There is a Timing News Research Group, comparing Dow Jones, MNSi, and, separately, Bloomberg – the last is actually done by Pricewaterhouse, because, for historical reasons, Reuters is not allowed to receive it directly. On 5 February Bloomberg beat Reuters by one second. Reason: its computers are quicker. The journalists at Reuters are hoping to get new terminals instead of the present Fast Alert Terminals, which are not working well.

The people in Treasury worry a great deal about timing; one of my

---

[9] In electronic financial markets, algorithmic trading or automated trading is also known as algo-trading or robo-trading. It consists of using computer programs for entering trading orders with the help of a computer algorithm. It is mostly used by hedge funds, pension funds, and mutual fund traders, and by other institutional investors. "A third of all EU and US stock trades in 2006 were driven by automatic programs... By 2010, that figure will reach 50 percent...". See http://en.wikipedia.org/wiki/Algorithmic_trading; last accessed 3 July 2011.

BOX 5.2   ALERT IS NOT ALERT

09.32 ALERT, 09.33 not alert

ADVISORY – PLEASE IGNORE ZEW ALERT WHICH SENT IN ERROR OFFICIAL NUMBER HAS NOT BEEN RELEASED (ZEW INSTITUTE FEB GERMAN ECONOMIC SENTIMENT INDEX) released at 09.27.

---

interlocutors collected the timing for the last two years. At first glance, it may be surprising. As I've noticed before, people at Reuters do not like performance targets, and yet they seem keen on competing with other agencies. Competing with people on the same team is likely to be counter-productive, however; competing with the speed of other agencies gives an adrenaline kick. Perhaps it was not accidental that the journalists at TT had horse racing results pinned up in their meeting room.

Although the speed of Alerts is everything, other types of news are timed slightly differently. Scheduled news, for example, is different from exclusive news. In scheduled news, Reuters competes with other agencies in minutes rather than seconds:

> There are different levels of speed required for different purposes. What is enough for one level may be not enough for another, even if they're intercon-nected. The journalists in the financial space are all driven by speed. They're aiming to get those Alerts when the bank interest changes, or a company announcement before Bloomberg does . . . these are measured in seconds, in milliseconds when it comes to reaching their customers . . . and we are working on driving down the latency for those kinds of Alerts. But there are a whole lot of things that don't require that kind of speed – anything from the stories they create to the pictures to the videos. . . If you think about it, speed is the time it takes to create the news. It may take a journalist five minutes to write an article, or ten minutes to write an article. . . (Int. 5/4)

Alerts can sometimes be wrong (Box 5.2).

A Brief is a kind of semi-automated short story that follows a Snap. It might have been made out of company statements that were sent to the Regulatory News Service at 07.00 in the morning. Whereas all big and well-known companies are well attended to, some statements may be inter-esting even if they come from a small and as yet unknown company. Box 5.3 shows one that earned itself a Brief and then an Update.

Though it was not a priority story, it was interesting, but it came late and, according to the target set by Company, it should be moved in five minutes: "there is time pressure the whole time" (Int. 5/1). The priority is decided by the selection of Top News, which, in turn, is decided during the morning meeting and then sent around.

In Box 5.4 is a story that is nice though not typical.

BOX 5.3   COMPANY THAT EARNED A BRIEF AND AN UPDATE

09:10GMT 16Feb2009 – Ark Therapeutics up on French approval

Shares in Ark Therapeutics rise 9 percent after its brain cancer drug Cerepro is approved for use on a named patient basis in France.

"This approval may trigger other regulatory agencies, under pressure from physicians, to approve the product under the same route", analysts at Piper Jaffray say in a note to clients.

For more click on [nLG510005]

Reuters messaging rm://ben.deighton.reuters.com@reuters.net

BOX 5.4   AN UNUSUAL STORY

LONDON, Feb 16 (Reuters) – Two nuclear-armed submarines, one British and one French, have collided while on separate exercises in the Atlantic Ocean, British newspaper reports said on Monday.

The nuclear-power submarines were badly damaged in the underwater collision earlier this month, the *Daily Telegraph* said. No one was injured in the accident, and there was no damage to the vessels' weapons, the *Daily Mirror* said.

Neither the British nor the French defence ministries would confirm that the collision had taken place, but both issued statements on their nuclear marine force.

...*The Sun* newspaper said modern anti-sonar technology is so good that it is possible that neither submarine detected the other in time.

Story code: QnL G611527

13.40. Britain's First Sea Lord Admiral Jonathon [sic] Band, head of the Royal Navy confirmed the collision of the two submarines.

An Update may not result from the new events, but from a decision by Taster, who takes a look at a story and decides that some things need to be done to it. Taster may send it back to the correspondent or to the subeditor who was "subbing" the story. Box 5.5 shows is one such Update, in which reactions from appropriate sources have been demanded by Taster.

In the parentheses after "BMW AG", there are links to Factboxes that tell the interested client how BMW is doing on the stock market, what it specializes in right now, and what research is being done there – all this information is accessible via a click.

If the subeditor edited the story, he or she sends it to the correspondent.

BOX 5.5   UPDATE REQUESTED BY TASTER

UPDATE 3-BMW to cut 850 jobs at UK Mini plant
Mon Feb 16, 2009 9:06pm IST
(Adds reaction from PM spokesman and Conservatives)
By John Bowker

LONDON, Feb 16 (Reuters) – German car manufacturer BMW AG (BMWG.DE: Quote, Profile, Research) is shedding around 850 jobs at its Mini plant in Oxford, central England, as it cuts back production in the wake of a 35 percent slump in sales.

The company, which produced 235,000 cars at the plant last year – its only Mini factory worldwide – said in a statement it would now be operating five days a week instead of seven.

"While Mini has been weathering the economic downturn, it is not immune from the challenges of the current situation", the company said in a statement on Monday.

Sales of the Mini, made famous in the 1969 Michael Caine movie *The Italian Job*, slumped 34.5 percent in January to just over 10 100 worldwide, according to data supplied by the company.

The news brings the total number of announced job cuts by Britain's struggling car industry close to 4,000 over just a few months.

"Clearly this is very disappointing news. The government is doing and will do everything it can in order to help those affected," a spokesman for Prime Minister Gordon Brown said.

Trade union Unite described the production cuts as scandalous and criticised BMW for sacking agency workers who cannot claim redundancy pay.

If the correspondent has left and can't be contacted, it becomes difficult, but the policy is to discuss changes with the correspondent. I'll tell you why: I've made what I thought were very minor changes in stories from time to time, and it turned out that I misunderstood what they meant. It also happens often that a correspondent disagrees with that change, even if it's a minor change. (Int. 5/1)

There can be also an RPT, that is, news repeated. Corrections are usually minor (Box 5.6). Nevertheless, Reuters has a strict correction policy: they correct even the slightest mistake.

Boxes 5.7 to 5.10 show the sequence of a news development.

And here is Update 2 in Box 5.10 (to facilitate reading, the text that repeats the Brief or the Update 1 is in italics).

BOX 5.6   CORRECTIONS

10.15 CORRECTED – Shooting shakes Equatorial Guinea Capital (Corrects day to Tuesday)
10.25 CORRECTED – Asia-Naphta-Reliance March exports seen at 240 400 T
(Corrects paragraph 1 to 240,00 tonnes, not 160,000 tonnes, and corrects the last paragraph to at least 486,000 tonnes, not 455,500 tonnes).

BOX 5.7   ALERT

06:19 18Feb2009 RTRS – POLISH C. BANK HEAD SAYS POLAND NOT READY FOR EURO, NO ECONOMIC REASON TO ENTER ERM-2 THIS YEAR – REPORT

While the changes from Alert to Brief and from Brief to the story are clearly visible (more details), the changes between two Updates illustrate well the idea of making the narrative more coherent. More details are added, as new press releases have been issued, but it also means that quotes from less important actors are partly replaced by those from more important actors: the Prime Minister, for instance. Some local details are removed, and more of a wider (in time and space) context is added, together with the comments of the economists and Reuters analysts – a survey poll had already been conducted during the two hours that passed. Metaphors are added – cold water, walloping, antechamber. Somewhat surprisingly, and

---

BOX 5.8 BRIEF

06:25 18Feb2009 RTRS – Poland should not enter ERM-2 this year – c. bank head

WARSAW, Feb 18 (Reuters) – Poland is not ready for euro adoption at the moment and there are no economic reasons to enter the ERM-2 exchange mechanism this year, central bank head Slawomir Skrzypek was quoted as saying. Asked whether Poland is ready for euro adoption, Skrzypek told *Rzeczpospolita* daily, "We are not ready. The zloty exchange rate is not stable enough, therefore ERM-2 mechanism cannot be introduced".

(Reporting by Patryk Wasilewski; Editing by Kim Coghill)
((patryk.wasilewski@thomsonreuters.com; +48 22 653 9717: Reuters Messaging: patryk.wasilewski.reuters.com@reuters.net))
Keywords: POLAND EURO/

---

in my view incorrectly, "changes in constitution" were replaced by "constitutional changes". A new keyword – Financial – has been added. Thus, although the story is basically the same, it has changed visibly in form and in content. In fact, very few sentences were kept from the previous version.

Box 5.11 shows the advice the journalists are given on how to build their stories.

These instructions have been written for human collaborators only. It would be instructive to see how many of those recommendations can be changed into commands and incorporated into the software.

BOX 5.9 UPDATE 1

11:31 18Feb2009 RTRS – UPDATE 1 – Poland in talks with ECB on ERM – 2 entry – ruling party

(Adds quote, detail)
WARSAW, Feb 18 (Reuters) – Poland a few days ago started official talks with the European Central Bank on joining the pre-euro Exchange Rate Mechanism (ERM-2), a ruling party official was quoted as saying on Wednesday.

"Official talks with the ECB on Poland's ERM2 entry have been going on for a few days now," the ruling Civic Platform's parliamentary leader, Zbigniew Chlebowski, was quoted as saying by the PAP news agency.

Chlebowski also said Poland has decided to go ahead with ERM-2 entry without making constitutional changes related to the final adoption of the euro, which are opposed by the main opposition party Law and Justice.

"We decided to take this step knowing that Law and Justice does not agree to a change in constitution. We have taken the decision to enter the ERM-2 without a change in constitution," Chlebowski added.

The European Central Bank and the Polish finance ministry declined to comment.

Under a road-map drawn up by the government last year, Poland plans to enter the ERM-2 mechanism in the first half of 2009 and the euro zone in 2012.

A candidate country must keep its currency in the ERM-2 grid, where it trades within a fixed band against the euro, for at least two years prior to adoption of the common currency.

Many analysts doubt that the plan is realistic, and say that the spreading global crisis, the sharply weakening zloty and high market volatility would make ERM-2 entry much too risky for the economy.

Poland faces an additional political obstacle to euro adoption.

The government has failed to secure the required support of the eurosceptical main opposition party Law and Justice (PiS) to amend Poland's constitution, a move required to enter the euro zone but not ERM-2.

The constitution now stipulates that only the National Bank of Poland can set monetary policy and issue money. The European Central Bank takes over these responsibilities in the euro zone.

The zloty <EURPLN=> gained 0.4 percent against the euro immediately after Chlebowski's comments.

At 1118 GMT zloty traded at 4.8300 zlotys per euro.

Writing by Karolina Slowikowska; editing by Patrick Graham)
((karolina.slowikowska@reuters.com; +48 22 653 9725; Reuters Messaging: karolina.slowikowska.reuters.com@reuters.net))
Keywords: POLAND ERM2/

BOX 5.10   UPDATE 2

11:31 18Feb2009 RTRS – UPDATE 2 – Poland starts ERM-2 talks with ECB, c. bank unconvinced

By Karolina Slowikowska

WARSAW, Feb 18 (Reuters) – *Poland has started talks* to enter *the pre-euro ERM-2 mechanism, an official* said *on Wednesday*, pressing on with a goal to adopt the single currency in 2012 in the face of political barriers and a sceptical central bank.

The debate over joining the euro zone has taken centre stage after a tumble in the zloty due to the economic crisis. Economists forecast more turbulence ahead, with some warning Warsaw could get bounced out of the ERM-2 waiting room like Britain in 1992 if it did join.

The head of Prime Minister Donald Tusk's centre-right *Civic Platform party, Zbigniew Chlebowski*, said *Poland had started official talks on euro adoption with the European Central Bank*, sending the *zloty <EURPLN=> 0.4 percent higher* against the euro.

"Official talks with the ECB on Poland's ERM-2 entry have been going on for a few days now," the ruling Civic Platform's parliamentary leader, Zbigniew Chlebowski, was quoted as saying by the PAP news agency.

Tusk added he was ready *to enter ERM-2 without* making constitutional changes needed to join the euro itself, postponing a battle between his government and the conservative opposition.

The conservative opposition, whose votes are needed to make the changes to the constitution and pave the way for the euro entry, has already said no to switching zlotys for euros in 2012.

"The prerequisite for this (adopting the euro) is the ERM-2. Since they (the opposition) don't want to help, we have to do it now without the constitutional changes," Tusk told reporters.

The European Central Bank and the Polish finance ministry declined to comment.

Despite the government's plan for 2012, most analysts surveyed in a Reuters poll expect ERM-2 entry only next year, not this summer as Tusk plans, with euro adoption in 2013.

RISKY

A candidate country must keep its currency in the ERM-2 grid, where it trades within a fixed plus or minus 15 percent *band against the euro, for at least two years prior to adoption of the common currency.*

Even the most staunch euro supporters on Poland's Monetary Policy Council have voiced concern that pushing for ERM-2 now could endanger the economy.

Echoing those concerns, Central Bank governor Slawomir Skrzypek poured cold water on the idea on Wednesday and pointed to market conditions that have walloped the zloty, causing it to lose about a third of its value to the euro since last July.

"There are no economic reasons to enter the ERM-2 mechanism this year," *Skrzypek told daily Rzeczypospolita. "We are not ready. The zloty exchange rate is not stable enough, therefore ERM-2 mechanism cannot be introduced."*

Even if *Poland* agrees with the European Central Bank on joining the ERM-2, it still *faces* a big *additional political obstacle to euro adoption.*

The government has failed to secure the required support of the eurosceptical main opposition party Law and Justice (PiS) to amend Poland's constitutions, a move required to enter the euro zone but not the ERM-2 antechamber.

Some analysts say the failure to make changes in the constitution before ERM-2 entry could trigger speculative attacks on the zloty while in the grid.

The constitution now stipulates that only the National Bank of Poland can set monetary policy and issue money. The European Central Bank takes over these responsibilities in the euro zone.

Writing by Karolina Slowikowska; editing by Patrick Graham)
((karolina.slowikowska@reuters.com; +48 22 653 9725; Reuters Messaging: karolina.slowikowska.reuters.com@reuters.net))
Keywords: FINANCIAL POLAND ERM2/

BOX 5.11   ADVICE FOR JOURNALISTS

BITE CRITERIA
These are the main points we will be looking for (in brief and in detail):
1. What's new? Tell me something I don't know.
2. So what? Tell me why I should go on reading.
3. Did you question that? Is this the real story? Don't just parrot the official line.
4. Says who? Tell me how you know, make it authoritative and relevant to the client.
5. Can I cut it? Give me all I need at the top, don't ramble.
6. So what's next? Point me to the future.
7. Does it sing? Give me a golden quote or flash of colour.

1. We want the "who, what, where, why and how." We want it fast, first and exclusive. The opening paragraph must strip the facts bare to uncover the story that they signify but sometimes obscure.
2. It's all about the context. For some new stories the context is obvious. For others it isn't. We must show the reader why the story is significant. Sometimes you can do it by inserting a "nut graf"[10] high up that binds the new to what is already known.
3. Take a critical look at what is being said and challenge it by including context, background, opposing views and facts. Don't let the spin doctors take over your file.
4. What is the source of the information you are giving? You can polish a story as much as you like but it's useless if the reader cannot trust you. In the era of information overload it's all about trust. That means accuracy and balance. Say where the news and opinions are coming from. Make it as authoritative as possible and relevant to the client. We have to display proper knowledge of a specialist subject.

---

[10] A nut graf is a paragraph, particularly in a Feature story, that explains the news value of the story. The term is a contraction of the expression "nutshell paragraph", dating at least to the nineteenth century. In most news stories, the essential facts of a story are included in the lead, the first sentence or two of the story. Feature stories will often begin in a more narrative manner – introducing the background or the context, for instance. The nut graf, which will start in the third or fourth paragraph, will explain what the story is about. See http://en.wikipedia.org/wiki/Nut_graph; last accessed 4 July 2011.

5. Build an inverted pyramid. Give the facts in a logical sequence according to their relative importance so that the reader gets the guts of the story on one screen. Keep it simple.
6. Take the reader beyond the event. Point to what could happen next. In the corporate world, for example, what will news mean for a company's share price, for that sector, for rival companies?
7. Make your story sing. Avoid the tired quotes that state the obvious. Strive for the quote or true colour that sheds light on the event. Tell the news through people and when necessary spell out what the impact of the event could be on people's lives.

Branching Out (and Embedding)

The stories do not only proceed linearly; in the process, the "trunk" of a story becomes enriched by a variety of Factboxes, tables, and graphs.

Factboxes may, for example, contain "Key events in Venezuela during Chavez's decade in power, 1998–2009" or "Five facts about Kate Winslett".

Though Alerts, or Snaps, are the most important, as they signal breaking the news, Reuters is trying to branch out into "Analyses" – stories that explain the meaning of events announced by Alerts. This has to do with the fact that prior to the merger with Thomson, the main clients were traders, banks, and dealers. Since the merger, the clients are more mixed: there are also investment advisers, who have a longer time horizon than dealers, and the newsroom must now serve them both. Different types of information – Alerts based on company releases, central bank declarations, exchange situation and Analyses – need to be balanced. The analysts are journalists, but specialists, knowing how to assess and how to present economic information. Their job is to be as close as possible to the marketplace and to notice what is shaping its behavior. They are translating for the general public the meaning of economic policies. Box 5.12 gives an example of an Analysis.

Observe the irreverent tone, typical of British reporting; while it is less visible in the formulation of news, it is much more obvious in Analyses and Features. Whereas both the media scholars and the journalists in TT and ANSA were speaking of the recent "in-formalization" of the languages of their news, my impression was that Reuters was always maintaining this irreverent tone of reporting.

Another story format is Buy&Sell, a bullet-point list reviewing the pros and cons of buying or selling a specific share.

BOX 5.12 AN ANALYSIS

110:02 18Feb2009 RTRS – ANALYSIS – Crisis, what crisis? Italy is hardly noticing
By Gavin Jones

ROME, Feb 18 (Reuters) – Europe may be reeling from the worst recession in living memory, but in Italy you can barely tell.

As leaders around the continent suffer the backlash from factory closures and job losses, Prime Minister Silvio Berlusconi is more popular than ever, there is not a hint of social unrest and unemployment remains close to record lows.

It's not that the euro zone's third largest economy is flourishing, far from it. But Italy has been the area's most sluggish performer for well over a decade so Italians are inured to the crisis and they can finally enjoy seeing others doing even worse.

"You'll see that we improve our position in this crisis, even if it's because other nations are going backward faster," Economy Minister Giulio Tremonti told reporters last month.

He may well be right. The European Commission expects Italy's economy to contract by 2 percent this year, far less than Britain, Ireland and Germany and broadly in line with the average performance of the euro zone for the first time in years.

Long before a global credit crunch sent the world into recession, Italian media pundits were wringing their hands about rising poverty and national decline. Now the same pundits focus on the European and American crisis more than the Italian one.

"Italy is used to a stagnant economy and society feels the difference of going from zero growth to –2 percent far less than going from 3 percent growth to –3 or –4 percent as is happening in other places," said Unicredit analyst Marco Valli in Milan.

That may explain why dismal figures on industrial output and gross domestic product have produced negligible popular protests and no appreciable change in the national mood.

Retail sales data shows spending has been stagnant for years. It has recently got even worse but restaurants in the centre and the outskirts of Rome and Milan appear as full as ever.

"For us there has been a crisis since 2001 but not much has changed in the last year," said Alessandra Fiengo, who sells newspapers, books and toys from her kiosk in Rome.

There is clearly a mismatch between what the experts tell us and public opinion," said Paolo Pizzoli of ING bank in Milan.

This is borne out by consumer confidence data from the ISAE think-tank and the European Commission which shows Italians' morale, although depressed, has fallen far less than the euro zone average.

LOW GROWTH, LOW RISK

Italy's traditionally low-growth but low-risk economic structure is a source of strength in the current crisis.

Italian banks' more conservative lending practices mean they have suffered less from the crisis than their European peers.

Credit card and household debt is a fraction of that in the United States, Britain and Ireland and is also well below that of mainland European economies like Germany and the Netherlands.

"Italian families have relatively high savings and low debt, that is important at a time of crisis because it gives citizens a bit of breathing room," said union leader Guglielmo Epifani.

Most Italians have no mortgage and live in houses fully paid for at the time of purchase. House prices never boomed as in Britain, Ireland or Spain and show no sign of a similar bust.

Italy's labour laws have become more flexible over the last decade, but for firms of more than 15 employees they still offer considerable worker protection.

As a result unemployment, which hit a record low of 6.0 percent in the second quarter of 2007, has edged up only gradually to 6.7 percent, still unthinkably low compared with rates of above 12 percent a decade ago.

BERLUSCONI AHEAD

Berlusconi's response to the crisis has been to express constant optimism and generally act as if it didn't exist.

The government was widely criticised by economists for producing stimulus packages a fraction of the size of those of other large countries, and yet the prime minister's minimalist approach appears to be bearing fruit politically.

He remains far ahead in opinion polls and after a handsome government victory this week in a closely watched regional vote on the island of Sardinia, opposition leader Walter Veltroni resigned, leaving Berlusconi looking even stronger.

Analysts say it is only matter of time before the output slump takes a bigger toll on jobs, yet the same economists point out Italian employment levels are traditionally stickier than elsewhere in Europe and correlate less closely to GDP changes.

For Italy, the most frightening aspect of the current crisis is what happens when it ends, said a top Treasury official who asked not to be named.

"The crisis will be less acute here and you won't see social unrest, but our structural weaknesses are all still there and when the other countries recover we will recover less. Then we will go back to being the sick man of Europe."

((editing by Ian Jones; Rome newsroom; gavin.jones@reuters. com; Phone: + 39-06-8522-4232))
Keywords: ITALY CRISIS

Another initiative in the course of development is Newsmakers, to which Reuters invites the top-notch personas, politicians or CEOs, for instance, who, in a televised interview or a speech, break some kind of news. The plans are to make Newsmakers into a brand of its own (there is a whole unit at Reuters dedicated to branding). The Newsmakers is seen as an important initiative because, it is felt that it helps Reuters to avoid "being regurgitators" (Obs. 5/23).

The Commentary is a new unit that is developing a new kind of operation: "of course we cannot give opinions, and all our news is unbiased and impartial, but a commentary is needed – there's so much of it, that you can't be reporting in 2009 and not have columnists" (Int. 5/3). The columnists will be blogging. Apart from this, over the last five years or so all journalists have been encouraged to ventilate their passions through blogs, on which readers can comment.

Much of the background information necessary for embedding a story can be taken from EDREF (Editorial Reference), or from the EDREF Baskets when EDREF is closed or unstaffed. In Box 5.13 is the list of such Baskets (from February 2008).

Features are articles with no analytical ambition – stories that merely describe an interesting phenomenon. "Many people write a lot about nothing much in Features" was one critical comment about this form (Obs. 5/23). I have watched the writing of one Feature, which, interestingly enough, also ran under the general headline "Crisis, what crisis?" but was not an Analysis:

NE: I'll look at your Feature, M.
M: Yeah, great.
Feature: For many Brits, the recession is good news.
NE: It reads very well. We may need to be slightly careful if we're sending it to Feature Editor, because she may say that we need a case study.
M: I thought of that, as this guy is just giving an example. But it could be better to have more. . . at the end of the day, he's just one person. . . .

NE returns to Feature on recession being good for Brits (not for the shareholders and not for the unemployed – but for the rest). "Money is to be spent, not kept in banks" – thus more travel trips.

NE: Can we get a para in, something along the lines that one of the concerns about recession is that it has become self-fulfilling?. . .
Newsplanner teleconference:
NE: There's M's Feature: Crisis, what crisis? It's interesting because of the contrarian view. It says that except for the unemployed, people are having a good time. . .
I: Yes, very interesting. You see queues for restaurants. And the banks are thrilled at being nationalized, because right now their employees are demoralized. But how does UK compare to Ireland?
NE: I think it's the same. But it's a good idea to compare it. (Obs. 5/23)

And in Box 5.14 is the Feature in its final version.

It can be seen that the text acquired more and more details and examples (with "additional reporting", probably required by the Feature Editor). In general, the conviction is that branching out is important, because the trunk of the story can be in common with other media, but the "branches" must be original, unique insights (Obs. 5/23).

Analyses, Features and the forthcoming Comments are all a part of a balancing act: an attempt to counterweigh the requirement for speed with the requirement for detailed information.

BOX 5.13   EDREF BASKETS

GENERAL BASKETS:
BACKGROUND: Contains items on COUNTRIES and their chronologies, tables, lists etc.
LISTS: Xmitted boxes/chronos on SUBJECTS which cut across national borders such as AIDS, air crashes etc.

SUBJECT BASKETS:
GULF: contains boxes related to IRAQ. Also contains background from Gulf War/Profiles etc.
POPE: all information/boxes on the Pope
MANDELA: all information/boxes on Mandela

PEOPLE:
NEWSMAKER: Contains   PROFILES,   NEWSMAKERS/ CHRONOLOGIES/BOXES on individuals in alphabetical order
NOTE: The aim eventually is to clear out the Newsmaker Basket and have all profiles in PROFILE A–Z baskets

COUNTRIES:
GOVT LIST: Lists of some 22 countries cabinets and governments
CTRY PROOF: A–Z list of key facts of countries

BOX 5.14   CRISIS, WHAT CRISIS? FINAL VERSION

RPT-FEATURE – Falling costs a boon for many Britons
Wed Feb 25, 2009 1:04pm GMT

21 percent "comfortable and confident" – survey
* Mortgage repayments drop for some homeowners
* Retailers compete on prices to attract shoppers
By Michael Holden

LONDON, Feb 25 (Reuters) – Beyond store closures, shortened factory hours and longer lines of job-seekers in Britain is a reality that doesn't make front pages: a significant number of people are doing well out of efforts to stimulate the economy.

Falling prices and negligible interest rates are supporting consumption and borrowing, and discouraging saving: it's the opposite of what experts say the economy needs in the long term, but their confidence may lift the short-term mood.

Lower mortgage repayments for those homeowners whose loans track falling interest rates, and a falling cost of living as retailers compete on price are among factors prompting more than one in five people to say they felt positive in a survey last month by market research firm Mintel.

"It cannot be ignored that 21 percent are 'comfortable and confident' and do not feel that their finances have really been badly affected by the worsening economy," said Toby Clark, head of Mintel's Financial Research.

"For most, the economic downturn has been fairly manageable. Some will even be feeling better off, with more money to spend as inflation falls and interest rates reach a new low."

Self-employed driving instructor Bill Lord is one example. A 60-year-old who works in Bromley, southeast of London, he says he has seen his standard of living rise.

His mortgage repayments have tracked interest rates down, other bills have fallen and, with auto retailers struggling to attract customers, he has been able to negotiate good terms with car dealers for the vehicles he needs for his business.

"Every recession is different . . . but it looks very healthy from our point of view," he told Reuters by phone from his busy office.

The Bank of England has cut interest rates to a record low of 1 percent, leading to a significant drop in mortgage repayments for some home owners.

Prime Minister Gordon Brown has cut Value Added Tax, a sales tax, by 2.5 percent. Although criticised – notably by French President Nicolas Sarkozy who scoffed at the cut as achieving "absolutely nothing" – it has cut prices in shops.

With the British economy forecast to contract by as much as 3.3 percent this year and unemployment to reach almost 3 million in 2010, according to the Confederation of British Industry, those who are still spending are not a meaningless minority.

"There will be a significant number of households in the UK who will benefit from the current economic conditions," Philip Shaw, chief UK economist at Investec, told Reuters.

"There are big losers – namely people who have lost their jobs and also those people who are dependent on some sort of variable rate savings income – but there are also big winners."

"BEST MOVE I MADE"
Driving instructor Lord said work was booming as those seeking jobs saw a driving licence as an easy qualification to help find employment: "I came into this industry 20 years ago because there

was a recession on and I lost my job. It's done well for me, it's the best move I ever made."

He is expecting his income to increase by 20 percent over the year, while the main school he works with is looking to take on 15 more instructors in addition to the 90 it already employs.

One concern expressed by retailers and commentators is that negative reports in the media would damage consumer confidence and hold back spending, aggravating the recession.

Lord said he did not plan any belt tightening.

"I'm certainly not going to start cancelling holidays. Money is for spending – it's not for sticking in the bank."

Manufacturing and financial services have suffered from the credit crunch, but many, such as those with secure public sector jobs, still feel less likely to be hit.

"Workwise and personally I have not been affected," civil engineer John Smythe, 53, told Reuters while working on a major improvement project for construction company Balfour Beatty at London's Blackfriars railway station.

"I've been through recessions before in civil engineering. There is always a 'Plan B' by the government which will provide funding for our long-term projects."

Far from being encouraged to pay back debt, Shaw said Britons with large mortgages would particularly benefit as the standard variable interest rate for repayments has dropped to about 4.25 percent from 7 percent last year.

That could make someone with a mortgage of 100,000 pounds ($142,200) 167 pounds a month better off.

"Providing you have a job, you have a variable interest rate mortgage and you are an energy consumer, then your purchasing power will increase perceptively compared with 2008," he said.

UNTHINKABLE OPPORTUNITIES

For some, including about 40 percent of borrowers who, according to the Council of Mortgage Lenders, have loans that track rates in the broader economy, this has provided opportunities that had been unthinkable.

Mark Osland, an independent financial adviser, said one client had discussed with him the option of quitting work because her family was better off now.

"In her particular case, the mortgage has come down so much they could consider the lady actually giving up work to spend time with her children," he said.

With more cash to spend and savings rates offering little incentive for people to put money aside, businesses as well as individuals could eventually see the benefits.

Both the government and Bank of England, which have for years tried to persuade Britons to save for their retirement, now say spending is more important.

"This is the paradox of policy at present – almost any policy measure that is desirable now appears diametrically opposite to the direction in which we need to go in the long term," BoE Governor Mervyn King said in a speech last month.

"Spending now supports the economy, but in the long run we need to save more and borrow less."

For driving instructor Lord, the only downside of the recession so far has been a sense of guilt.

"You always feel a little bit ashamed here because we're dealing with a lot of people who have lost their jobs, he said. "But every cloud has a silver lining."

(Additional reporting by Martina Fuchs; editing by Sara Ledwith and Andrew Dobbie)

Coding (and Interlinking)

Journalists admit that it is a problem that Reuters sends an enormous wave of news – producing overflow for the clients – so they are doing their best to help the clients to manage this overflow. This is done primarily through classification and coding.

Forms

To begin with, there are different forms of news, some of which have already been listed. Furthermore, there are packages such as Front Page. There is also a program called Reuters Top News Packager, in which it is possible to cut and paste for Multimedia Top News, and that overwrites all previous versions.

Front Page, prepared by the Top News Desk, is formatted like a newspaper, which runs parallel to the media wire. Front Page is sent to banks

---

BOX 5.15   FRONT PAGE HEADLINES

FRONT PAGE:
"Japan sentiment". . .

Clinton calls for coordinated economic response. Risk dumped as Asia stocks drop, US dollar jumps

E. Europe crisis weighs on bank ratings – Moody's Vienna, Feb 17 (Reuters) The recession in emerging Europe will be more severe than elsewhere due to large imbalances, and will put financial strength ratings of local banks and their western partners under pressure, Moody's said on Tuesday

Vale, Xstrata, Rio bid for $ 2 bln Mongolian mine

China fund seeks partner to buy $ 8 bln AIG unit

GM talks with unions progress, Tues deadline for bailout plans

OPEC should cut again if market imbalanced – Iraq

"Killing Fields" torture chief goes on trial

---

and similar clients; the newswire goes to the media. The news in Front Page is formed according to the classic pyramid: "Who? What? Where? Why? How?" And the first paragraph is more informative, because some people read only that. There are Front Pages for European companies, Asian companies, and US companies, but the main one is Global Economy, which stays on all the time, whereas the others are time-zone related. Box 5.15 gives examples of Front Page headlines.

There are also Schedules: World News Schedule and Business News Schedule, similar to Front Page, but cheaper, and sent to the media clients. Schedules contain a Slug line (the first line of the Alert); they say if there will be pictures or not, when it will be done, what it is all about, and how long it will be.

There is also something called Snapshot (short information bits), which, at the time of my study, had the following titles: Financial Crisis, News, Markets, Quotes, Events/Diary/Data. Take a Look is similar.

Diaries, which come at 09.00 and at 16.00, announce upcoming events: "Political and General News Events from February 16 to May 17", for example.

Codes

As I suggested in the heading of this section, codes are of particular importance. They have historical tradition. At the turn of the previous century, all Reuters bureaus were equipped with enormous – and identical – code books (Read, 1992). The purpose of these codes was different from the present purpose: they made telegrams shorter, thus saving Reuters money; they hid sensitive issues; and they made telegrams undecipherable to others.[11] An especially efficient code was designed before World War I by Reuters Assistant Manager Samuel Casey Clements, who boasted that he was able to turn the fortunes of Reuters in this way (Read, 1992: 120).

The centrality of coding remains, but at present its purpose is overflow management. To begin, there are Address codes (which wire it should go to; Addr/Prod) and Content or Topic codes, here related to Top News:

- Front Page (TOP/NEWS)
- Global Economy (TOP/MACRO)
- Financial Services [TOP/FIN]
- US Companies [TOP/EQU]
- Asian Companies [TOP/EQA]
- Government Debt [TOP/DBT]
- Commmods & Energy [TOP/CE]
- Tech, Media, Telecoms [TOP/TMT]
- Consumer Goods [TOP/RETAIL]

- Politics & General [TOP/G]
- Corporate Finance [TOP/DEALS]
- Fund Mgmt [TOP/FUND]
- European Companies [TOP/EQE]
- Foreign Exchange [TOP/FRX]
- Corporate Credit [TOP/CREDIT]
- Emerging Markets [TOP/EMRG]
- Basic Industries [TOP/BASIC]
- Healthcare [TOP/HEALTH]

---

[11] In 1877, G.P. Williams composed a "Political Code", to be used by Reuters correspondents filing to London. In 1889, a printed code in French was issued for the use between St. Petersburg and London. At the time of the assassination of Tsar Alexander II in 1881, *Vendez à trente-huit* was to mean that the bomb had killed the tsar, and *Annulez commande papeterie* meant that the bomb coup had failed (Read, 1992: 98).

- Sports
  [TOP/SPORTS]
- Must Read Features
  [TOP/FEA]

- Lifestyle
  [TOP/LIFE]
- Directory [TOP/]
- Directory [TOP/]

There are Country codes, Company codes, Language codes, and many others, with an amazing intercontextuality between them. The code of a company gives the reader stocks, relates stories, Reuters "company views" with pictures – all of which is updated in real time.

Clients subscribe to a given service depending on their needs. In order to learn codes, they have the Help Desk and training people. But, my interviewees claimed, most of them know only a couple of codes at the most (BNK for Banks, MRG for Mergers & Acquisitions). As for the editors, Julius contains the lists of Tags, Codes, and Slugs, but sooner or later the desks learn "their" codes. Some codes are easy to guess, but some are mysterious. One example is WDW – story withdrawals or "kills": these are stories that are entirely wrong – either because the source was wrong, or because Reuters was wrong. This seldom happens. There is a warning first, and the story is withdrawn, but it always causes inquiry. A new code, RiNVM (Reinvestment), has caused many protests, as it was seen as too cryptic (Obs. 5/17). Still, compared to the problems of Italian journalists who have to decipher and memorize English acronyms, the situation of journalists at Reuters is much easier.

A recent addition is autocoding: a system that recognizes certain codes and associates appropriate topics with it:

> The system itself is going to insert some codes regardless of what we do. But other codes. . . If, for example, it's a story about a merger – and a lot of investment bankers know only this one code – MRG – because they only need that one. So there are codes like that, describing the thing in the story that is necessarily associated with the lead, because not every story about carmakers is going to be about mergers, right? So we have to be sure that all relevant codes are in. Because if I'm a client, an investment banker, and I want to know what happens with mergers and acquisitions, I hit MRG, and I expect a relevant story to be there. (Int. 5/1)

Autocoding has not been decided upon within Editorial. The decision was made by Company, on the assumption of "better safe than sorry" (Int. 5/11), whereas the editors preferred to determine for themselves which codes should be associated with the lead. Now the system does it for them.

Coding is the main tool for managing the overflow of information that is being constantly created by Reuters, and this is a tool that it gives to its clients. Coding is not browsing (which is also possible using Keywords):

calling upon codes links to other types of news related to the code, whether it uses the same words or not. Here is an example related to the Polish currency story:

10.54 16 Feb 09 RTRS Polish Central Bank's euro entry presentation –
hard to find arguments for ERM2 entry in current conditions.
Related news:
[M] [T] [E] [D] [PX] [PL] [CEEU] [EMRG] [EUROPE] [CEN] [INT]
[GVD] [DBT] [ECB] [POL] [LEN] [RTRS]

Although some codes are obvious, some are less so: LEN, for example, is Language English. I double-clicked on PL, which is obviously "Poland" and it produced eight later and more than 200 earlier news items including, for some reason, a news item about the movie *Milk*. They were obviously all news items from Poland – not only those related to the euro.

Many links can be reached automatically. If a client right-clicks on the price of a commodity, for example, various options appear: price indexes, profiles of companies – like in the case of BMW (these are called "clicky links").

The clicky links and the autocoding further support my thesis of the ongoing cybernization and cyborgization of news production. Whereas in the case of ANSA, the codes were still used as classificatory devices, here the operation of classification is accomplished practically unnoticed; the codes are added to the text, as it were, rather than text being portioned into categories, and sometimes they are piled on it ("better safe than sorry"). The introduction of international categories is a clear sign that all agencies are moving in this direction, but Reuters is clearly leading the way.

Why safe, and why sorry? As Bowker (2006) pointed out, what is not classified becomes invisible, and the effects are ambiguous:

> The negative telling is that things that are not classified are not considered of economic, aesthetic, or philosophical importance. . . The positive telling is that our databases provide a very good representation of our political economy, broadly conceived. . . This is one of the ways in which the world converges (messily, partially) with its representation. (Bowker, 2006: 153)

Bowker was discussing scientific databases, but his observation fits news agencies even better. What is not coded may disappear, thus better more than fewer codes. No coding system can cover everything, however; thus, the events to be represented must be limited to those that fit the codes, even if new codes are constantly being added. I return to this phenomenon in the last chapter.

THE MATRIX REVISITED

Although the matrix metaphor is meant to summarize my findings, it must be said that the physical location of Reuters News is in itself conducive to such an association. In the underground station, even before the building is in view, the futuristic landscape dominates (Photo 5.11).

Add to that a Keanu Reeves look-alike poster on one of the pillars (Photo 5.12).[12]

In this frame of mind, the Reuters building, which is the first sight one sees upon exiting the underground, does indeed have a futuristic, or perhaps old-fashioned futuristic look, just like the movie, *The Matrix* (Photo 5.13).

But it is much more than the buildings that evoke the association with the Matrix in the film. Inside the buildings, there are collections of machines that look old and fatigued (with the exception of the boiling hot and icy cold water faucet), and yet they all work. Furthermore, the introduction of the new system, as presented in the interviews, seems to be covering all the aspects of known prescriptions for the correct introduction of new technologies (as was the case with TT and ANSA). Usually, such ideal description raises the suspicion that the interviewed persons were geared toward impression management. In the case of news agencies, I believed the descriptions, because it was obvious to me that the new system *had to work* – otherwise it would be abandoned.

Photo 5.11   The exit of Canary Wharf underground station

---

[12] In another text (Czarniawska, 2011) I ponder over the impact of these visuals on my choice of metaphors.

Photo 5.12   Keanu Reeves look-alike

More similarities result from looking at the work and the collaboration of people and machines. Heath and Nicholls (1997), who studied news-making at Reuters, noted that there is an established image of journalists working individually, yet they are, in fact, constantly coordinating their actions and collaborating on the smallest details of their work. This can be said of all professional work, perhaps, but what is striking in Reuters, however, is that the cooperation is based on an incredibly complex infra-structure, where actions of people and artifacts blend. Thus, the Matrix.

Photo 5.13   Canary Wharf – the landscape

Reuters is a macro actor (Latour, 2005), not merely an assembly of cyborgs and machines: a human-computer network. People work for computers, which work for the human beings, and together they deliver an amazing output. I have had trouble locating information about the units that Reuters consists of in its entirety – probably because there is no such information. Like the Matrix, Reuters is not visible in its entirety – probably, to anyone:

> One of the difficult things about explaining all this is its constant state of evolution. And there are those people who are working behind the scenes the whole time, who are changing how these things work. So the whole thing gets unbelievably complicated. (Int. 5/1)

There is also a semantic confusion. The very names of the units, for example, are used in a mixture of formal labels and everyday abbreviations, and a mixture of British and American English: there are divisions, departments, sections, offices, rooms, bureaus. . . The change of ownership caused further problems: "Are we Thomson Reuters or are we Reuters? Are we Thomson News or are we Reuters Media? And everybody got confused in the middle" (Int. 5/3).

Such confusion is even more acutely felt by an external observer like I was. Internally, they communicate without trouble, but it has been confirmed again and again that there are many operations that are hidden from any one person's point of view, and that it is unnecessary for everyone to know everything. "Unbelievably complicated" and "quite confusing" were the expressions often used by my interlocutors in trying to explain to me how Reuters works. Reuters clients cannot grasp the variety of its products, either, but, again, they have no need to do so. The coding system helps them to navigate within their relevant services and databases.

The navigation metaphor returned often:

> [I]t's like a well-oiled machine, so nobody ever sees anybody else paddling ferociously to keep their heads out of water. If a worldwide disaster happens, it just becomes an all-hands-on-deck kind of thing. (Int. 5/3)

This further strengthens the analogy with the activity of navigating a large ship, as described by Hutchins (1995), and that I have been evoking in previous chapters. But I am suggesting an even more complicated machinery – a whole world of Matrix, as it were. In *The Matrix*, the movie, the characters also navigate ships, even if these are space ships. Thus, Reuters especially, and the two other news agencies to a lesser extent, are like the Matrix, because they consist of an enormous cognitive network performing operations that practically nobody within it is able to grasp, and because they are populated by cyborgs. I consider the consequences of this metaphor in the next chapter.

6. How news is produced

In this chapter I summarize my findings, revealing a picture of a complex action net extending far beyond the news agencies. It is not news that news production is circular, but circuits described in earlier studies were limited to human links (see, e.g, Gans, 1979/2004). The need to manage the overflow of information at the input and output requires more collaboration from non-human producers – thus, the ongoing cybernization and cyborgization of the process. The contribution of the non-humans, especially unintended contribution, deserves more scrutiny than it receives in media studies.

DIFFERENCES AND SIMILARITIES AMONG THE THREE AGENCIES

The mechanisms of production are similar in all three agencies. The difference is in size – the size of the "factory" and the range of its products. How can one tell the difference among these three agencies, I wondered?

> The way of functioning is the same, because it's exactly the specificity of news agencies that they work in a certain way. You can tell the difference among the agencies by looking at the way they lay out their news. The agencies need to communicate with their clients, and therefore introduce a layout that's useful to their clients. This is the way each agency tries to raise its own flag. (Int. 4/2)

TT has economic news under "Economy", for instance, which is the traditional part of Swedish newspapers. Reuters, with clients outside the newspaper world, has three internal units covering economic issues: Treasury, Commodities & Energy, and Corporate. This organization evolved partly because of the volume of Reuters' products and partly because of its adaptation to the interests of its clients. Additionally, the agencies have had to compete with other agencies on their own terrain. TT is the main Swedish agency, but Reuters, Bloomberg, and AFP have their own bureaus in Sweden, and nobody can prevent TT's clients from contracting with them. In the eyes of my interlocutors from ANSA, this problem is especially acute in Italy:

Just imagine being a journalist at a newspaper in Italy, and seeing hundreds and hundreds of news items arriving each hour on your computer screen. In France, Great Britain, and Germany, there's a national agency, and you work with it. We're the national agency in Italy, but there are other agencies that dispatch news. There's a plurality of news, and the newspapers stand in front of enormously rich material. We're helping them to sort it out, therefore, by sending the list of "The News of the Day", "Front Page", and then various packages tailored to the needs of radio or local television. Thus, on the one hand, we have to produce news, but on the other hand, we need to help our clients orientate themselves within those thousands and thousands of news items by establishing their priority order. (Int. 4/2)

What was intended to highlight a difference actually emphasizes another similarity. The national competition problem may indeed be more acute in Italy, but all the agencies help their clients to "sort through those thousands and thousands of news items". In fact, these are the ways of managing overflow, which I describe in greater detail later.

The similarities among agencies was generally recognized, and explained by their similar origins:

The history of the agencies is similar. They were born with the same purpose in mind, and they are using more or less the same method. They have the same original sin in common; they were all born with the help of those in power, and were trying to become independent. At present they all try to answer to the challenge of the market, because the Internet equalized everything, so that agencies now look for new ways of differentiating themselves. It's a flotilla, in which some ships are very big, and others are very small; but the course they run is very much the same. (Int. 5/2)

As for original sin, perhaps Reuters should be excluded; it started as a small private agency and continues as a large private agency, in the sense of not being state-owned – although it has often been "helped out" by the state. There is another strong similarity: technology (although perhaps this was included in the concept of "method" in the previous quote). They all buy machines and basic software from external suppliers, and then adapt them for their own use – in a similar way.

There are some differences in the method, as well, likely due to the size of the newsroom. Mail and chat rooms have replaced many meetings at Reuters. The editors say that this is an important change, as there used to be many more meetings. And although TT and ANSA dedicate their morning meetings to an evaluation of the previous day's work, meetings at Reuters have coordination as their main purpose, so the desks know what the others desks are doing. The coordination problem was not acutely felt at TT, but it was at ANSA, which is halfway between Reuters and TT in size, and ANSA will likely be moving toward a solution similar to that of Reuters.

There are few surprises or long discussions at Reuters morning meetings; the editors have already sent their Top News to the Top News Desk, which has, in turn, already compiled a list. Other news is sent directly to the wire by the editors; there is no Central Desk, as there is at TT and ANSA. Local bureaus sometimes send news directly to the wire, as well. That may happen when there are time pressures at Reuters, or it may happen as a part of an attempt by TT and ANSA to give the local bureaus greater independence. Many of Reuters meetings take the form of teleconferences.

Common sense, emphasized in this report in relation to ANSA, is of central importance everywhere. Everywhere, too, common sense is close to expertise, even with people who do not have a distinct specialty. As a woman at Reuters who moved between the desks told me, she felt that she was doing first a degree in Stocks & Markets, and then in Commodities & Energy (Chapter 5).

Even if agencies are – to a certain degree – like fish markets, another aspect of the analogy can be stressed: at different places, fish with the same name are always different.

One can begin with the language: both TT and ANSA use English and English terms to an increasing degree. Much to my surprise, however, these are not the same terms. At Reuters, there are no "takes", which are central in TT, and there are no "Flashes", which are central at ANSA. Some terms used by TT and ANSA had been used previously at Reuters: "Alerts" were still called "Flashes" in Reuters when Read wrote his history in 1992. Borrowing also goes via various routes; sometimes these are US terms, sometimes British, and sometimes they are coined locally, even if they are still in global language.

Furthermore, both TT and ANSA reported that the language was becoming more informal – a phenomenon not observed at Reuters, where it was informal to begin with. Yet, both agencies try to keep their language different from the language used by the newspapers. As I pointed out in another context (Czarniawska, 2004), the Italian newspapers, probably following the example of the Anglo-Saxon ones, try to increasingly dramatize their news (Edelman, 1988). In order to create a spectacle, they use exaggerated metaphors. But ANSA suggests avoiding "the abuse of metaphors, useless Anglicisms, hermetic jargon, hackneyed expressions, platitudes and verbs not in common use". According to a chapter of ANSA's *Code of Work* entitled "The contents and the language of ANSA", the agency has a duty to maintain strict respect for "the rules of objectivity, thoroughness and clarity of information". If this means a rigid language, as the critics of TT have claimed, too bad. It is up to their clients to give color to the language, to play with polysemy. "To make an article alive [or, as the Reuters' guide puts it, "to make your text sing"] . . . it is not necessary to write in a precious or literary language, but in a way that is as simple and clear as possible".

It seems that "informalization" occurred much earlier at Reuters than at TT and ANSA. Engländer, Reuter's assistant, thus commented on developments in 1889:

> "I inaugurated myself, nearly 30 years ago, the present service of sober, naked statements of facts for our services, but at that time the newspapers published only a few sober telegraphic announcements of facts, and telegraphy itself was in its infancy: – but your Editors still shrink from developing any light and colour in the service, and believe the dull skeleton telegrams alone to be acceptable." (Quoted in Read, 1992: 103)

Thus, what was seen by TT's historians as "officialese" (Hadenius and Weibull, 1999), the historian of Reuters sees as "cablese": a simplified language enforced first by the cost of telegrams, then supported by the newspapers' use of it. Herbert William Jeans, Chief Editor[1] at Reuters said at the World Press Congress in Geneva in 1926 that progress in communication technology and the fall of prices for telegraphing meant that a correspondent could now "'telegraph his story in his own words with all its lights and shades'" (Read, 1992: 196). As Read pointed out, it is noteworthy that he used the term "story" rather than telegram, message, or information. Reporters could now send stories, or material for stories, to editors who composed them further.

Nevertheless, there is a strong belief in all three agencies in a special mission of agencies, which should deliver news that, in TT's version, must be "objective and unbiased" (Hadenius, 1971: 57) and in Reuters' version "independent, unbiased and impartial" (Read, 1992: 197). Objectivity, also used in Reuters, did not mean neutrality, "but rather the absence of emotion in vocabulary, so that events may be judged dispassionately, at least as far as the account of them is concerned" (Read, 1992: 371).

To summarize this issue of language, one could say that TT and ANSA have gone in the same direction that Reuters took earlier – a relatively informal language, albeit simple, clear, and to the point. But is there a difference in the contents of the news?

> Here in Italy it's not like the Anglo-Saxon countries, where politics is always and only a matter of the official communication. With us, the communication is practically always informal, and the way the politicians talk to journalists is like that, too. Thus, if it's difficult to find "gossip" with a political content in London – that is, there's a lot of gossip about politicians but not when they do

---

[1] The change of name to "Editor-in-Chief" came later (Read, 1992: 204).

politics – in Italy politics is run by different rules. You need to wait until the end of a meeting to decide what a given politician has actually said. At the end of a meeting of several politicians there are many journalists outside. One politician talks to one journalist; another talks to another journalist. One politician makes one declaration; another makes another declaration. There are formal press conferences, but, in reality, half of the information is created beyond the formal occasions. It's a bit like that in Brussels, too: a large portion of the information is created through those encounters, from these talks, from this mixture of politicians and journalists.[2] (Int. 4/2)

Indeed, at Reuters they "consider gossip but not report it" (Obs. 5/16). A similar order rules at TT, in the sense that even if journalists wait to speak with politicians after the official press conference, these are not chats – reserved for the evening newspapers – but rather explications and explanations of what has been said. One of my interlocutors at Reuters explained the meaning of a rumor to me: "King [the head of the Bank of England] has been shot" is a rumor, but "sterling fell because of the rumor that King has been shot" describes a market move, and will be reported (Obs. 5/18). In fact, Reuters has a strong anti-rumor policy. Clients complain, but "if you did rumors, you wouldn't be doing anything else". There are lots of rumors and many are actionable on legal grounds. After Reuters mistakenly reported Khrushchev's death in 1984, its then Editor-in-Chief issued the following note:

"Rumours and unconfirmed reports can cause financial collapse, panics, riots and revolution. . . The credit does not go to an agency which first reports a rumour. It goes to the agency which can first report the FACT". (Quoted in Read, 1992: 376)

Further differences concern the authorship of articles. Although a Reuters byline is quoted in the non-British papers that use its services, the British papers – with the exception of *The Independent* and *The Guardian* – do not do that. Reuters did complain, but it is an established custom, and difficult to change. Reuters wants branding, but unlike other agencies, the newspapers are not its main clients. Bylines of TT and ANSA are inserted by their clients, sometimes with the addition of the name of the newspaper journalist who expanded the text.

The agencies and their work are similar, though, and the most striking similarity is the circularity of news production.

---

[2] A fascinating description of European news agencies located in Brussels can be found in Bastin (2003).

CIRCULARITY

The traditional image of a factory as an open system already suggests a
certain circularity of production processes; its products incite a response
that returns to the producers: the so-called feedback loop. This type of circular connection does exist and is described here, but it is not central to the
production of news. Pierre Bourdieu spoke of "the circular circulation of
information" (1998: 23) in journalism, condemning it as a narcissist game
of mirrors, leading to mental closure. I chose to see it as part of a greater
circuit of culture, as described by Richard Johnson (1986–87), whose
model I adapted to depict the circularity of news production[3] (Figure 6.1).

The circuit runs in a two-dimensional space: one extends between official representations to private lives and the other extends between concrete experiences and their abstract versions. Events happen in this space,
assume a specific cultural form, and result in the production of cultural
artifacts, with texts being one type of artifact. Texts are then read and
interpreted, thereby contributing to the lived culture.

Johnson's model can be quite literally applied to the phenomenon of
news production, but in this text I wish to give it a more specific meaning,

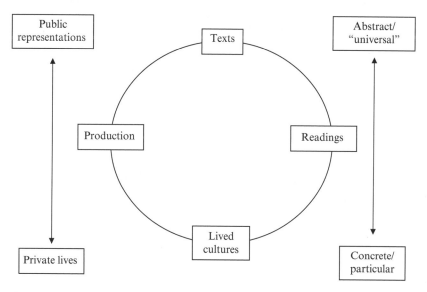

Figure 6.1   A circuit of culture, based on Johnson (1986–87, p. 47)

---

[3] Scholars within cultural studies postulated the abolishment of a distinction between production and consumption in the 1980s. For a recent summary, see Jackson et al. (2001).

by describing concrete circuits that are part of the greater circuit of culture.

Circuit 1: Clients Who Are Producers, Producers Who Are Clients

There were few direct contacts with the clients, mainly the newspapers, at TT:

> It's strange that we have as few contacts with our clients as we do . . . very little. This is one of the most important issues for us – how to receive reactions from our clients. We have no good solution for that yet. (Int. 3/2)

> If [clients] think something is missing, they should let us know. Unfortunately, that happens only too rarely. I don't know what it depends on – because they're so pleased or because they're so dejected? (Int. 4/4)

In this situation I decided to take the matter into my own hands and ask one of the clients, on hearing a complaint about Lunch News Bill:

> 3/12: It's obvious that we have to have the meeting with the EU committee, where Fredrik Reinfeldt [Swedish Prime Minister] will talk about what he is going to say in Brussels during the weekend. I also know that these meetings are always covered by X at TT, and I know that he's reliable, writes well and faultlessly. But it wasn't in the bill. And if you're a News Editor at a newspaper, and happen not to know that the committee meets today, you can be somewhat unpleasantly surprised when the texts come after 15.00. But I don't bother to call them in Stockholm and ask, "Why don't you have this?" Because it's meaningless. They're not going to say more than, "Of course we will have it", so I know the answer already, and don't want to risk sounding like a stupid fusspot, especially if I called them everyday. . .
> BC: But you're a paying client?
> 3/12: Hmm.

As we have seen in Chapter 4, ANSA's clients have no such fears – they call quite often. But apart from that, each agency actively collects feedback by checking how much of their material has been used by the clients. This is easier for TT than for the other news agencies, because clients do give TT a byline, which happens rarely with Reuters, even if the agency tries to fight against being quoted anonymously. This measure is not appreciated by everyone, exactly because of its circularity:

> This is how one always measured our success – how well what we did has been used by the newspapers and other media that are our clients – how pleased our clients are. (Int. 3/1)

My interlocutor was critical toward this way of measuring success; isn't it mostly a conformity check? Somebody else, with the same criteria, evaluates what has already been evaluated by the same criteria. Where is the room for innovation, for originality, for breaking with the old ways? Yet this kind of feedback is good for the individual journalists who otherwise cannot see their names in print.

It is not the main aspect of this circuit that I wanted to emphasize, however. My point is that the clients of the agencies are themselves sources of news reported by the agencies:

> It can be that we read the top news in *Dagens Nyheter*, for example, because we already get it in the evening, and it may happen that we say, "This news item is very good", so we refer to it and send it in the middle of the night, and then of course the radio news at 06.00 will have received it, and will repeat it. So it goes round and round . . . [Laughs]. (Int. 3/8)

According to Pablo Boczkowski (2009a: 40), who studied newsmakers on paper and online, this kind of what he calls imitation is nothing new in news production. What changed, though, thanks to the new technologies, is the opportunity to monitor what others are doing (Boczkowski, 2010; see also Chapter 2). In the old days apparently, journalists tried to figure out what the others were writing by sounding out their colleagues in face-to-face encounters. Now they can save themselves the ordeal, as well as the uncertainty about whether the information they gathered was correct or not. The screen will tell them soon enough. Indeed, the question "X has A, why don't we?" was a standard one at editorial meetings.

Although the results of my study are in perfect consonance with those of Boczkowski (2010), I did not choose, for several reasons, to interpret them through the notion of imitation as he did. In the first place, it is important to cast in relief the non-imitation of work processes that I noted in the agencies. One could imagine, somewhat counterfactually, that the agencies could monitor the production processes by visiting other agencies, or by employing consultants specializing in such matters. One could imagine a sole producer of specialized news agency software. Yet, probably because of a felt need for differentiation, they hardly know what the work at other agencies looks like, and they carefully reconstruct the process and the software from the visible product that they can easily monitor.

It needs to be added, though, that as the brief histories in Chapter 2 revealed, the agencies imitated one another in the beginning. Also, as a result of competition won, they quite often appropriate personnel from agencies that lost the battle for survival. It could be that the non-imitation and re-creation of production processes by deducing them from the product is a new phenomenon, forced by speed and enabled by the Internet.

It cannot be said that agencies imitate their clients, either – and here I mean the newspapers and other media. They adapt their product to the product of their client, but constantly emphasize how different their work is from that of other journalists. The newspapers do not imitate agencies, either; they replicate their product.

Finally, I do not use the concept of imitation, because, unlike Boczkowski, I do not see it as a negative phenomenon. Like Gabriel Tarde (Tarde, 1901/2003; Czarniawska, 2009b) I believe imitation to be one of our central social mechanisms. Nevertheless, it is correct that "technologies of imitation" change in time and, as Boczkowski (2010) says, there is a growing homogenization of news, in spite of the multiplication of its producers.

Boczkowski was aware that his definition of imitation differed from Tarde's:

> I adopt a more restricted notion of imitation that is conceptualized as the act that occurs when one actor, based on knowledge of another actor's behavior or output, decides to completely or partially reproduce this behavior or output instead of pursuing a different course of action. (2010: 16)

Yet, as Luhmann (1998) pointed out, Tarde's concept helps us to understand that order is possible without knowledge. Also, if applied literally, Boczkowski's definition would be contradicted by my material, which shows that both news agencies and their clients do choose to act differently, and yet the results are still almost identical.

What is more, the source of news is not limited to the agencies' own clients; news items can also be supplied by other agencies that they collaborate with:

> This is Bloomberg. We take many things from Bloomberg, which is enormously bigger than we are, and we have a collaboration contract with them. So we report how things are on the stock market, and then try to understand why they are as they are. (Int. 4/1)

Thus, Bloomberg provides data, but ANSA must interpret them, although Bloomberg has already produced these data from information gleaned from other sources, such as the organs of finance. After ANSA has made its interpretation, Bloomberg can quote it in order to explain the situation on the Italian market, and so on. Although I have already suggested that news agencies produce "semi-manufactured products", it must be added that the differences among "raw material", "semi-manufactured products", and a ready "product" is arbitrary in the production of news, because it is a circuit. Perhaps there are no "data", only "capta" as Ronald Laing (1967) called it, as there is nobody to "give" us the knowledge of the world; it must be produced. As Alfred Schütz (1953/1973: 5) expressed it: "Strictly speaking, there are no such things as facts, pure and simple. All facts are from the outset facts selected from a universal context by the activities of our mind". In speaking of "our mind", Schütz was referring to the individual person, but he could have been speaking of news agencies. It is the activities of their minds and their machines, their collective cognition that is selecting and elaborating the "facts". Thus, "the facts" have not disappeared, as the Italian journalist Marco Travaglio (2006) fears, because they were never there.

The circuit between the producers and their clients also means that the clients can become competitors of the agencies. The British newspapers do not give Reuters bylines, and the Swedish ones attempt a contrasting selection:

> Most newspapers fight for exclusivity, so it may happen when I receive a report that I find boring and irrelevant, that *Dagens Nyheter* picks it up just because we wrote nothing about it. It will become an argument in their selection: let's do something that TT didn't do. They do another evaluation just to be different from TT. (Int. 3/4)

The circuit means that it is not only clients that compete with TT; TT also competes with its clients:

> 3/7: We live in a big media world. There are websites, newspapers, TV, and of course we compare ourselves with them. And if we see that we're slower or that we miss some things, we do everything to catch up.
> BC: You don't compare yourselves to other agencies?
> 3/7: No, it's strange, but we compare ourselves with newspapers, radio, and TV . . . that is, our clients. Our main goal is to serve them, not to compete with them, but it's only natural that one compares a text with what they have written; perhaps we could have done it better. "Look, the Swedish Radio has done a follow-up of our news that was actually much sharper than ours".
> BC: So perhaps it's not so much competition as a race?
> 3/7: It lies in the nature of the whole news industry . . . race . . . yes, it's a kind of race. Everybody wants to be fast and good. Write well. Be first. This is the way the news is produced.

Reuters compares itself with other agencies of the same character that are not their clients (Chapter 5), but the element of racing is present everywhere. The whole circuit exemplifies an observation made many times – that the borders among the various media become effaced – but this depends primarily on the fact that they all use the same kind of technical platforms (Ekdahl and Wigstrand, 2006). And although the fact of cooperation among competitors was acknowledged some time ago (Anderson et al., 1994; Brandenburger and Nalebuff, 1998), here is variation of this phenomenon: competition within cooperation. Even this variation is not new, however. The agreement made by Reuters with Associated Press in 1942 was summarized by one of the Reuters managers as concluded under the motto "Compete and cooperate" (Read, 1992: 250).

Circuit 2: The Experienced Teach the Newcomers

The generally accepted assumption that the skills of news production can be acquired only through news production made me hypothesize another circuit here. From where does innovation come?

> 3/3: Experience is absolutely necessary to develop the kind of judgment that's required in news production.
> BC: Isn't it very conservative? What has been done before will decide what is to be done now. How can anything change?
> 3/3: By experience I mean the skill of avoiding errors. Avoiding errors is completely different from doing the right things, and from doing new things. This new but right thing can come from some other place. We receive many stimuli, not least from our clients, who constantly demand that we do something new or different. They may want a lighter type of text, and then it's my duty to prioritize this type of text and avoid long and boring ones. For this, you don't have to have much experience, but for avoiding errors, yes. You must either have done them yourself or have seen others do them.

That innovations often come from the outside is also well known, but one could assume that, as in case of other companies, they would come from other agencies or from consultants. But it seems that there are no news agency consultants, and the agencies have little contact with other agencies, except via products, and the innovations can come from there. Otherwise, it is back to Circuit 1: producers learn from clients, and clients learn from producers. But there is also a great deal of confidence in the internal creativity potential:

> We have tried to find new forms of texts and other things . . . such things don't arise from the daily management of inflow and the daily assignment duties, but from inside each of us. We constantly try new things, and sometimes they work, and sometimes they don't. . . But I don't think that's in conflict with experience, because an experienced person feels much more secure and can therefore dare to experiment. On the contrary, you're conservative when you're insecure, because you're afraid of making errors, so you try to do what everybody else does. (Int. 3/4)

Reuters has introduced a promising innovation, deviating from the circuit somewhat. It is not only the most experienced journalists who have the task of teaching the newcomers. The teaching duties rotate; even young collaborators are sent for a time to perform introductory duties. Thus, the newcomers not only learn the traditional ways of doing things, but are kept up to date with various attempts to experiment and to innovate.

One commonly quoted obstacle for experimentation and creative thinking is the demand for speed. An experiment can misfire and waste time. The solution, as one of the respondents from ANSA pointed out in describing the changes in technical infrastructure (Chapter 4) is to deviate from the usual way of experimenting. Instead of running an experiment and evaluating the results after it is finished, the changes and the innovations are introduced while the machine is running. Then it may have to be slowed down for a minute, but no longer.

Without casting any doubt on the creativity of news producers, I believe that the biggest innovations are the result of technological inventions. From the outset, news agencies were dependent upon the progress of communication technologies – from e-mail to placing the telegraph cable under the Channel – and this is still the field where most things happen. Johnson has not mentioned technology in his circuit of culture, but it has a central place in the lived culture, and in both the production and the consumption of cultural artifacts.

Circuit 3: Sources Try to Impact News Production

Molotch and Lester (1974) differentiated among three groups of news producers: *news promoters, news assemblers* (the media), and *news consumers*. In their opinion, each of those groups actually produces the news. The sources attempt to formulate their information in the way that is advantageous to them; the media apply professional production methods; and the readers interpret them and thereby produce them once more for their private use. They all play their roles from what the phenomenologist Alfred Schütz called a *purpose-at-hand* (1953/1973), meaning that they all try to select and formulate the news in a way that suits them – with varying success. It is unlikely that those in power form a conspiracy in order to exert a systematic pressure on the media.[4] It is highly likely, however, that the existing routines bear traces of previous power relationships that became stabilized in objects, technology, and procedures (Molotch and Lester, 1975; see also next section). Even the readers try to influence the news, thereby closing the circuit, which can be seen in Molotch

---

[4] Not that they are not trying, but it does not mean that they succeed. A recent critique of AFP by Sarkozy (Girard, 2008) has met with strong protests from the French journalists association.

and Lester's model as a line. "Consumers" also try to be "promoters", although not everybody succeeds in such attempts.

This picture contrasts with the thesis that was a starting point for Gaye Tuchman's study reported in *Making News. A Study in the Construction of Reality* (1978). She claimed that the "news media set the frame in which citizens discuss public events" (p. ix). Not alone, certainly. News agencies, together with other media, do form the public discourse, but from the inside, by filling it with forms dictated by their software – software that, to a certain extent, decides the contents.

If everybody tries to influence the news, but not everybody succeeds, what decides success or failure? I would say that it is *knowledge of the rules of the game* that separates less successful from more successful attempts. As for sources, one can say that this circuit becomes better and better balanced as more and more of the people who work in press offices and other information units are journalists (Engwall, 2006; 2008). During my study I happened to read in my local newspaper, *Göteborgs-Posten,* that its News Editor was taking the position of Head of Communication in the Municipality of Göteberg: "Are you changing sides now?"

"You can see it like that, or at least traditionally one would see it like that. But I think that the job of both a journalist and a Head of Communication consists of providing the citizens with correct information" (*Göteborgs-Posten,* 25 September 2008). This is one of the signs that homogenization proceeds within the circuit.

But one may ask, "What means do non-journalists have to influence news agencies?" The authorities can place an embargo on the news, making information available in advance, so journalists can familiarize themselves with it, with the restriction that the news cannot be sent on wire before an indicated hour. According to Read (1992: 25), the first known case of an official embargo was the one imposed on Reuters by the French government in 1859. It concerned the full text of the speech of Napoleon III at the opening of the French Chambers – a text that was sent in advance with instructions to withhold it until the speech had actually been made. At present, EU and many international agencies work that way.

As discussed in Chapter 5, the official financial news is released in a similar manner, by actually holding journalists under lock and key until the specified hour. This seems to be one of many indicators that the circuits run both ways. According to Read (1992: 12), this ingenious system was invented by Julius Reuter in Aachen. He kept his subscribers locked in his office when stock market and commodity news was expected, so they would all receive it at the same time.

Apart from an official embargo, there are many attempts to attain advantageous timing: "If a company has bad news, they often do it at

20.00 on a Friday evening, so it may pass unnoticed for a while at least" (Int. 3/5). Furthermore, submitting many news items simultaneously can quickly switch attention to some other matter; this tactic has its counterpart in the "rationing" of news – a favorite method of politicians.

News agencies seldom receive comments and suggestions from the final readers or listeners; suggestions are much more likely to be directed at newspapers. There is a great deal of talk now about "interactive journalism", but, as Nygren (2008b) pointed out, many journalists are skeptical about the value of readers' comments. Journalists who blog at Reuters do not read the comments to their blogs. Yet, some readers or, more often, some formal or informal organizations, may intervene:

> 3/2: There are some persons and some interest groups that don't like the way we write about them. There are some people engaged in the Middle East conflict who think that we're pro-Palestinian. Our clients, who, after all, employ specialists in those questions, don't think so, but some readers have very decisive opinions on this complex and inflamed issue, and are simply trying to use us. They focus on single statements in what we write, to prove that they reveal a systematic bias of which we're guilty. It's very difficult to defend oneself against such an accusation. There is absolutely no systematic pattern in the way we're describing one side or the other. The way we write about each of them is decided by what we see as being stimulated by the news of the day.
> BC: But if I understood it correctly, they don't call you, but try to create a public debate around you. Is that right? [I have seen it happening on the Internet].
> 3/2: Yes, this is how it was in this specific case. But in other cases it could be that they address us directly. One such example was the Balkan War. During the battles it could have happened that persons on one side called to scold us for a specific text, saying that we represented their enemy. An hour later, someone from the opposite side would call us to scold us for the same text – because it represented the interests of the other side.[5] This is how it goes.
> Of course it can happen that . . . we went too fast, were sometimes a bit naive, and described some event in a way that affected some person in a negative way. Then they called us. There's a handful of such cases per year. Sometimes they're right; we have been careless. Then we try to put it right afterwards – and we apologize.

Ericson et al. (1989) conducted a unique study of news sources, albeit for the newspapers, but the dynamics are the same. They pointed out that, especially with letters to the editor, the sources become reporters themselves. "What a letter writer submits is highly structured by the newspaper, in the same way that the newspaper structures what its own reporters submit" (Ericson et al., 1989: 339).

---

[5] It seems that foreigners and immigrants are more likely to come up with direct feedback in Sweden. Less afraid of being perceived as "fusspots", as one of the TT clients put it?

Circuit 4: News Producers Cause the Events that Become News

This circuit is most obvious in the case of Reuters; by sending certain Alerts, they cause robo-trading. In this sense, Reuters *performs* economy – literally and directly, not indirectly, as the economic models do (MacKenzie et al., 2007). It triggers the events on which and on the consequences of which they will later be reporting. In the words of my interlocutors, it is a continuous push–pull effect (Obs. 5/17). The introduction of dealing services by Reuters is the most obvious element of this circuit, the ambiguity of which was the subject of a great deal of discussion at the time. In 1975, Michael Nelson, then Head of Commercial Services, commented on the Reuters Monitor Dealing Service proposal:

> "A dealing system is different from Reuters' present business. It is information handling, but makes Reuters an instrument in the execution of a transaction which we have never been before. At least one senior executive believes that we should not do it because it will affect our relationships with our sources since we shall become a part of an actual trading operation". (Quoted in Read, 1992: 308)

By 1991, both the critique and the Reuters stand on the matter had crystallized, as evidenced in a speech by Peter Job, then Managing Director, Royal Institute of International Affairs:

> "Periodic snapshots of economies at fixed exchange rates had to give way to a moving video. . . It was here that Reuters was the agent of change. Utilising computer technology harnessed to information flow, it was possible to give instant valuations of a country's exchange rate to a broad spectrum of users across the world. . . Using such systems the experts in the banking industry could take a real-time look at national pretensions, and by taking a speculative view of the future, start to use fast information flows to discount what might happen in the following hours, days, weeks or months. I think it is arguable that in this very specialised and highly focused area, we were among the first to exploit the freedom to alter and adjust the known values of the world". (Quoted in Read, 1992: 398)

Furthermore, although the ANSA journalists claimed that Reuters and Bloomberg merely provide numbers that must then be interpreted by humans,[6] the ambitions of robo-trading include interpretation:

> Computers are now being used to generate news stories about company earnings results or economic statistics as they are released. And this almost instan-

---

[6] Similarly, Beunza and Stark (2009) suggested that the main value of traders' work lies in the interpretation of the information they collect.

taneous information forms a direct feed into other computers which trade on the news. . . . "There is a real interest in moving the process of interpreting news from the humans to the machines", says Kristi Suutani, global business manager of algorithmic trading at Reuters. "More of our customers are finding ways to use news content to make money". (*Financial Times*, 16 April 2007: 1)

News agencies can be said to cause – or at least to trigger – political actions as well: "When we send a news item to mobile phones, every member of parliament and every senator who subscribes to [mobile services] will receive it. If the news item is wrong or mangled, it will directly affect their actions" (Int. 4/2). Such causality was probably even stronger in the past. Here are some examples taken from the history of Reuters:

- In 1861, during the US Civil War, the Federals kidnapped the Confederates' envoys to Europe. "Reuter personally took the story to Lord Palmerston, who, on the strength of Reuter's report alone, called an emergency Cabinet meeting" (Read, 1992: 37).
- When Britain had decided to give up the Gold Standard in 1931, the Viceroy of India took appropriate actions on the basis of Reuters news (Read, 1992: 201).
- "Hitler had shot himself. . . after hearing, courtesy of Reuters, that Himmler was treating with the Allies. . . . He had always trusted the accuracy of Reuters news" (Read, 1992: 227).
- Khrushchev's message from 1962 proposing a deal resolving the Cuban missile crisis reached Kennedy via his Reuters printer (Read, 1992: 376).

There is also a circuit effect that they call snowballing. Here is an example from Reuters:

Two nights ago, the German Finmin [Minister of Finance], at a speech in Düsseldorf, spoke about the ECB [European Central Bank] and its monetary policy on long-term inflation, mentioning Ireland in the speech. Reuters sent Alerts on Tuesday night. The bureau in Berlin decided to lead with its story about inflation. London decided, instead, that the more interesting news was the stuff about not supporting the euro zone member in trouble: Ireland This snowballed. Bloomberg's team in Ireland called the Finmin, and Berlin Reuters team returned to the minister for comments. It has become a big issue in Dublin, and Finmarket's analysts were commenting all over. This caused damage control from everybody. [The German minister said that he was speaking in abstract terms.] (Obs. 5/18)

News Circuits

Let me now reconstruct the way the circuits turn. The sources try to influence the news producers; the news producers follow each others' ways in which the news is produced, but also cause events that lead to the news, and produce news themselves; the clients choose what they think is relevant and fits their purpose. The lay readers and listeners then interpret the news in their private worlds, and from this interpretation try to formulate news that can be transmitted to the news producers.

But the circuit, or circuits, also run in the opposite direction: readers, spectators, and listeners do or do not buy the newspapers, access the websites,[7] listen to the radio, or watch TV. The newspapers and other media try to deduce the dominant preferences from these behaviors, and transmit this image to the news agencies, demanding adaptation; the important clients declare their preferences directly. As Tarde (1901/2003) pointed out, readers are unaware of the extent to which they are being influenced by other readers. This awareness is blocked by a feeling of community – or what Tarde called a virtual crowd – of simultaneous readers; one tends to forget that previous readings influenced the present text. Also, news producers educate their reporters directly and their sources indirectly, teaching them to look for a certain type of event. And even more indirectly, they educate the final recipients of the media.

This circularity leads, in the first place, to increasing standardization, but both technical inventions and unexpected big events can disturb a circuit and change the production processes. But such changes do not take place via significant reforms and dramatic restructurings resulting from ownership and company management changes; they occur through a continuous adaptation that changes the production, millimeter by millimeter, exactly as Hutchins (1995: 374) described in his study of navigators. Even when new technologies are invented or acquired, they are meshed into the production process at Editorial, so as not to disturb the flow. The production of news develops in time through partial solutions to recurring problems, and these partial solutions are tested by repetition before being stabilized in technical artifacts and routines – thus, the piecemeal introduction of new systems and new software.

Like navigation instruments and the ship itself, the instruments of news production are created partly on the spot by home IT specialists and partly

---

[7] Rogers (2001) claimed that the media on the Web receive much more feedback from their audience than the traditional media do. Although it may be so, it is easy to agree with Boczkowski that reader participation "is possible but not likely in the case of online news" (2010: 183). Feedback areas may have a cathartic function for the readers, but are unlikely to influence news production.

by the specialized suppliers – not by the news producers. Does this have any impact on the production of the news? Yes, because technical norms that rule the behavior of machines also rule the actions of human beings (Joerges and Czarniawska, 1998). In part, this impact is direct. SEAN Editorial, DEWAR, and Coyote control many things. They may limit the number of words permissible in the heading or even in the entire text, or they may ask: "Do you really want to send this text now?", suggesting, politely but firmly that there is something wrong with it. In part, control happens indirectly, through the rules of the functioning of machines. If you push "Send", the message is dispatched, and you cannot get it back; there are special procedures for correcting erroneous information. There is irrevocability in news production, as dictated by the machines.

Technical rules are not set accidentally, of course. It would be easy to produce a conspiracy theory according to which data designers – by themselves or in cahoots with people in power – try to steer the news production. This is not how it is, though, for two reasons. First, the uses of artifacts (including software) are always wider than and different from the intentions of the designers and programmers (Czarniawska, 2009a). The users are often creative and always disobedient. Second, the designers project into their creations more than they know themselves, because they inadvertently follow the institutional rules of their time, which they take for granted (even if they consciously oppose some other institutional rules of which they are aware). This is why many programs that are meant to be innovative are, in fact, conserving the existing work order – something that the programmers at ANSA thought was good and the programmers at Reuters have vowed to avoid. The role of technology in the production of news is not a common theme for reflection, however, because:

> [t]echnical norms tend to operate out of awareness of their habitual readers. Smoothly and reliably prescribed machine-technical operations and assemblies become more or less sealed-off from ongoing representations of organizational life. . . . Technical norms are the institutional structure of machinery. (Joerges and Czarniawska, 1998: 381)

Thus, the circular moves of the news-producing machine, although realized now and then, are, for the most part, hidden from the attention of the news producers – and their clients.

This statement goes against another of Gaye Tuchman's claims: that "news is an interchange among politicians and policymakers, news workers, and their organizational superiors, and that the rest of us are eavesdroppers on that ongoing conversation" (1978: x). As Boczkowski so appropriately commented:

political economy and institutional perspectives usually focus on the power of news organizations and elites. However, they often do not pay as much attention to how ordinary patterns of action among journalists contribute to imitation and homogenization dynamics. . . . Because social processes cannot remain forceful without being anchored in routines of actors at all relevant levels of organizational decision making, not just of those at the top, failure to understand the agency of the rank and file hinders the ability of these perspectives to grasp the obduracy of these dynamics and to devise realistic change strategies. (Boczkowski, 2010: 185)

One should stress that "the rank and file" contains a great many objects, quasi-objects, and machines, thus making the "obduracy of these dynamics" even more difficult to decipher.

I end this section with another quote from Molotch and Lester (1974: 101), which to me explains in a convincing way why news is so important for everybody, and why its production is unavoidably circular:

Everyone needs news. In everyday life, news tells us what we do not experience directly and thus renders otherwise remote happenings observable and meaningful. Conversely, we fill each other in with news. Although those who make their living at newswork (reporters, copy editors, publishers, typesetters etc.) have additional need for news, all individuals, by virtue of the ways they attend to and give accounts of what they believe to be a pregiven world, are daily newsmakers. News is thus the result of this invariant need for accounts of the unobserved, this capacity for filling-in others, and the production work of those in the media.

Everybody wants news, and everybody contributes to its production. This is not to deny that journalists and their IT collaborators decide the form of news, and that they listen more to some parties than to others. It may be the case, however, that they listen to their software more than they listen to anybody else.

MANAGING OVERFLOW AT INPUT AND AT OUTPUT

Managing the Input Overflow: Routines and Software

Information is practically endless in cyberspace and this creates an abstract need for control of information that can never in fact be satisfied, though the provision of ever more complex technologies at times dulls the information hunger.
Jordan, 2007: 598

Input overflow is not perceived as a problem for two reasons. In the first place, it is the opposite – a scarcity of information – that is perceived as a potential problem (viz. Sundays, when weather receives exaggerated attention). Furthermore, there are a great many mechanisms in place, old as well as new, that help to manage the overflow relatively smoothly.

Filtration is one such mechanism, and it was developed by the agencies practically at the outset. Nevertheless, there are new forms and new devices. The net provider can enforce mechanical stops of inflowing information, as in the case of the zombie attack described by respondents in ANSA. Furthermore, computerization allowed the incoming information to become more uniform, making comparisons easier. There are still faxes in ANSA, and they are dealt with manually, as described in Chapter 4, but in the other two agencies all information specifically addressed to the agency comes through e-mail. Here is another innovation: spam and junk filters. And although the spam filter at my workplace usually throws out any messages of importance to me, my respondents trusted their spam filters, and some of them did not even check the items in quarantine (Chapter 3). The last step in filtration is close to accreditation: judging the credibility and importance of the source. Even this can be done partly by software that recognizes domains and addresses.

Accreditation has two aspects: credibility of the source and credibility (correctness) of the contents of the news. Some sources are trustworthy by definition; other agencies consider Reuters to be trustworthy and almost everyone sees the *Financial Times* as trustworthy. What may seem like blind faith in the power of the brand is probably just an assumption that the trustworthy sources have already earned accreditation for their trustworthiness. In other cases, the sources are checked against one another. Here, a new complication consists of multiple sources from the Internet. The news producers deal with the so-called "Babel problem" (Benkler, 2006) in ways similar to those ascribed by Benkler to individual users of the Internet; they establish the trustworthiness of a source by comparing judgments (within the agency, but also across the media) and by establishing a historical record.

Accrediting the contents of the news (verification) is a process that partly requires the accreditation of sources. But there are two types of news that ring alarm bells, no matter what the source: big news and improbable news. It has been repeated by many media and individuals alike, that it took some time to believe the 9/11 news. If time permits, big news and improbable news are checked and rechecked. Still, the traditional journalist conflict remains: is this a landmine to step on, or a scoop?

Of all the processes of managing input overflow, validation remains the least mechanical, and most intersubjective – in contrast to what Latour (1996), called "interobjective", in order to emphasize the role of objects. Which news has priority in time and space? What can wait? When asked

about critical incidents and near-misses, the journalists most often mentioned errors of this type: a news item judged unimportant by the agency
became front page news in other media or a news item judged unimportant
today became the main news tomorrow. Here, the demand of speed is the
main obstacle.

In his merciless analysis of the mass media, Niklas Luhmann (2000)
emphasized the fact that both scientific research and journalism look for
"things that are true", but that journalists do it under limiting conditions that differ from the limiting conditions of the scientist. Both professions reduce and simplify – a map cannot be identical to the territory
– but in a different manner. Speaking specifically of news production,
Luhmann listed such internally created mechanisms as differentiation, a break with external determination, and operational closure. In
Luhmann's vocabulary, the system needs to impose limits on itself: "the
point is to introduce into a determined, even if unknown, world an area
of self-determination which can then be dealt with in the system itself as
being determined by its own structures", (Luhmann, 2000: 27). As long
as the actors (in this case, the news producers) remain in the system,
they are unable to see those mechanisms visible to observers. This is why
news producers do not experience input overflow: selection is included
in the profession of journalism, in the organization of agencies, and in
the software used.[8]

Managing the Output Overflow, or Code is the King[9]

Managing the overflow of outgoing information is indeed a new challenge,
as there is no mechanical limit to the number of news items that can be sent
on the newswire. The only limit is speed, and whereas the speed of newswire at TT is impressive, at Reuters it is breathtaking. Thus, news producers are not so much gatekeepers as active contributors to information flow
– and overflow. Being aware of this, they try to control it, and in this sense
they are perhaps the gatekeepers after all – internal gatekeepers. But even

---

[8] Luhmann (2000: 27–35) offered a list of selection criteria: (1) surprise, (2) conflict, (3)
    quantities, (4) local relevance, (5) norm violations, (6) events provoking moral judgments,
    (7) events presented as actions of individuals, (8) topicality, and (9) provocative opinions.
    I have chosen to apply Benkler's (2006) categories of filtration and accreditation, because,
    being more general, they allow for specification with the terms used by my interlocutors.
    Media scholars have been establishing such lists almost constantly (see, for example,
    Galtung and Ruge, 1965 and Harcup and O'Neill, 2001).
[9] Although this subtitle is an allusion to Lessig's (1999) statements concerning the impor-
    tance of the code, I do not mean the cybercode here, but the verbal code used to classify
    information on the wire.

here the floodgate is a better analogy than a city gate. The mechanisms operating the floodgates are many.

First, there are News Bills, meant for the media clients, to help them plan their own work. Second, there is "Top News", or "News of the Day", which prioritizes the contents of the newswire for all the clients. Third, the newswire itself is divided into regional, national, and global, and even according to the type of news it carries. Fourth, and in my opinion most important, is classification and coding. As Bowker (2006: 140) pointed out, "you cannot develop a database without having some means of putting data into pigeonholes of some kind or another; you can't store data without a classification system". No archive without classification.

What in ANSA was still a classification in the sense of situating a news item into a certain category (pigeonhole), at Reuters it became something else: codes are additions to the contents of the news, and are stapled onto one another, under the assumption of "better safe than sorry". Such coding can therefore be seen as an act of framing – an operation of overflow management – halfway between classification (sorting the text into categories) and indexing,[10] the Web operation that permits browsing a database by keywords.

The system does the coding for the journalists, and the journalists add even more to it. The only problem seems to be wrong coding (see Chapter 4) – never too much coding. Thus, a paradox arises: a device meant to frame overflow can itself produce overflow, as in the case of the Reuters news item in which the code for Poland brought me information about the movie *Milk* (Chapter 5). This confirms Callon's (1998) observation that framing itself can cause overflow, and is consistent with Jordan's (2007) description of what he has called a "technopower spiral", consisting of information overflow, managing overflow with a tool, and a recourse to information overflow.

It needs to be added that this paradoxical effect does not have to be perceived as a defect that should be removed. In contrast to economics, the constructivist sociology to which I adhere takes the constant re-emergence of overflows for granted: "overflowing is the rule: . . . framing – when present at all – is a rare and expensive outcome [that] is very costly to set up" (Callon, 1998: 252). This is because, exactly as in the case of news agencies, the very tools applied are potential – and actual – conduits for overflow, which also means enrichment. To paraphrase Callon, a totally successful frame would condemn the news to the sterile reiteration

---

[10] Also called "parsing" and "tokenization", (see http://wikipedia.org/wiki/Index_(search–engine); last accessed 5 July 2011.

of existing knowledge (1998: 255). A complete set of categories, covering all types of news, could be learned by all the users, but such a situation is patently absurd. No such set can exist. New categories are constantly added, and some of the old fade away. The management of the overflow of categories is left to the clients. It seems that they solve this problem by learning to recognize only one or two codes.

Overflow and its management are therefore stable elements of news production, and are seen as challenging but not problematic by the news producers. I now move to other themes that emerged from my three field studies – themes that can be seen as new and at least potentially problematic.

SPEED, STANDARDIZATION, AND SOFTWARE

The main developments characterizing the news world, as my study revealed, were *cybernization* (the increased role of technology in control of production), *cyborgization* (an ever-closer association between people and machines), and *marketization* (the conviction that the market offers the most effective form of organizing, and that its demands must therefore be followed). These concepts are related to each other, and together produce several effects; among others, is an emphasis on speed and the growing standardization of products. Opinions on these developments and their effects are divided, but there is no doubt that the software plays an increasingly central role in all of these developments.

Speed

"Acceleration is a formula for dissolution and breakdown in any organization", claimed McLuhan (1964: 226), and many people agree with him. But he was not always right. Yet there is no doubt that the requirements for the speedy distribution of news have increased. In the eyes of the news producers, however, acceleration lies in the nature of their profession. Speed is the result of trying to be first, and new technologies simply permit faster distribution of the news.

In his insightful text, dedicated to the emphasis on speed in contemporary societies, Christopher Grey (2009) pointed out its obvious but neglected connection to the characteristics of contemporary capitalism. This connection is nowhere as obvious as in the case of Reuters, with a delivery of news connected to robo-trading. It is all a matter of milliseconds, or nanoseconds, as they put it. The question is, as usual, is this acceleration good or bad – for the producers of news and for the consumers of news? Although noting that the motto of present times seems to be "Speed is good", Grey made a historical observation:

> It is noteworthy that for much of the twentieth century the expectation was that the fruits of greater prosperity and mechanization would be a more leisured and reflective existence (Russell, 1935/2001). This continued to be a cardinal assumption in, at least, Western societies, right up to the 1970s. What in fact has happened is that we have a much more frenetic and pressurised world. (Grey, 2009: 33)

Grey considered two types of effects of this acceleration: for companies (and work) and for individuals (and leisure). In the case of companies, he quoted examples of corporations famous for the speed of their decision-making – organizations that became equally famous for the spectacular mistakes they had made. In the case of individuals and communities, he quoted a list of well-known negative consequences, and considered the opposition movement: slow food and slow living. The poet of slowness, Milan Kundera, put it this way:

> There is a secret bond between slowness and memory, between speed and forgetting.
> A man is walking down the street. At a certain moment, he tries to recall something, but the recollection escapes him. Automatically, he slows down.
> Meanwhile, a person who wants to forget a disagreeable incident he has just lived through starts unconsciously to speed up his pace, as if he were trying to distance himself from a thing still too close to him in time.
> The degree of slowness is directly proportional to the intensity of memory; the degree of speed is directly proportional to the intensity of forgetting. (1993/1997: 34)

But Kundera never stands for simple conclusions, and as he has often noted (see for example, Kundera, 1988), he tends to be misinterpreted, not least on the issue of forgetfulness. Forgetting is as important as remembering, as it allows forward movement, to continue living in spite of the traumatic past, exactly as in the Kundera quote. Indeed, speed has been celebrated from the outset as a synonym of progress (Grey, 2009). So the issue is not if speed as such is good or bad, but, just like overflow, to whom is it good or bad, and under what circumstances? In this case the question is: is the speed requirement good or bad for news agencies?

I do not have a straightforward answer to this question, which is why research reports rarely make the news. Thomas Hylland Eriksen (2006: 19) reported the case of an interview with another Norwegian anthropologist, who believed that a journalist had faultily interpreted her words. Considering possible responses, she excluded sending a letter to the editor in question, as "[t]he fast media . . . were simply unable to accommodate the kind of data necessary in an account which had to take all the relevant facts into consideration". Instead, she wrote a popular book. Eriksen did not condemn the media, merely stated that "the fast media are simply unable" to report fully.

Speed is required in the race to be first, which contributes to the pressure felt by the news producers; but even they admit that racing gives them adrenaline kicks. Furthermore, forgetting – not only traumatic events, but any events – is, in the case of the news producers, balanced by their collective memory. Yet, they do complain about not having enough time for reflection:

> Our problem is that in our daily work we have so little time for discussion and reflection over the forms of our products. We do quickly discuss a concrete text that just arrived to the desk. Is this the best angle? Are the comments relevant? But nothing more general.
>
> We've tried to encourage the reporters to do such "nerdy readings" of each other's texts, slowly and with attention. Some do it, I know; others think it's not much fun. We sometimes organize meetings as well, where we discuss not so much forms as contents. Are we choosing the right subjects? What should we write more about? What new angles can we find? But again, there's so little time during the day for such things. We have such enormous input and so few reporters and generally quite tense situations all the time. (Int. 3/4)

The idea of organized moments of reflection that could be decoupled from pressing production matters were expressed in many utterances, but it was obvious that the united forces of speed requirements and constant budget restrictions rendered that possibility unrealistic. According to Scott Lash, this has to do with the very nature of a cyberfactory or, as he has called it, "technological forms of life":[11]

> In "simple" forms of life, we have narratives and meta-narratives. A certain pace of movement of time is conducive to such narratives and meta-narratives. Just about the right pace for reflection. Technological forms of life are too fast for reflection and too fast for linearity. They not only compress linearity; they outpace it. In speed-up culture becomes increasingly ephemeral. The monument lasts for centuries, if not millennia; the novel for generations; a scholarly book a decade. The newspaper article has value for just a day. The pyramids took centuries to build; the scholarly discourse of a treatise – entailing reflection – takes, say, four years. The newspaper report on the latest Arsenal football match must be written and wired within 90 minutes of the end of the match. This leaves no time for reflection, and scarce dedicated space as we compose

---

[11] Lash refuses the idea of cyborgization, claiming that it is a matter of interfaces, not of merging. Apparently, he has been spared the experience of prosthetic surgery.

messages in trains, on planes and read our email on mobile phones. (Lash, 2001: 110–11)

It is incorrect to assume, however, that the speed requirement is new for news agencies. The race for Beats was always there. The Normandy landings were reported on 6 June 1944: "Reuters, 06.33 a.m.; BUP, 06.35; AP, 06.38" (Read, 1992: 224). Similarly, the time and place compression in late modernity (Harvey, 1989) is not a new phenomenon in media or finances. Julius Reuter's office in Paris was erected opposite the main post office, so that the last financial newssheet could be printed just in time for the last post of the day (Read, 1992). The brokers who set their offices near the Bank of England (Chapter 5) have a long tradition behind them.

From the point of view of news consumers, however, one can ask if there could be a demand for "slow but correct" news? Perhaps, as with slow food, it is an opportunity for small and specialized companies. Standardization of the news in general speaks against such a possibility in the case of large agencies.

Standardization

The demands of speedy news encourages growing standardization, helped by the fact that desk programs are similar to one another, and are consciously made similar to one another in order to accelerate the process of taking in external news and dispatching one's own news. The Internet teaches everybody how to write – no matter what they are writing about. News agencies produce news in the same way, not because, like other companies, they imitate each other's production processes, but because they have access to the same standardized product – the news – which dictates the organization of production. In turn, similar production processes make the products still more similar. And as standards become global (Brunsson and Jacobsson, 2000), the standardization of news can eventually win over any attempts to differentiate them. W. Lance Bennett summarized this state of affairs:

> Standardized news is safe. Management in news organizations must constantly compare their product with that of their competition and defend risky departures from the reporting norm. . . . Other organizational arrangements also strongly influence standardized reporting. Among the most powerful standardizing forces are daily news production routines. (Bennett, 2007: 168–9)

Many unintended and undesirable effects of standardization exist; but in this section I address the (perhaps unexpected) positive side-effects of standardization. Albert O. Hirschman (1992) noted that, in certain production tasks, standardization leads to a positive effect that he called "lack of latitude" in standards of performance (i.e., tolerance for poor performance):

> When this latitude is narrow the corresponding task has to be performed *just right*; otherwise, it cannot be performed at all or is exposed to an unacceptable level of risk (for example, high probability of crash in the case of poorly maintained or poorly operated airplanes). Lack of latitude therefore brings powerful pressures for efficiency, quality performance, good maintenance habits, and so on. It thus substitutes for inadequately formed motivations and attitudes, which will be *induced* and generated by the narrow-latitude task instead of presiding over it. (Hirschman, 1992: 19; italics in original)

Applying Hirschman's reasoning to the production of news in the agencies, it can be surmised that the journalists working in the agency do not have to be "highly motivated" and "inspired"; the task at hand will do it for them. After all, "narrow-latitude tasks will, if performed poorly and (ex hypothesi) disastrously, give rise to a strong public concern and outcry – to voice" (Hirschman, 1992: 20).

It could be, however, that it is not only news as the product and news production that becomes more and more standardized. The speed requirement means that news producers encourage their sources to report; or perhaps they are already trained to perceive the world in categories of formatted news, in which the editorial software dictates the format. As Bowker (2006: 111–12) put it, "[i]t is not just the bits and bytes that get hustled into standard form in order for technical infrastructure to work. People's discursive and work practices get hustled into standard form as well".

This development may be more pervasive in news agencies than in other media, because, by definition, their product is to be "just news", without adjectives, opinions, and commentaries. Such "stripped-down" news can be standardized much easier than interpretations can. Thus, after having left "cablese" and "officialese" behind them, the news agencies may hardly notice that they are entering the era of "standardese".

News producers are worried that speed requirements will diminish the trustworthiness and correctness of the news, but they seem to be unaware of the influence of form on content, and unaware that the standardization of procedures leads to a further standardization of products and the other way around. In my opinion, this is because too little attention is paid to the software.

Software

In 1964, Marshall McLuhan declared that "The medium is the message", thus attracting attention to the role of hardware in news production. It seems that the time is ripe to pay as much attention to the role of software.

Nigel Thrift (2005: 153) emphasized "software's ability to act as means of producing a new and complex form of automated spatiality". This ability has not been the subject of enough study, in his opinion, for at least four reasons. (1) Software does not occupy much space; for the most part it is invisible, whereas hardware attracts much of our attention. (2) Software is deferred; although it may have political and aesthetic consequences when used, these are rarely if ever considered at the time of its construction. (3) Software is in-between hardware and the final product; both detract attention from it. (4) People are schooled in ignoring software, as they are schooled to ignore standards and classifications. Software is "a non-representational form of action . . . for its text is about words doing things" (Thrift, 2005: 157)

Elena Esposito, who used a Luhmannian perspective in her analysis of the media, concluded "[t]hat the informatic programs rather than the structures of language and of communication decide which forms are impressed in the medium of the available data is a novelty on which we can only now begin to reflect" (2004: 10). In the same vein, Saskia Sassen (2007: 583) suggested that the Internet should be regarded "as a space produced and marked through the software that gives it its features and the particular aspects of the hardware mobilized by the software". There are many traits of hardware that are not utilized by the software programmers. In her research on changes in the Internet, Sassen always begins by tracing changes in the software.

This is a new idea, not only because of the four reasons listed by Thrift, but also because, as historian Hayden White pointed out in *The Content of the Form* (1987), Western culture harbors a strong conviction that content is independent of form – a conviction that he powerfully contested. The difference in the contents – after all, apart from global news, there are many things that happen every day in Sweden that do not happen in Italy or England – obscures the fact that the Swedish, Italian, and British news is formatted in practically the same way. Speed requirements answer for the fact that "rightly formulated" news is preferred to complicated translations aimed at rendering the nuances of different languages, jargons, and dialects. This standardization is strengthened by the increasing dominance of English. What was earlier a massive translation from "local" languages to the "global" one and the other way around, is now being reduced to a direct formulation of news in some kind of "broken English", as Czech film director Milos Forman once called it.[12] Fortunately, standardization is always followed by variation-producing processes, due to simple errors in imitation or to the differences that still exist between the language of the news agencies and the language of other media.

Is the central role of software a reason for concern? As with many other questions, the answers vary. The news producers would like to have more and better software. The commentators are not convinced:

> The news of the day is a figment of our technological imagination. . . We attend to fragments of events from all over the world because we have multiple media whose forms are well suited to fragmented conversation. . . . Without a medium to create its form the news of the day does not exist. (Postman, 1995: 8)

Postman's intention was most likely critical, but it is possible to treat his words merely as a correct observation. News items are "figments of our technological imagination", but they have always been just that. Only technologies have varied (see, for example, Darnton, 2000, in which he claims that the Internet, or rather its low-tech equivalent, already existed in the sixteenth century in the form of gossip, local newspapers and private letters etc.). The question is, rather, if our forms of conversation have become adapted to the existing media, or if changes in the media followed changes in forms of conversation. To be on the safe side, it is best to assume that the influence went both ways. Whereas other authors take up the (allegedly dying) art of conversation (see, for example, Miller, 2006), I discuss in what follows the consequences of the circularity of news production.

Indeed, until now my reasoning, in spite of all protestations, seemed to rely on a kind of "city-within-the-walls" or a factory distinctly separated from its environment: this is definitely not the case with news agencies, even if they sit in separate buildings. After all, they are in – and on – the net.

THE CYBORGS AND THE MATRIX

> The world of the future will be an ever more demanding struggle against the limitations of our intelligence, not a comfortable hammock in which we can lie down to be waited upon by our robot slaves. (Norbert Wiener, 1963: 69)

In 1960, two NASA researchers, Manfred Clynes and Nathan Kline, predicted a new era, in which cyborgs would make their appearance.

---

[12] More about the impoverished language resulting from translations between the local languages and global language can be found in MacIntyre (1988).

For them, a cyborg was a hybrid between a human being and a machine, in which the mechanical parts automatically and without involving consciousness, solve smaller mechanical problems, thereby freeing the human part to investigate, create, reflect, and feel. The neologism was swiftly adopted by science fiction writers, and in time has been thoroughly analyzed by social scientists, the most quoted being the discussion by Donna Haraway (1991). In time, a whole "cyborgology" has evolved (see, for example, Gray et al., 1995; Downey and Dumit, 1997; Bell and Kennedy, 2007). Authors in both domains concluded that people are already cyborgized to a large degree, through mechanical parts of their body (eye glasses being first on the list, and pacemakers being one of the later additions).

A cyborg – a cybernetic organism – is a being composed of biological flesh and machine parts. Thus, the cyborgs from news agencies can have a gut feeling, but their right hand is a computer, and their left hand a cell phone.[13] What about the brain? It is collective: part human brain and part machine, as I have claimed. And as noted before, the role of the mechanical parts is ambiguous; on the one hand, they permit new and original things that have never been done before; on the other hand, their construction tends to repeat and therefore stabilize previously existing institutional orders (Joerges and Czarniawska, 1998). Much attention is traditionally directed to the first aspect, and almost none to the second. Machines are seen as the synonym of progress – desirable or threatening – but rarely as a conserving element in society.

Seeing this ambiguity in practice has become an unpleasant surprise to everyone who believed that, by surpassing the limitations of the organic body, cyborgs, as depicted in Haraway's (1991) vision[14] would be harbingers of liberation – particularly for women. The media depiction of cyborgs, in the movie *The Matrix*, for example, revealed that the mechanical additions could be used for the extension and even the strengthening of conventional gender roles (Czarniawska and Gustavsson, 2005). Cyborgized human beings can be imprisoned by their mechanical parts, or can even be forced to limit some of their bodily functions, as McLuhan suggested. Tobias Engberg (2009) claims, for example, that ergonomic improvements in our offices led to workers spending more time in unhealthy positions – thus the increase of back and joint problems.

How does this relate to news agencies? My study led me to see them as

---

[13] Unless they are left handed, of course.
[14] Even if Haraway saw cyborgs as a metaphor for the discursive codes that rule the biological existence (Wilson, 2002).

factories employing cyborgs.[15] The editors have computers with editorial software as the dominant hand and telephones as the non-dominant hand. For reporters, it is the opposite: the dominant hand is the telephone and the other hand is the computer. Their brains are connected to one another and to the Internet's virtual brain, to the news archive's virtual memory, and to the constantly talking newswire. As feelings are located in the guts, the heart can stand for the central pump, and the server can be seen as the agency's heart. When the server stops, everything stops. Satellites are their eyes and ears. All this does not mean that they are will-less machines: cyborgization and a growing net of connections increases rather than diminishes the ability of both individuals and collectives.

If this picture seems exaggerated, it may be useful to recall that the very idea of a news agency was invented in relation to a machine that could transmit information. As my interlocutors reminded me, it was human beings who once dispatched news by wandering from village to village. Later, the local authorities employed specific persons to dispatch the news to the population – so-called town criers. It was the invention of the telegraph that made news agencies possible, and it is the satellite, the telephone, and the computer that make them possible now. A news agency could function for a while without people, but it could not function without machines.

My interlocutors were fully aware of this fact. In their talk, however, humans and human brains are complemented by the systems (Obs. 5/18). But perhaps it is the systems that are complemented by human brains? After all, the idea of the cyborg was to mechanize the monotonous part of work to liberate the creative potential of humans. Has it happened? It does not seem so; increased mechanization means more and more new duties, and greater and greater speed. The news producers could probably exert greater influence over the programmers, for example, or they could extend the use of the programs in many new and innovative ways, if they had time to do so. In contrast to young hackers, who can spend days and nights tinkering about with software, the news producers are adult family members with normal lives, and their working time is structured foremost by the demand of speed. "I wish we had more time to reflect", sighed one of my interlocutors at TT, but speed is everything, or almost everything. Let me also remind you about an utterance of an ANSA journalist:

---

[15] Martin Parker (1998) would argue, and rightly so, that all work organizations are "cyborganizations". My emphasis on news agencies as "cyberfactories" has to do with the fact that the professional journalist has been cyborgized as well.

Now we have fewer journalists, but the job has been augmented enormously. Because there are websites, because there's e-mail, because a flood of mail arrives every day – actually, checking mails is the most tiring job in Editorial. Then shortening items is even more tiring, because you have to read all of it. The end result is that many things are unnecessarily long, but it takes too much effort to do something about it . . . that's Internet for you. . . . (Int. 4/3)

An appropriate if somewhat unexpected analogy could be the mechanizing of kitchen duties. The purpose was to liberate homemakers from monotonous and strenuous jobs. Indeed, as demonstrated by Ruth Schwartz Cowan (1985), this is what happened in the case of men and children who, before mechanization, had had many duties related to the home. These were not duties carried out by women, however. In the case of women, the effect of mechanization was the opposite. It allowed standards to be raised, so that, instead of spending time at leisure and creation, the housewives began to clean their houses more often and do more laundry. Something similar may be happening at the news agencies: automation multiplies mechanical jobs, and sets higher standards.

One interpretation would be that cybernization, like the mechanization of housework, did not fulfill its promise because the technology was faulty and should be improved. An alternative has been suggested by sociologists of science and technology, who question the idea that tools are but extensions of human organs: "all technologies incite around them [a] whirlwind of new worlds. Far from primarily fulfilling a purpose, they start by exploring heterogeneous universes that nothing, up to that point, could have foreseen and behind which trail new functions" (Latour, 2002: 250). Although this statement applies to all tools, the computer and the cell phone are perhaps the most obvious and the most convincing examples of the phenomenon. The purpose of cyborgization might have been the liberation of human creativity from the burden of mundane duties, but the effects are heterogeneous, in part unexpected, and in part contrary to the original purpose. New functions – of humans and of machines – appear all the time.

Connectivity in the Matrix

It is not a row of instruments, software, persons, or even cyborgs that produces news. Production occurs through their interconnections, which are not limited to newsrooms. Globalization theoretician Saskia Sassen has suggested that one of the phenomena caused by ongoing globalization is increased connectivity: more and more places become connected to one another, and more quickly (Sassen, 2001). Her main examples are financial markets (Sassen, 2005). In fact, there are many similarities between work in finance and work in news agencies, even apart from the fact that, especially in the case of Reuters, these are closely and directly connected.

Those who work with finance are also cyborgs, equipped in the same way with phones and computers, and connected to the global network. Karin Knorr Cetina and Urs Bruegger, who studied foreign exchange traders, concluded that the traders did not have any contact with the physical world other than via their computers. The world came to them "appresented"[16] on their Bloomberg screens, and trading occurred on the computer, so that not even telephones played a crucial role. Knorr Cetina and Bruegger (2002) concluded that foreign exchange traders were involved in a network of *post-social* connections – between human beings and electronic objects.

There is no doubt that the news producers are deeply connected in the network of human beings and electronic objects; nor is there any doubt of their extreme sociality in the traditional sense of interactions among human beings. In their study of Reuters, Heath and Nicholls (1997) thoroughly debunked the notion of the journalists' individual work. Journalists are almost always in contact with their neighbors and on the phone with their reporters. They can write or edit their texts and talk at the same time.

David Beunza and David Stark (2005; 2009; 2010) observed a trading room in a large investment bank in New York, and the picture they generated is closer to Heath and Nicholls' than to Knorr Cetina and Bruegger's. The traders talked on the phone with one another, there were a great many interactions between them and their clients, and they even cooperated while making deals. David Renemark (2007) found similar results in his study of everyday work in the Swedish financial sector, and MacKenzie and Hardie (2009) detected the same in their observation of hedge fund traders.[17] Both types of contacts were dense; the main observation was increased connectivity, as postulated by Saskia Sassen. Just as in the news agencies, the world was perceived through screens and outside the screen. In one of ANSA newsrooms, they had to open the windows to learn what was happening on the street nearby – a demonstration that they would otherwise have missed. Time and space might have been compressed in late modernity, as geographer David Harvey (1989) has acutely observed,

---

[16] A concept borrowed from Husserl's phenomenology.

[17] It would be fascinating to know if Knorr Cetina and Bruegger's conclusions revealed a phenomenon specific to Swiss trading, which they studied. Perhaps post-sociality is the future of trading, and the Swiss, experienced as they are in these matters, are already there? At any rate, as Donald MacKenzie (2009) observed, local customs play a critical and under-researched role – in news production as well as in finance.

but as everybody knows, even the astronomers need to look outside the telescope sometimes – to find their glasses, for example. In news agencies, as in finance companies, contacts with technical objects, contacts mediated by technical objects, and eye-to-eye contacts are blended with no difficulty and no reflection. If there is a difference between finance workers and news producers revealed by ethnographic studies, it is that news producers do not socialize after work. Working shifts and simple tiredness seemed to prevent it effectively. The news producers in this study did not socialize with their clients, either – most likely, their bosses at Company took care of that.

Although increased connectivity may be a universal phenomenon resulting from globalization and technological developments, it certainly has a specific function in news production. The collective cognition demands connectivity – and manufactures it simultaneously. The consequences of this development can spread outside of cyberfactories.

The News World and the World

> Whatever we know about our society, or indeed about the world in which we live, we know through the mass media. (Luhmann, 2000: 1)

One can imagine that in times of rapid cybernization,[18] when the circuits of culture run more and more quickly, the world will become one in which everybody exchanges news that is already formulated and formatted in the "right" way. Close to it is the dystopic possibility that people will, in time, perceive the world and their own lives in terms of their news value, and that different communication systems – which, according to Luhmann (1985), are incompatible – will become one. In Martin Amis's *London Fields*, Keith Talent reports darts tournaments in exactly the same way as the radio and TV reporters do. This is not, says the helpful narrator, because Keith imitates the reporters. No. He already sees the tournament this way.

Following this thought, it can be imagined that in the not-so-distant future we will all be providing information to an automatic news agency, where an algorithm designed specially for that purpose will select and edit texts thus produced. In contrast to the present situation, the commentators may be needed more than the news producers will be – this assuming

---

[18] Pierre Naville (1960), obviously writing under the influence of Norbert Wiener, inventor of cybernetics, saw in it a new form of civilization, based on the automatic (and therefore autonomous) modes of communication. Although the Wiener text that I quoted earlier is of a later date (1963), it clearly presents the idea of the "mechanicohuman" system.

that commentators will be able to produce varying comments, and not standardized, like everything else.

Neil Postman (1985) predicted such a dystopic development, using Aldous Huxley's *Brave New World* (1932) as its model. But Huxley's dystopia portrays the world created by bioengineering, Pavlovian conditioning, hypnopaedia (sleep learning), and drugs. *The Matrix* is not only more recent, but it portrays the world populated by cyborgs and machines – like our present one.

I am referring to the film, *The Matrix*, here – the first and best-known part of a trilogy by brothers Larry and Andy Wachowski (1999) – that attracted public attention, and that of critics and philosophers alike. It needs to be remembered, however, that the idea, and the very concept of cyberspace, was first coined in 1984 by sci-fi writer William Gibson in his *Neuromancer*:

> Cyberspace. A consensual hallucination experienced daily by billions of legitimate operators, in every nation, by children being taught mathematical concepts. . . A graphic representation of data abstracted from the banks of every computer in the human system. Unthinkable complexity. Lines of light ranged in the nonspace of the mind, clusters and constellation of data. (Gibson, 1984: 67)

It is this notion of the Matrix that is discussed in the book *Matrix and Philosophy* (edited by William Irwin, 2002). The volume addresses many of the issues present in the filmatic trilogy, but I focus on only one, relevant for my discussion: the relationship between knowledge and reality, or, in the present case, the news and the world.

To recall briefly the main elements of *The Matrix*, there are two worlds, one virtual (a complex computer program created by artificially intelligent machines) and the other real ("ugly, a world seared by war between humans and machines, where existence is meted out with only the barest means and life is lived in a constant threat of death"; Gracia and Sanford, 2002: 55–6). Neo, an incarnation of the first man who realized the unreality of the Matrix, is able to break free from illusion and thus help humans in their war against (some) machines.

As Gracia and Sanford pointed out, the movie is based on the Aristotelian categories of disjoint and complete: real–unreal, mind–body, human–machine (in contrast to the news agencies' categorizations that pile code upon code). However – and it is not certain if this is an inconsistency in the film or a pointer toward the only solution – there also are many elements belonging to the third category, the hybrids. Neo and Trinity are cyborgs, death is the same in both realms, and virtual pills are effective in both worlds "because the mind takes them to be part of the real world and commands the body to act accordingly. . . . Minds are real, and they have the power to produce unreality" (Gracia and Sanford, 2002: 64).

Ontologically speaking, the virtual world has a weaker status, because its existence depends upon things in the real world. It exists only as long as AI machines are able to run the program and send signals to human brains. Thus, the real world causes the Matrix, but the Matrix is not the cause of things in the real world. Or so it seems – if not for the mind's capacity to turn the unreal into the real. Thus, the fact that Reuters news is able to cause actual trading can be interpreted in two ways: either the news is real, not merely an appearance, or else it is causative in the sense that it provokes minds to act upon it. Philosophy allows for more interpretations, which cannot all find a place in one movie: that appearance is all there is (idealism) or that appearances, and various representations, are part of reality (pragmatism).

There is no doubt that news agencies contribute to the construction of reality, as Gaye Tuchman (1978) claimed, but so does everybody else, including animals and machines. There is equally no doubt that whereas constructivism is usually a marginal view, there exists and has always existed a strong belief in what Tuchman called "a pregiven world" – a world independent of human cognition – and an almost equally common belief that this world can be represented in one correct way. Everyone agrees, however, that there are a great many false representations, and therefore one question is eternally relevant: "Is everything we experience a mere appearance, or are these appearances manifestations of actual things which are more or less as they appear to be?" (Garcia and Sanford, 2002: 62). Or, in the present case, is the world as news agencies describe it, or do they invent it for us, driven by hidden (or not so hidden) forces? Did the Gulf War ever take place, asked French philosopher Jean Baudrillard (1991), and has anybody really landed on another planet, asked US film director, Peter Hyams (1979).[19] How are we to know?

Gracia and Sanford declared no interest in this epistemological question, noting that in *The Matrix*, the answer is that you must have a teacher. But then, *The Matrix* is a relatively conservative movie, in which much weight is allotted to authorities (Morpheus, Oracle) and in which women, even the main characters like Trinity, must sacrifice themselves for men's nobler pursuits (Czarniawska and Gustavsson, 2005). Mitsuo Nixon (2002) raised this issue in "The Matrix possibility: it's possible that I am (or you are) in the Matrix right now" (p. 28).

[19] *Capricorn One* tells the story of a studio-televised landing on Mars, but it is connected to the emergence of hoax theory of Apollo landing on the Moon, see http://en.wikipedia.org/wiki/Capricorn_One; last accessed 5 July 2011.

How can we figure that out? First, we need to decide if we believe in the existence of hidden forces: Descartes' malicious demon, a totalitarian regime, a conspiracy of evil, or hateful AI machines like those in *The Matrix*. If the decision is negative, we can move to a second alternative, presented by Mitsuo Nixon:

> The other sort of response goes like this: "If you look at how we actually use the word 'know' in the real world, you'll see that there are all kinds of circumstances in which we recognize the *possibility* of having a false belief but we still call it knowledge." In the real world . . . we almost *never* require that a belief be such that it is impossible to be false before we call it known. . . . The proper response to someone's telling me that my belief *could* be false is, "So what?" It's not *possibility* that matters, it's *probability*. So until you give me a good reason to think that my belief is not just *possibly* false, but *probably* false, I'm not changing anything about what I believe or what I think I know. (Mitsuo Nixon, 2002: 30, italics in original)

In other words, is the Matrix a possibility? Yes, it is, if the first alternative is accepted, but it is not highly probable. This reasoning is, in fact, close to what I have called "common sense" in describing news production (Chapter 4), and what Mitsuo Nixon called "ordinary knowledge". When evaluating news coming from news agencies (and their clients), we repeat – less systematically – the same procedure they use. Whatever we believe to be true can be false. Because there is no chance of superior knowledge, of absolute truth, we must rely on our ordinary knowledge and common sense. Does this news come from a trustworthy source? Is it probable? If not, can it be checked against other sources? We are all producers of news, although there are differences between lay people and professional producers. They know how to manufacture news in appropriate forms, and manufacture it quickly. We, on the other hand, have one advantage: more time, which makes room for reflection, and permits a closer inspection of the role of the non-human producers of news. The war between cyborgs and machines is not likely to start any time soon. Yet even Reuters historian Donald Read, echoing Gaye Tuchman, had some doubts, which he expressed in the final sentences of his book:

> Had Reuters unwittingly become a tool of the [capitalist] system . . .? Had it contributed to the rise of the materialistic "yuppie" culture of the 1980s? In Sweden and elsewhere the yuppie condition was defined as possession of "a fat salary, a red Porsche and a Reuters terminal". (1992: 404)

As to Read's first question, the answer is undoubtedly "yes", although not in the sense of being unwittingly used by the system, but by being part of it. As to the second question, however, the scrupulous historian was incorrect for once. The Swedish definition of a yuppie mentioned "a Bloomberg terminal". Reuters saved its reputation by preserving the political and general news, in spite of its occasional unprofitability.

THE FUTURE IS BRIGHT, OR IS IT?

> The financial crisis is taking a terrible toll on both financial-services firms and newspapers, so you might expect the news agencies that serve them to be in trouble too. Not so. Christoph Pleitgen, a senior Reuters executive, says the big newswires have been staffing up in the past year. The *Journal's* owner, News Corp, announced cuts at the newspaper earlier this month, but said that the Dow Jones newswire was adding journalists at its bureaus, especially in India. Likewise, Bloomberg's recent announcement of around 190 job cuts at its foreign-language television venture got more attention than its promise to create 1,000 jobs elsewhere, including in its news bureaus. And CNN, a television-news network, plans to set up a new international agency to rival AP and Reuters. (*The Economist*, 12 February 2009).

This observation is corroborated by Boczkowski's results; much as he deplores it, he sees "an increase in the relative contribution and prominence of wire service agencies" (2010: 180) as inevitable. Some newspapers in trouble stopped their subscriptions, others, having made cuts in their newsrooms, became even more dependent upon news agencies. The proliferation of websites and the new TV stations in developing regions boost the demand for ready-made news.

Perhaps most important is the increase of news delivery straight to individual consumers. It is actually impossible to remove the Stocks application from an iPhone. In the worst possible scenario – the Matrix becoming probable – the newspapers will vanish, all the consumers will become trained as providers, and speed requirements will cause everybody to communicate in a digi-language. But, as developments at Reuters seem to indicate, this scenario can be compensated for by both professional Analyses and Features, and by bloggers eager to explain the world. Furthermore, the present threat constituted by the Web can be compared to that constituted by the radio in the late 1930s and TV in the late 1950s. Newspapers survived both.[20]

It is more difficult to predict the form in which they will survive. "Welcome to the era of algorithm as editor", says Jeremy W. Peters in the "Business with Reuters" section of the *International Herald Tribune* (6 July, 2010). He does not speak of newspapers, though, but of the new

---

[20] For an optimistic view on the future of US newspapers, based on charging the viewers for the online version, see Massing (2009).

media. Yahoo! tracks issues that interest Web users, and then orders articles on such issues from journalists. There is also an ambition to provide
"tailor-made" newspapers, comprising parts of different newspapers
according to the orders of individual clients. In each case, however, the
role of hardware and software in the production of news increases. Still,
Nigel Thrift (2005) is accurate in his claim that much more attention has
been paid to the role of hardware in shaping our lives, whereas the software remains a gray eminence of sorts.

In ending I would like to quote one of the predictions of the future
offered to me in an interview:

> Three, four hundred years ago, people went from one village to another and
> told the news. If they were good storytellers and told stories that were interest-
> ing, funny, or moving, and true besides, they were given good food and permit-
> ted to sleep in the kitchen near the stove. If it was discovered that they were
> wrong, they were not let in, and they may even have been punished. At best they
> could sleep among the pigs. And nothing has changed, really. We do the same
> thing today. We need to tell something that's true and is either entertaining or
> moving or enlightening. And we must tell in a way that raises interest. . . .
>
> After the Internet has opened all the doors, it will be the best storytellers that
> survive. The public will choose them, rather than listening to the media com-
> panies and journalists telling them what they should want. Thus, I believe that
> we're going back to the origins of storytelling. One can have many opinions on
> whether this is good or bad, but I believe that this is going to happen. When all
> the monopolies have been destroyed by technological developments, the stories
> told will change, too. (Int. 3/3)

This prediction can be seen as overly optimistic, not to say naive, for
who decides which storyteller is best and by what criteria? Yet this utterance can be also read in another way, parallel to an observation made by
Walter Ong (1982), the renowned scholar of orality and literacy. Ong also
believed that the narrative – storytelling – accompanies human beings
across times and places. Furthermore, he admitted that – paradoxically
– the era of electronic processing of information reinstated much of the
orality that seems to have been lost with the invention of writing, and then
printing. But the most important point, which seems also to be present in
the previous quote, is that human beings are "beings whose thought processes do not grow out of simply natural powers but out of these powers
as structured, directly or indirectly, by the technology of writing" (Ong,
1982: 78). Whether or not any technology will be able to break down "all
the monopolies" remains to be seen, but it is certain that the technology of
writing influences what is being written. In a cyborg body, the body steers
the machine, but the machine has an impact on the body, as suggested by
the exercise programs supplied by the Reuters Intranet. Although most

writing in the contemporary world happens via computers, with the help of similar software, writing technology may have its greatest impact on the writing of the news. And for better and for worse, the stories told will follow changes in technology. In my opinion, therefore, the software needs watching.

Cyborgization, if done right – that is, to provide freedom from menial duties (such as a spell check) – could be helpful rather than an obstacle in such scrutiny. The requirement of speed may prevent it, however. Speed is not only a requirement coming from Company to Newsroom; a strong interest in racing other media existed before sport pictures were hung on the walls of Reuters. So perhaps, after all, we will all become news providers, and a Mighty Algorithm will sort things out.

References

Agre, Philip E. (1998), "Designing genres for new media: social, economic and political content", in Steven G. Jones (ed.), *Cybersociety 2.0. Revisiting Computer-mediated Communication and Community*, Thousand Oaks, CA: Sage, pp. 69–99.

Amis, Martin (1991), *London Fields*, London: Vintage.

Anderson, James C., Håkan Håkansson and Jan Johanson (1994), "Dyadic business relationships within a business network context", *The Journal of Marketing*, **58** (4), 1–15.

Bantz, Charles R., Suzanne McCorkle and Roberta C. Baade (1980), "The news factory", *Communication Research*, **7** (1), 45–68.

Bastin, Gills (2003), "L'Europe saisie par l'information (1952–2001): des professionels du journalisme engagé aux content coordinators", *Cahiers Politiques*, 19–41.

Baudrillard, Jean (1991), *La guerre du golfe n'a pas eu lieu*, Paris: Galilée; English version: (1995) *The Gulf War Did Not Take Place*, Bloomington, IN: Indiana University Press.

Bell, David and Barbara M. Kennedy (eds) (2007), *The Cybercultures Reader*, London: Routledge.

Benjamin, Walter (1935/1999), "The work of art in the age of mechanical reproduction", in Walter Benjamin (ed.), *Illuminations* (with introduction by Hannah Arendt), London: Pimlico, pp. 211–44.

Benkler, Yochai (2006), *The Wealth of Networks*, New Haven, CT: Yale University Press.

Bennett, W. Lance (2007), *News. The Politics of Illusion* (7th edn), New York: Pearson/Longman.

Beunza, Daniel and David Stark (2005), "How to recognize opportunities: heterarchical search in a trading room", in Karin Knorr Cetina and Alex Preda (eds), *The Sociology of Financial Markets*, Oxford: Oxford University Press, pp. 84–101.

Beunza, Daniel and David Stark (2009), "The cognitive ecology of the arbitrage trading room", in David Stark (ed.), *The Sense of Dissonance. Accounts of Worth in Economic Life*, Princeton, NJ: Princeton University Press, pp. 118–62.

Beunza, Daniel and David Stark (2010), *Models, Reflexivity, and Systemic*

Risk: A Critique of Behavioral Finance, accessed 28 June 2011 at SSRN: http://ssrn.com/abstract=1285054.

Boczkowski, Pablo J. (2009a), "Technology, monitoring and imitation in contemporary news work", *Communication, Culture & Critique*, **2** (1), 35–59.

Boczkowski, Pablo J. (2009b), "Rethinking hard and soft news production: from common ground to divergent paths", *Journal of Communication*, **59** (1), 98–116.

Boczkowski, Pablo J. (2010), *News at Work*, Chicago, IL: The University of Chicago Press.

Boudon, Raymond (1998), "Common sense and the human sciences", *International Sociology*, **3** (1), 1–22.

Bourdieu, Pierre (1998), *On Television*, New York: The New Press.

Bowker, Geoffrey C. (2006), *Memory Practices in the Sciences*, Cambridge, MA: MIT Press.

Bowker, Geoffrey C. and Susan Leigh Star (1999), *Sorting Things Out. Classification and its Consequences*, Cambridge, MA: The MIT Press.

Boyd-Barrett, Oliver and Terhi Rantanen (2001), "News agency foreign correspondents", in Jeremy Tunstall (ed.), *Media Occupations and Professions*, Oxford: Oxford University Press, pp. 127–43.

Brandenburger, Adam M. and Barry J. Nalebuff (1998), *Co-opetition: A Revolution Mindset that Combines Competition and Cooperation*, New York: Doubleday.

Brunsson, Nils and Bengt Jacobsson (eds) (2000), *A World of Standards*, Oxford: Oxford University Press.

Brunsson, Nils and Kerstin Sahlin-Andersson (2000), "Constructing organizations: the example of public sector reform", *Organization Studies*, **21** (4), 721–46.

Burenstam Linder, Staffan (1970), *The Harried Leisure Class*, New York: Columbia University Press.

Callon, Michel (1986), "Some elements of a sociology of translation: domestication of the scallops and the fishermen of St. Brieuc's Bay", in John Law (ed.), *Power, Action and Belief*, London: Routledge & Kegan Paul, pp. 196–229.

Callon, Michel (1998), "An essay on framing and overflowing: economic externalities revisited by sociology", in Michel Callon (ed.), *The Laws of the Markets*, Oxford: Blackwell, pp. 244–69.

Callon, Michel and Fabian Muniesa (2005), "Economic markets as calculative collective devices", *Organization Studies*, **26** (8), 1229–50.

Chambers, Deborah, Linda Steiner and Carole Fleming (2004), *Women and Journalism*, London: Routledge.

Clynes, Manfred E. and Nathan S. Kline (1960), "Cyborgs and space",

Astronautics, September, 29–31; accessed 3 July 2011 at: http://www. scribd.com/doc/2962194/Cyborgs-and-Space-Clynes-Kline.

Cooper, Geoff, Christine Hine, Janet Rachel and Steve Woolgar (1995), "Ethnography and human–computer interaction", in Peter J. Thomas (ed.), *The Social and Interactional Dimensions of Human–Computer Interfaces*", Cambridge: Cambridge University Press, pp. 11–36.

Cottle, Simon (2003), "Media organization and production: mapping the field", in Simon Cottle (ed.) *Media Organization and Production*, London: Sage, pp. 3–24.

Cowan, Ruth Schwartz (1985), *More Work for Mother. The Ironies of Household Technology from the Open Hearth to the Microwave*, New York: Basic Books.

Czarniawska, Barbara (2002), *A Tale of Three Cities*, Oxford: Oxford University Press.

Czarniawska, Barbara (2004), "Metaphors as enemies of organizing, or the advantages of a flat discourse", *International Journal of Sociology of Language*, **166**, 45–65.

Czarniawska, Barbara (2007), *Shadowing and Other Techniques for Doing Fieldwork in Modern Societies*, Malmö: Liber.

Czarniawska, Barbara (2008), *A Theory of Organizing*, Cheltenham, UK and Northampton, MA, USA: Edward Elgar.

Czarniawska, Barbara (2009a), "How institutions are inscribed in technical objects and what it may mean in the case of the Internet", in Francesco Contini and Giovan Francesco Lanzara (eds) *ICT and Innovation in the Public Sector. European Studies in the Making of E-government*, Basingstoke: Palgrave Macmillan, pp. 49–87.

Czarniawska, Barbara (2009b), "Gabriel Tarde and organization theory", in Paul Adler (ed.) *The Oxford Handbook of Sociology and Organization Studies: Classical Foundations*, Oxford: Oxford University Press, pp. 246–67.

Czarniawska, Barbara (2009c), *Den tysta fabriken. Om tillverkning av nyheter på TT*, Malmö: Liber.

Czarniawska, Barbara (2009d), *Analisi etnografica di un' agencia di stampa*, Rome: Carocci.

Czarniawska, Barbara (2011), "What comes first, the egg or the chicken? Or: where do the metaphors we use in our research come from?", in Arne Carlsen and Jane E. Dutton (eds) *Research Alive: Exploring Generative Moments in Doing Qualitative Research*, Malmö/Copenhagen/Oslo: Liber/CBS Press/Universitetsförlaget, pp. 50–58.

Czarniawska, Barbara and Eva Gustavsson (2005), "The (d)evolution of the cyberwoman?", *Organization*, **15** (5), 665–83.

Darnton, Robert (2000), "Paris: the early internet", *New York Review of Books*, 29 June, 42–7.

Darnton, Robert (2008), "The library in the new age", *New York Review of Books*, 12 June, 72–80.

Djerf-Pierre, Monika (2005), "Lonely at the top. Gendered media elites in Sweden", *Journalism*, **6** (3), 265–90.

Djerf-Pierre, Monika and Lennart Weibull (2001), *Spegla, granska, tolka. Aktualitetsjournalistik i svensk radio och TV under 1900-talet*, Stockholm: Prisma.

Dodier, Nicolas (1997), "Réseaux socio-techniques et conscience du collectif", *Sociologie du Travail*, **39** (2), 131–48.

Downey, Gary Lee and Joseph Dumit (eds) (1997), *Cyborgs & Citadels*, Santa Fe, NM: School of American Research.

Easterly, William (2008), "Foreign aid goes military", *The New York Review of Books*, 6 November.

Economist, The (2009), "High wires. With newspapers in crisis, newswires may learn to live without them", 12 February.

Edelman, Murray (1988), *Constructing the Political Spectacle*, Chicago, IL: The University of Chicago Press.

Ekdahl, Mats and Wigstrand, Hans (2006), *Detta är medieberedskap*, Stockholm: Styrelsen för psykologiskt försvar.

Engberg, Tobias (2009), "Small time breaks", in Barbara Czarniawska (ed.) *Organizing in the Face of Risk and Threat*, Cheltenham, UK and Northampton, MA, USA: Edward Elgar, pp. 235–54.

Engwall, Lars (1978), *Newspapers as Organizations*, Farnborough: Saxon House.

Engwall, Lars (2006), "Global enterprises in fields of governance", in Marie-Laure Djelic and Kerstin Sahlin-Andersson (eds) *Transnational Regulation in the Making*, Cambridge, UK: Cambridge University Press, pp. 161–79.

Engwall, Lars (2008), "Minerva and the media", in Carmelo Mazza, Paolo Quattrone and Angelo Riccaboni (eds) *European Universities in Transition: Issues, Models and Causes*, Cheltenham, UK and Northampton, MA, USA: Edward Elgar, pp. 31–48.

Epstein, Jason (2000), "The coming revolution", *New York Review of Books*, 2 November, pp. 5–12.

Ericson, Richard V., Patricia M. Baranek and Janet B.L. Chan (1989), *Negotiating Control: A Study of News Sources*, Toronto, CA: University of Toronto Press.

Eriksen, Thomas Hylland (2006), "Diversity versus difference: neoliberalism in the minority-debate", in Richard Rottenburg, Burkhard Schnapel and Shingo Shimada (eds), *The Making and Unmaking of Differences*, Bielefeld: Transcript, pp. 13–26.

Esposito, Elena (2004), "The arts of contingency", *Critical Inquiry*, **31**, accessed 25 June 2011 at www.uchicago.edu/research/jnl-critinq/features/artsstatements/arts.esposito.html.

Ewertsson, Lena (2001), "The triumph of technology over politics?", *Linköping Studies in Arts and Sciences*, **232**, accessed 5 July 2011 at: http://liu.divaportal.org/smash/record.jsf?pid=diva2:20704.

Farr, Robert M. (1993), "Common sense, science and social representations", *Public Understanding of Science*, **2** (3), 189–204.

Financial Times (2002), Carlos Grande: "How a media organization famed for being first with the news is struggling to keep pace with the market", 17 October, p. 15.

Financial Times (2007), Aline van Duyn: "City trusts computers to keep up with the news", 16 April, p. 1.

Financial Times (2009), Andrew Edgecliffe-Johnson: "Thomson Reuters merger effective", 7 August, p. 17.

Flanagan, John C. (1954), "The critical incident technique", *Psychological Bulletin*, **51** (4), 327–58.

Galbraith, John K. (1958), *The Affluent Society*, Boston, MA: Houghton Mifflin.

Galtung, Johan and Mari Holmboe Ruge (1965), "The structure of foreign news", *Journal of Peace Research*, **2** (1), 64–91.

Gans, Herbert J. (1979/2004), *Deciding What's News: A Study of CBS Evening News, NBC Nightly News, Newsweek, and Time*, Evanston, IL: Northwestern University Press.

Gibson, William (1984), *Neuromancer*, London: Victor Gollancz.

Gieber, Walter (1956), "Across the desk: a study of 16 telegraph editors", *Journalism Quarterly*, **33** (4), 423–32.

Girard, Laurence (2008), "L'AFP sus le feu nouri des critiques de la majorité", *Le Monde*, 13 May.

Glaser, Barney G. (1978), *Theoretical Sensitivity: Advances in the Methodology of Grounded Theory*, Mill Valley, CA: Sociology Press.

Gracia, Jorge E. and Jonathan J. Sanford (2002), "The metaphysics of *The Matrix*", in William Irwin (ed.) *The Matrix and Philosophy. Welcome to the Desert of the Real*, Chicago, IL: Open Court, pp. 55–65.

Grafström, Maria, Jaan Grünberg, Josef Pallas and Karolina Windell (2006), *Ekonominyhetens väg från kvartalsrapporter till ekonominyheter*, Stockholm: SNS Förlag.

Gray, Chris Hables, Steven Mentor and Heidi Figueroa-Sarriera (eds) (1995), *The Cyborg Handbook*, Thousand Oaks, CA: Sage.

Grey, Chris (2009), "Speed", in Philip Hancock and André Spicer (eds), *Understanding Corporate Life*, London: Sage, pp. 27–45.

Gustavsson, Eva (2005), "Virtual servants: stereotyping female front-office employees on the internet", *Gender, Work and Organization*, **12** (5), 400–419.

Hadenius, Stig (1971), *Nyheter från TT. Studier i 50 års nyhetsförmedling*, Stockholm: Bonniers.

Hadenius, Stig and Lennart Weibull (1999), *Massmedier. Press, radio & tv i förvandling* (7th edn), Stockholm: Albert Bonniers Förlag.

Hadenius, Stig, Lennart Weibull and Ingela Wadbring (2008), *Massmedier. Press, radio & tv i den digitala tidsåldern*, Stockholm: Ekerlids Förlag.

Hannerz, Ulf (1996), *Transnational Connections*, London: Routledge.

Haraway, Donna J. (1991), *Simians, Cyborgs and Women. The Reinvention of Nature*, London: Free Association Books.

Harcup, Tony and Deirdre O'Neill (2001), "What is news? Galtung and Ruge revisited", *Journalism Studies*, **2** (2), 261–80.

Harvey, David (1989), *The Condition of Postmodernity: An Inquiry into the Origins of Cultural Change*, Cambridge, MA: Blackwell.

Hayles, N. Katherine (2007), "Computing the human", in David Bell and Barbara M. Kennedy (eds), *The Cybercultures Reader*, London: Routledge, pp. 557–73.

Heath, Christian and Gillian Nicholls (1997), "Animated texts: selective rendition production of news stories", in Lauren B. Resnick, Roger Säljö, Clotilde Pontecorvo and Barbara Burge (eds), *Discourse, Tools and Reasoning: Essays on Situated Cognition*, Berlin: Springer-Verlag, pp. 63–86.

Hine, Christine (2000), *Virtual Ethnography*, London: Sage.

Hirschman, Albert O. (1992), *Rival Views of Market Society*, Cambridge, MA: Harvard University Press.

Horgan, John (2005), "In defense of common sense", *The New York Times*, 12 August, accessed 2 July 2011 at www.edge.org/3rd_culture/horgan05/horgan05_index.html.

Hutchins, Edwin (1995), *Cognition in the Wild*, Cambridge, MA: The MIT Press.

Huxley, Aldous (1932), *Brave New World*, London: Chatto and Windus.

Ingold, Tim (2007), *Lines. A Brief History*, London: Routledge.

Ingold, Tim (2008), "Stories against classification", in James Leach and Sandra Bamford (eds) *Genealogy Beyond Kinship*, Oxford: Berghahn Books.

Irwin, William (ed.) (2002), *The Matrix and Philosophy: Welcome to the Desert of the Real*, Chicago, IL: Open Court.

Jackson, Peter A., Michelle Lowe, Daniel Miller and Frank Mort (2001), "Introduction: transcending dualisms", in Peter A. Jackson, Michelle Lowe, Daniel Miller and Frank Mort (eds), *Commercial Cultures. Economies, Practices, Spaces*, Oxford: Berg, pp. 1–6.

Jemielniak, Dariusz and Jerzy Kociatkiewicz (eds) (2009), *Management Practices in High-tech Environments*, IGI Global: Premier Reference Source.

Joerges, Bernward and Barbara Czarniawska (1998), "The question of technology, or how organizations inscribe the world", *Organization Studies*, **19** (3), 363–85.

Johansson, Bengt (2008), *Vid nyhetsdesken. En studie av nyhetsvärdering vid svenska nyhetsredaktioner*, Sundsvall: Demokratiinstitutet.

Johnson, Richard (1986–87), "What is cultural studies anyway?", *Social Text*, **16**, 38–80.

Jordan, Tim (2007), "Technopower and its cyberfutures", in David Bell and Barbara M. Kennedy (eds), *The Cybercultures Reader*, London: Routledge, pp. 594–601.

Kerr, Walter (1962), *The Decline of Pleasure*, Virginia Beach, VA: Time-Life Books.

Knorr Cetina, Karin and Urs Bruegger (2002), "Trader's engagement with markets. A postsocial relationship", *Theory, Culture & Society*, **19** (5/6), 905–50.

Korneliussen, Tor and Fabrizio Panozzo (2005), "From 'nature' to 'economy' and 'culture': how stockfish travels and constructs an action net", in Barbara Czarniawska and Guje Sevón (eds), *Global Ideas. How Ideas, Objects and Practices Travel in the Global Economy*, Malmö/Copenhagen: Liber/CBS Press, pp. 106–25.

Kundera, Milan (1988), *The Art of the Novel*, London: Faber and Faber.

Kundera, Milan (1993/1997), *Slowness*, New York: Faber and Faber.

Laing, Ronald (1967), *The Politics of Experience*, New York: Pantheon Books.

Lanchester, John (2010), *I.O.U. Why Everyone Owes Everyone and No One Can Pay*, New York: Simon & Schuster.

Lash, Scott (2001), "Technological forms of life", *Theory, Culture & Society*, **18** (1), 105–20.

Latour, Bruno (1996), "On interobjectivity", *Mind, Culture, and Activity*, **3** (4), 246–51.

Latour, Bruno (1998), *Artefaktens återkomst*, Stockholm: Nerenius & Santérus.

Latour, Bruno (2005), *Reassembling the Social*, Oxford: Oxford University Press.

Le Monde (2002), Marc Roche: "Les difficultés de l'agence de presse Reuters, victime de la crise des marchés", 5 November, p. 23.

Lessig, Lawrence (1999), *Code and Other Laws of Cyberspace*, New York: Basic Books.

Lewin, Kurt (1947), "Frontiers in group dynamics: II. Channels of group life: social planning and action research", *Human Relations*, **1** (2), 143–53.

Löfgren Nilsson, Monica (1999), *På Bladet, Allehanda och Kuriren. Om journalistiska ideal och organiseringsprinciper i den redaktionella vardagen*, Gothenburg: JMG.

Luhmann, Niklas (1985), *Social Systems*, Stanford, CA: Stanford University Press.

Luhmann, Niklas (1998), *Observations on Modernity*, Stanford, CA: Stanford University Press.

Luhmann, Niklas (2000), *The Reality of the Mass Media*, Oxford: Polity Press.

MacIntyre, Alisdair (1988), *Whose Justice? Which Rationality?*, London: Duckworth Press.

MacKenzie, Donald (2009), *Material Markets. How Economic Agents are Constructed*, Oxford: Oxford University Press.

MacKenzie, Donald and Hardie, Iain (2009), "Assembling an economic actor", in Donald MacKenzie (ed.), *Material Markets. How Economic Agents are Constructed*, Oxford: Oxford University Press, pp. 37–62.

MacKenzie, Donald, Fabian Muniesa and Lucia Siu (eds) (2007), *Do Economists Make Markets? On the Performativity of Economics*, Princeton, NJ: Princeton University Press.

Massing, Michael (2009), "A new horizon for the news", *New York Review of Books*, **56** (14).

McLuhan, Marshall (1964), *Understanding Media: The Extensions of Man*, New York: Signet Books.

Miller, Steven (2006), *Conversation. A History of a Declining Art*, New Haven, CT: Yale University Press.

Mitsuo Nixon, David (2002), "The Matrix possibility", in William Irwin (ed.), *The Matrix and Philosophy. Welcome to the Desert of the Real*, Chicago, IL: Open Court, pp. 28–40.

Mol, Annemarie (2002), *The Body Multiple: Ontology in Medical Practice*, Durham, NC: Duke University Press.

Molotch, Harvey and Marilyn Lester (1974), "News as purposive behavior: on the strategic use of routine events, accidents, and scandals", *American Sociological Review*, **39** (1), 101–12.

Molotch, Harvey and Marilyn Lester (1975), "Accidental news: the great oil spill as local occurrence and national event", *The American Journal of Sociology*, **81** (2), 235–60.

Naville, Pierre (1960), "Vers l'automatisme social", *Revue française de sociologie*, **1** (3), 275–85.

Nygren, Gunnar (2008a), "Multikompetens, mobilitet och ständig deadline", in Gunnar Nygren (ed.), *Nyhetsfabriken. Journalistiska yrkesroller i en förändrad medievärld*, Lund: Studentlitteratur, pp. 11–23.

Nygren, Gunnar (2008b), "Det förändrade journalistiska arbetet", in Gunnar Nygren (ed.), *Nyhetsfabriken. Journalistiska yrkesroller i en förändrad medievärld*, Lund: Studentlitteratur, pp. 267–89.

Ong, Walter J. (1982), *Orality and Literacy. The Technologizing of the World*, London: Routledge.

Parenti, Michael (1986), *Inventing Reality. The Politics of the Mass Media*, New York: St. Martin's Press.

Parker, Martin (1998), "Judgment day: cyborganization, humanism and postmodern ethics", *Organization*, **5** (4), 503–18.

Peters, Jeremy W. (2010), "A digital twist on old argument over who should decide what is news", *The International Herald Tribune*, 6 July.

Postman, Neil (1985), *Amusing Ourselves to Death. Public Discourse in the Age of Show Business*, New York: Penguin.

Protetti, Cesare and Stefano Polli (2007), *E l'agenzia, bella! Storie, teorie e tecniche del giornalismo di agenzia*, Rome: Centro di documentazione giornalistica.

Raviola, Elena (2010), "Paper meets web: how the institution of news production works on paper and online", dissertation 2010-065. Jönköping: Jönköping International Business School.

Read, Donald (1992), *The Power of News: The History of Reuters, 1849–1989*, Oxford: Oxford University Press.

Renemark, David (2007), *Varför arbetar så få kvinnor med finanser? – en studie av vardagen i finanssektorn*, Gothenburg: BAS.

Riesman, David (1953/2001), *The Lonely Crowd*, New Haven, CT: Yale University Press.

Rogers, Elizabeth (2001), "Audience and online news delivery: the impact of technology on editorial gatekeeping", *MIT Communication Forum*, 1 September 2010.

Sassen, Saskia (2001), *The Global City*, Princeton, NJ: Princeton University Press.

Sassen, Saskia (2005), "The embeddedness of electronic markets: the case of global capital markets", in Karin Knorr Cetina and Alex Preda (eds) *The Sociology of Financial Markets*, Oxford: Oxford University Press, pp. 17–37.

Sassen, Saskia (2007), "Digital networks and the state", in David Bell and Barbara M. Kennedy (eds), *The Cybercultures Reader*, London: Routledge, pp. 582–93.

Scarbrough, Harry, Maxine J. Robertson and Jacky A. Swan (2005), "Professional media in management fashion", *Scandinavian Journal of Management*, **21** (2), 197–208.

Schütz, Alfred (1953/1973), "Common-sense and scientific interpretation of human action", in Alfred Schütz (ed.), *Collected Papers I*, The Hague: Martinus Nijhoft, pp. 3–47.

Shanahan, Murray (2005), preface to Erik T. Mueller, *Commonsense Reasoning*, Oxford: Elsevier.

Shirky, Clay (2008), *Here Comes Everybody. The Power of Organizing Without Organizations*, London: Allen Lane.

Shoemaker, Pamela J. and Timothy Vos (2008), *Gatekeeping Theory*, New York: Routledge.

Spradley, James P. (1979), *The Ethnographic Interview*, New York: Holt, Rinehart and Winston.

Stone, Allucquere Rosanne (2007), "Will the real body please stand up?", in David Bell and Barbara M. Kennedy (eds), *The Cybercultures Reader*, London: Routledge, pp. 434–55.

Stothard, Peter (2009), "Harold Evans: memoirs of the future. The spike, Mr. Bow-Tie and other Fleet Street legends", *Times Literary Supplement*, 16 September.

Swales, John M. (1990), *Genre Analysis: English in Academic and Research Settings*, New York: Cambridge University Press.

Tarde, Gabriel (1901/2003), *L'opinion et la foule*, Chicoutimi, QC, accessed 26 June 2011 at: http://classiques.uqac.ca/classiques/tarde_gabriel/opinion_et_la_foule/opinion_et_foule.html.

Thrift, Nigel (2005), *Knowing Capitalism*, London: Sage.

Todorov, Tzvetan (1971/1977), *The Poetics of Prose*, Oxford: Blackwell.

Travaglio, Marco (2006), *La scomparsa dei fatti*, Milan: Saggiatore.

Tuchman, Gaye (1978), *Making News. A Study in the Construction of Reality*, New York: Free Press.

Tunstall, Jeremy (1970), *Journalists at Work*, London: Constable.

Veblen, Thorstein (1889), *The Theory of the Leisure Class*, New York: Macmillan.

White, David Manning (1950), "The 'gate keeper': a case study in the selection of news", *Journalism Quarterly*, **27** (1), 383–90.

White, Hayden (1987), *The Content of the Form. Narrative Discourse and Historical Representation*, Baltimore, MD: Johns Hopkins University Press.

Wiener, Norbert (1963), *God and Golem, Inc.*, Cambridge, MA: MIT Press.

Wilson, Robert Rawdon (2002), *The Hydra's Tale. Imagining Disgust*, Edmonton, AB: University of Alberta Press.

Index